Machine Learning

A Journey from Beginner to Advanced Including Deep Learning, Scikit-learn, and Tensorflow [2nd Edition]

Table of Contents

Introduction

If there is one innovation that is going to shape the world and to shape our future more than any other it is artificial intelligence. If you don't have a clue about artificial intelligence, or AI as it is known, you need to bone up on it otherwise you will be left behind and you will wake one morning to a world that you don't understand.

The rate that AI is growing is perhaps too fast to understand. The last 40 years have seen a few false starts but, in the last decade, we've seen huge advances in the processing power of computers and in data storage. All of a sudden, the game has changed in a big way.

Back in 2015, an AI conversational agent was developed by Google. This agent was very convincing in the interaction with human beings as a member of a tech support helpdesk team. It was able to answer questions so long as they were general knowledge and fact-based, could express an opinion and talk about morality.

In the same year, another agent was developed by DeepMind. Set to playing Atari games, the agent was well above humans in terms of performance in 49 of the games. In the meantime, an agent called AlphaGo played and beat one of the best Go players in the world, which was impressive considering Go had been a human-dominated game for 20 years following machines managing to conquer the game of Chess. Many of the masters were unable to grasp how a machine could play a game that had thousands of possible moves.

March 2017 saw OpenAI create agents that were able to invent a language that helped them cooperate and meet their goals. In August of the same year, OpenAI broke another milestone by beating the top professionals in the world on a 1 to 1 basis in the multiplayer online game called Dota 2.

These days, much of the technology we depend on and rely on daily is powered by AI. Take Google Translate, for example; next time you see something in another language, point your phone camera at it and Google Translate will translate it for you – instantly.

These days, AI is being used to design treatment plans (evidence-based) for cancer sufferers, analyzing medical results instantly so a patient is sent to the right specialist quickly, and helping in research for drug recovery.

In this guide, we will be exploring machine learning, the concepts that run these technologies and by the time you get to the end you will have more knowledge than many and will be equipped to start building your own applications.

So, what is this artificial intelligence? In a nutshell, it is a study of agents, of how they perceive things, come up with plans, and make specific decisions to reach specific goals. The foundations of AI are logic, math, probability, philosophy, neuroscience, linguistics, and decision theory. Other fields that come under the AI umbrella are natural language processing, robotics, computer vision, and, of course, machine learning.

Machine learning is classified as a subfield of AI and the goal of it is to give the computer the ability to learn without human intervention. The learning algorithm for a machine is what allows it to observe data and identify patterns, to build a model that can explain the world and, without needing any models or rules pre-programmed, to make predictions.

Good, strong AI is what will change the world as we know it and to understand how that will happen starts with understanding machine learning.

The technologies mentioned earlier are ANI examples, Artificial Narrow Intelligence, able to perform tasks that are narrowly defined. But things are moving on already and great advances are being made in AGI, human-level artificial general intelligence, which is what is known as strong AI. An AGI is an agent of artificial intelligence that can carry out any of the intellectual tasks that a human can and that includes planning, learning, and making decisions under conditions of uncertainty, communicating using natural languages, joking, stock-trading, and reprogramming itself.

That last one, reprogramming, is a huge deal. Once an AI is created that can make improvements to itself, a cycle of self-improvement will be unlocked and that, in time, could lead to an explosion of intelligence over decades or a single day. You may well already have heard of this as being termed "singularity", a name taken from a gravitational singularity occurring in the middle of a black hole. It is a one-dimensional point where the laws of physics that are known begin breaking down.

Recently, the Future of Humanity Institute issued a report of the findings of a study. AI researchers were asked their views on the AGI timelines and most believed in a 50% chance of AI outperforming the human race in every type of task possible in less than 45 years.

If ASI, or artificial super intelligence, of a higher level than humans ever comes to fruition, it could be the best or it could be the absolute worst thing that could happen to the human species. ASI brings a huge challenge – that of specifying what AI will want in a human-friendly manner.

We have no way of knowing what is in the future, but we do know one thing – now is as good a time as any to start understanding the way that machines think. We must learn to see how the world is viewed by a machine; we need to understand what machines "want", whether they have biases or modes of failure, quirks, and all this must be in the same vein as we learn to understand how the human race learns, makes decisions, and acts and feels.

The path of our journey to AGI runs right through the center of machine learning and, as time goes by, every industry will be changed. In short, AI is going to have a massive impact on the way our lives run and that is why you've made the best start possible in reading this book – you will be ahead of the game when it comes to understanding machine learning.

A quick note – this book has been written assuming that you have knowledge of the Python computer programming language. If you don't, go and learn the basics first.

Chapter 1: Let Your Computer Learn from Data

Machine learning is both the application and the science of algorithms that can make some sense out of data. It is an incredibly exciting part of the computer sciences arena and, like it or not, it's here to stay. The world today is full of data and using algorithms that have the capacity to learn. This means that this data can be used to create knowledge. In the last few years, there have been quite a few open-source libraries developed, some of them incredibly powerful, and that means we are probably at the peak time to start truly understanding machine learning, to start learning how to use these algorithms to find data patterns and predict future events.

In this first chapter of this machine learning bible, we'll discuss the concepts of machine learning and the three main types. You will learn some of the basic terms and you will be set for using machine learning to solve problems. Here's an overview of what this chapter will include:

- Machine learning concepts
- Three types of machine learning
- Basic terms
- What you need to design a machine learning system
- How to install Python and set it up for machine learning and data analysis

Turning Data into Knowledge

We live in a modern world filled with technology. Every day, we hear that the planet is being stripped of its resources but there is one resource that continues to grow, a resource that we have plenty of – data, both structured and unstructured. In the last 50 years of the 20th century, machine learning began to evolve. It was an AI subfield that used algorithms that could learn; algorithms that could derive knowledge from the data and use this knowledge to make predictions for the future. Where once a human being would have been needed to manually make the rules and build the models by analyzing vast amounts of data, machine learning does it much quicker and more efficiently. Machine learning allows us to capture the data, turn it into knowledge, and make improvements to how predictive modeling performed; the result of this is decisions driven by data.

So, you can see how important machine learning is in terms of computer sciences research, but do you realize just how often it features in everyday life? Think about the strong spam filters on your email, voice recognition on your computers and mobile devices, convenient text, decent search engines on the web, computerized Chess games and, in the future, safe self-drive cars. All of this is thanks to the advances made in machine learning.

Three Types of Machine Learning

In this part of the chapter, we will look in detail at the three machine learning types. They are:

- Supervised learning

- Unsupervised learning
- Reinforcement Learning

We'll describe the basic differences between the three and explain the practicalities of applying the principles.

Supervised Learning – Predicting the Future

Supervised learning has one basic goal – to learn a specified model from "labeled" data for training purposes so that predictions can be made about future data or unseen data. It is called "supervised" because the labels, or the output signals that we want, are known already.

Think about your email, about the spam filter in place. We could use supervised machine learning to train a model. The data would be labeled – emails already marked correctly as spam, those marked correctly as not spam – and the model would be trained to recognize to which group new emails belong. When you have supervised tasks such as this, using class labels, we call it a "classification task".

Predicting Class Labels Using Classification

So, classification is a subcategory with a goal of predicting under which class label new instances would be placed. This is based on previous data. The labels are discrete with values in no order that can be understood to be memberships of the instances. The example of spam filters is representative of a binary type of classification task – the algorithm will learn the rules so that it can work out the difference between potential classes – spam and not spam.

Although this is a binary classification task, the class labels are not required to be binary in nature. The learning algorithm will determine a predictive model that can then assign any of the labels from the dataset to a new instance that has no label. One example of this type of multiclass classification is recognition of handwritten characters. We could have a dataset that has the letters of the alphabet written in several different handwriting styles. If the user were to use an input device to give a new character, the predictive model could predict which letter of the alphabet it was with accuracy. However, the system could not recognize any digit from 0 to 9 because they would not be in the dataset used for training purposes.

Let's say that we have 30 pieces of sample data – 15 of them are labeled as a positive class with a plus sign (+) and 15 are labeled as a negative class with a minus sign (-). The dataset is called a two-dimensional dataset, meaning that each of the samples has two possible values, $x1$ and $x2$. Supervised learning algorithms could be used to learn the rule that a dashed line is used to represent the decision boundary and this rule is used to separate the classes and put any new data into one of the categories depending on the $x1$ and $x2$ values.

Continuous Outcome Prediction Using Regression

We know now that classification tasks are used for assigning unordered, categorical labels to instances. There is another type of supervised learning called regression analysis, and this is used for the prediction of continuous outcomes. With regression analysis, we have several explanatory or predictor variables, along with a variable for a continuous response. We can predict outcomes by finding relationships between the variables.

Let me give an example. We have a class of students and we want to try to predict their SAT scores. If we can find a link between how long each student studied and their scores, we could then use that data to learn models that can use the length of time studied to predict the score achieved by future students.

Reinforcement Learning – Solving Interactive Problems

Reinforcement Learning is another area of machine learning and the goal here is to develop an agent or system that can improve its performance. This improvement is based on how the agent interacts with its environment. Information that details the current environmental state tends to include a reward-signal, so this kind of machine learning can be considered a part of supervised learning. However, the feedback in Reinforcement Learning is not the right value or truth label; rather, it is an indication of how the reward function related to the action. By interacting with its environment, the agent learns several actions to maximize the reward. By using Reinforcement Learning, the agent will go through an approach of either deliberate planning or trial and error to get the reward.

A Chess engine is a great example of this type of machine learning. The agent will decide on the moves it will make, dependent on the environment (the board) and the reward is defined as winning or losing when the game is over.

Reinforcement Learning has a number of subtypes but, in general, the agent will carry out several environmental interactions in an attempt to get the maximum reward. Each of the states is associated with a negative or a positive reward – the reward is defined by achieving a specific goal, in this case, losing or winning the game of Chess. For example, in a game of Chess, the outcome of a move is a state of that environment.

Let's go a bit deeper into this. Take the locations of each square on the Chess board. Visiting them could be given a positive reward association – you take an opponent's piece or put his king or queen under threat, for example. Other locations have a negative reward association – losing one of your pieces by having your own king or queen put under threat in the next turn. Not every game turn will end with a piece being removed from the board so where does Reinforcement Learning come into this? Quite simply, it is about learning the series of steps that are needed by ensuring the maximum reward based on feedback – immediate and delayed.

This really is as far as we can go on Reinforcement Learning. We can only give you a basic overview because applications for this type of learning are way beyond the scope of this guide which is focusing on clustering, classification, and regression analysis.

Unsupervised Learning – Discovering Hidden Structures

With supervised learning, we already know the answer we want when the model is being trained. With Reinforcement Learning, we provide a reward measured by specific actions performed by the agent. With unsupervised learning, we are going one step further by using unlabeled data – data with unknown structure. By using these techniques, we can explore the data structure to get meaningful information without needing to be guided by a reward or by a variable with a known outcome.

Use Clustering to Find Subgroups

Clustering is a technique of exploratory data analysis which lets us organize a great amount of data into subgroups or clusters. We do not have any upfront knowledge about the group memberships. Each of the clusters identified from the analysis will define a specific group of objects that are similar to a certain degree but are not quite so similar to objects that are in the other clusters. This is why you often hear clustering being termed as "unsupervised classification". Clustering is absolutely one of the best techniques we have for providing a structure to a set of information and determining meaningful relationships from the information. For example, think of marketers. They can use clustering to determine specific customer groups by their interests so that they can devise a targeted marketing program.

Dimensionality Reduction

This is another subfield of the unsupervised machine learning area. More often than not, high-dimensionality data is used. This means that each observation has several measurements. This presents a bit of a challenge where storage space is limited and affects the performance of the learning algorithms. Dimensionality reduction, in terms of unsupervised machine learning, is used quite often in feature preprocessing, to remove the noise from the data. This noise can cause degradation in the predictive performance of some algorithms. It is also commonly used to compress data so it fits into a smaller subspace while keeping the relevant information intact.

Occasionally, we can also use dimensionality reduction for visualizing data. For example, we could project a high-dimensionality feature set onto 1, 2, or 3D feature spaces – this would allow us to see that feature set through 2D or 3D histograms or scatterplots. This will be covered in a later chapter.

Basic Terminology and Notations

We know what the three machine learning types are – supervised, reinforcement, and unsupervised. Now it's time to look at some of the basic terminologies. The Iris dataset is the common training dataset for machine learning. In the dataset there are measurements for 150 different types of iris flower, all from three separate species:

- Setosa
- Versicolor
- Virginica

Each of the samples is representative of a single row in the dataset and the measurements, all in centimeters, are the columns. These are known as the dataset features. We want the notation to be simple and the implementation to be efficient, so we use basic features of linear algebra. In the chapters that follow this, we will look at using vector and matrix notations to reference the data, using common conventions as a way of representing each sample as an individual row in an X matrix – each feature will be stored as its own column.

For the Iris dataset, with its 150 samples and its four features, we would write it as a 150 x 4 matrix.

Note

Taking the Iris dataset, each row in the matrix is representative of a single instance of a flower and is written as a 4D row vector. Each of the feature dimensions is written as a 150D column vector. In the same way, target variables or class labels are stored as 150D column vectors.

Machine Learning Systems – Building a Roadmap

Up to this point, we have looked at the basic machine learning concepts and the different machine learning types. Now we need to look at the rest of a machine learning system, the important parts that go with the algorithm. There are three important subsections to consider.

Preprocessing

Preprocessing is the act of getting our data into shape. Raw data is very rarely in the right format or shape required for the learning algorithm to work properly. So, we need to preprocess the data, and this is probably the most important step in any machine learning application. Again, we will use the Iris dataset as an example. The images of the flowers are the raw data from which we will be looking for meaningful features. Those features could be color, intensity, hue, height, length of flower, the width of flower, and so on. A lot of machine learning algorithms will also require the chosen features to be on identical scales for the best performance and this is achieved by transforming features in a range or by using standard distribution with "zero mean and unit variance" – more about this in later chapters.

Some of the features selected may be correlated and that means, to a certain extent, they are redundant. In these cases, we can use the dimensionality reduction to compress those features down to a lower subspace. By doing this, we don't need as much storage space and the algorithm is significantly faster. In some cases, reduction can also make the predictive model performance more efficient, especially if the dataset has got multiple instances of noise (features that are not relevant) – you will often see this as having a low ratio of signal to noise.

To see if the algorithm is performing as it should on the training dataset while reacting positively to new data, we will need to divide the dataset randomly into two sets – training and test. The training dataset trains the model and optimizes performance, while the test set is used last to evaluate the finished model.

Training and Choosing Predictive Models

You will see throughout this guide that many of the algorithms are designed to solve specific problems. There is one important thing to remember – learning is not free. This concept can easily be related to another popular saying by Abraham Maslow in 1966 – "I suppose it is tempting, if the only tool you have is a hammer, to treat everything as if it were a nail". Let's put this into context. Every one of the classification algorithms has got biases built into it. No one classification model is superior to any other provided we make no assumptions regarding the task. In practical terms, it is vital that several algorithms are compared so that the best model can be selected and trained. However, before we can do this, we need to decide which metric we are using to measure the performance. One of the most common metrics is classification accuracy and this is defined as a set proportion of instances that have been classified correctly.

But, and this is a legitimate question, how will we know which of the models will perform the best on the final test and on real-world data if the test set is used ONLY for the final evaluation and NOT on the model selection tests? To address this issue, we can use multiple techniques for cross-validation – the training dataset is split into two subsets: training and validation. This is done so that the model's generalization performance can be estimated. Lastly, although many software libraries offer learning algorithms, we should not take it for granted that the default parameters of these algorithms will fit the specific problem we are trying to solve. Instead, we will use techniques called hyperparameter optimization to fine-tune our model's performance and we'll see how this is done later. Basically, the hyperparameters can be thought of as parameters that cannot be learned from the dataset but instead, they represent dials that we can turn to improve the performance of the model. Believe me, when I say, this will all be clearer to you later in this guide.

Model Evaluation and Prediction of Unseen Data Instances

Once we have our model, the test dataset can be used to estimate how the model performs on unseen data. In this way, we can gain an estimation of the generalization error percentage. If we are happy with the way the model performs, we can use it for predicting future data. Be aware of one thing – it is vital that the parameters for the procedures we talked about, like dimensionality reduction and feature scaling, are obtained ONLY from the training dataset and are then applied to the test dataset to transform it. They are also applied to new samples of data. If we don't adhere to this, the test data may produce an overly-optimistic performance measurement.

Python and Machine Learning

Python is the most popular of all the computer programming languages and is the most used in the data science field. Because of this, it has the add-on libraries that we need that have been developed by a fantastic community and the Python developers.

You may be thinking that interpreted languages like Python are not as good for heavy computational tasks as the lower-level languages and you would, in theory, be correct. However, Python has several extension libraries, like SciPy and NumPy, that build on the low-level C and Fortran implementation to allow us to do fast operations that are vectorized on multi-dimensional arrays.

As far as machine learning goes, we will be mostly using scikit-learn, one of the most popular libraries and one of the most accessible.

Installing Python and Python Packages

Python can be installed on three of the biggest operating systems – Linux, Mac OS X, and Windows. You can get the installer and all the official documentation from the official website https://www.python.org.

For the purposes of this guide, we are using Python 3.5.2 or above, so install the most current version of Python 3. Some examples are backward compatible with Python 2.7.13 or above and, if you opt to use Python 2.8, you must make sure that you understand the differences between the two versions. If you are doing a clean install of Python, it is simpler just to download the latest version.

There are additional packages that you will need, and these are easiest to install using the pip installer – a standard part of the Python library since v3.3 was released. So, go ahead and install Python – all the instructions are on the website and then you can install the packages.

Open a terminal window – how you do this will depend on the operating system you are using.

Mac:

Go to your Applications folder and open Utilities. Then you can open Terminal. Alternatively, open Spotlight, type in Terminal and click the relevant result.

Windows:

Go to your Start menu and open Program Files>Accessories>Command Prompt. Alternatively, in the search bar, type in 'cmd' (without the quote marks). Right click on CMD and choose 'Run as Administrator' and then click 'Yes', A terminal window will open.

Linux:

On your keyboard, press CTRL + ALT + T at the same time – the terminal window will open.

Once your terminal is open, at the command prompt type the following:

```
pip install
```

followed by the name of the package – list to come later

if you already have Python and you need to update the packages, type in

```
pip install (name of package) -upgrade
```

Using Anaconda Distribution

Anaconda is highly recommended as a Python alternative and it comes from Continuum Analytics. Like Python, it is free, and it has all the relevant packages for math, data science, and engineering together on a single cross-platform distribution. To download this, go to http://continuum.io/downloads.

To install packages in Anaconda, at your command prompt, type in

```
conda install (name of package)
```

If you already use Anaconda and you need to update them, type in

```
conda update (name of package)
```

Packages You Need

For the most part, we will be using the multi-dimensional arrays from NumPy for the storage and manipulation of data. However, on occasion we use pandas, a NumPy library that gives us extra high-level tools for data manipulation – these make it much easier to work with tabular data. And, to help us visualize the quantitative data and boost our learning experience, we will be using the Matplotlib library, which is very customizable.

When you download your packages, make sure that you download the correct version numbers – listed below – or a higher version number. Never choose a lower one because you will have compatibility issues.

- Matplotlib 2.0.2
- pandas 0.20.1
- SciPy 0.19.0
- scikit-learn 0.18.1
- NumPy 1.12.1
- Jupyter 5.5.0

Chapter 2: Classification Systems

We talked previously about supervised learning and two of the most used tasks are classification (class prediction) and regression (value prediction). In this chapter, we are going to concentrate on classification systems.

MNIST Dataset

We will be making use of the MNIST dataset. This is a set of small images, each containing handwritten digits, each image labeled with the representing digit. The dataset contains 70,000 of these images and is the most studied dataset in the world of machine learning. Using scikit-learn you can fetch the MNIST dataset using the following code:

```
>>> from sklearn.datasets import fetch_mldata

>>> mnist = fetch_mldata('MNIST original')

>>> mnist
{'COL_NAMES': ['label', 'data'],

'DESCR': 'mldata.org dataset: mnist-original',

'data': array([[0, 0, 0, ..., 0, 0, 0],

[0, 0, 0, ..., 0, 0, 0],

[0, 0, 0, ..., 0, 0, 0],

...,

[0, 0, 0, ..., 0, 0, 0],

[0, 0, 0, ..., 0, 0, 0],

[0, 0, 0, ..., 0, 0, 0]], dtype=uint8),

'target': array([ 0., 0., 0., ..., 9., 9., 9.])}
```

You will find that scikit-learn datasets all tend to have a similar structure:

- **DESCR Key** – this describes the dataset
- **Data key** – this contains an array that has a row for each instance and a column for each feature
- **Target key** – this has an array that contains the labels

Let's have a closer look at the arrays:

```
>>> X, y = mnist["data"], mnist["target"]

>>> X.shape

(70000, 784)

>>> y.shape

(70000,)
```

Each of the 70,000 images is 28 by 28 pixels and has 784 features, each one representing the density of a pixel – this ranges from 0 for white up to 255 for black. Now we'll look at a single digit from this dataset; to do this, we get a feature for an instance vector, change the shape to an array of 28 by 28 and then use the imshow() function in Matplotlib to display it:

```
%matplotlib inline

import matplotlib

import matplotlib.pyplot as plt

some_digit = X[36000]

some_digit_image = some_digit.reshape(28, 28)

plt.imshow(some_digit_image, cmap = matplotlib.cm.binary,

interpolation="nearest")

plt.axis("off")

plt.show()
```

The result looks much like a number 5 and that is what the label confirms:

```
>>> y[36000]

5.0
```

Hold your fire though! It is important that a test set is always created and set to one side before you inspect the data. The MNIST dataset has already been split for us into a training set of 60,000 images and a test set of 10,000 images.

```
X_train, X_test, y_train, y_test = X[:60000], X[60000:], y[:60000],
y[60000:]
```

What we want to do next is give the training data a shuffle so that all the cross-validation folds are similar and are not missing any digits. Not only that, some of the learning algorithms are somewhat sensitive where the order of instances is concerned, and they don't like it if there are too many similar ones together shuffling stops this from happening:

```
import numpy as np

shuffle_index = np.random.permutation(60000)

X_train, y_train = X_train[shuffle_index], y_train[shuffle_index]
```

Training Binary Classifiers

For now, we'll keep things simple and stick to identifying a single digit, let's say the number 5, and we'll create a "5-detector". This is a binary classifier and it has the ability to tell the difference between the two classes – 5 and not-5. Creating target vectors for the classification is as simple as using the following code:

```
y_train_5 = (y_train == 5) # True for 5s, False for other digits.

y_test_5 = (y_test == 5)
```

Next, we need to decide on the classifier we are using and train it. The best places to begin is with the SGD (Stochastic Gradient Descent) classifier and we get this using the SGDClassifier class in scikit-learn. This classifier can efficiently handle big datasets because the idea behind SGB is to train each instance independently of one another – this also means that SGD is good for online learning and we'll talk more on that later. For now, we are going to create the SGDClassifier and then train it on the entire dataset:

```
from sklearn.linear_model import SGDClassifier

sgd_clf = SGDClassifier(random_state=42)

sgd_clf.fit(X_train, y_train_5)
```

Tip

It is worth noting that the SGDClassifier requires a certain degree of randomness during the training and this is why it is called 'stochastic". If you want your results to be reproducible, you need to set a parameter called random_state.

You can use this to detect all images with the number 5:

```
>>> sgd_clf.predict([some_digit])

array([ True], dtype=bool)
```

The classifier will make a guess that the number 4 is represented by the image and, in this case, it guessed correctly. Now we need to see how it performed.

Performance Measures

Classifier evaluation is quite tricky, far more so than regressor evaluation so that is what we will be discussing in the rest of this chapter. There are multiple measures of performance; so get your pen and notebook ready:

Cross-Validation

Cross-validation is one of the best methods of evaluation. You can use the function cross_val_score() or other functions like it but these don't always offer you the control that you need. In that case, you could implement cross-validation manually. It is easy to do and the code below does much the same as the other functions and the result is the same:

```
from sklearn.model_selection import StratifiedKFold

from sklearn.base import clone

skfolds = StratifiedKFold(n_splits=3, random_state=42)

for train_index, test_index in skfolds.split(X_train, y_train_45:

clone_clf = clone(sgd_clf)

X_train_folds = X_train[train_index]

y_train_folds = (y_train_5[train_index])

X_test_fold = X_train[test_index]

y_test_fold = (y_train_5[test_index])

clone_clf.fit(X_train_folds, y_train_folds)

y_pred = clone_clf.predict(X_test_fold)

n_correct = sum(y_pred == y_test_fold)

print(n_correct / len(y_pred))
```

So what does the StratifiedKFold class do? It carries out stratified sampling so that we get folds that contain a representing ratio of each of the classes. When it comes time for iteration, the code clones the classifier, the clone is trained on the training folds and then makes predictions on the test folds – this happens with each iteration. The correct predictions are then counted and the ratio of predictions that are correct is then output.

We're going to evaluate our SGDClassifier model with K-fold cross-validation. We'll use cross_val_score() to do this and K-fold will have three folds. K-fold cross-validation results in the training set being split into K-folds, three for this example; predictions are then made and evaluated on each of the folds making use of a model that has been trained on the rest of the folds.

```
>>> from sklearn.model_selection import cross_val_score

>>> cross_val_score(sgd_clf, X_train, y_train_5, cv=3,
scoring="accuracy")

array([ 0.9502 , 0.96565, 0.96495])
```

The accuracy or the ratio of right predictions is over 95% on all of the cross-validation folds but, before you get over-excited, we need to examine a dumb classifier – this one will classify pretty much all images that fall into the "not-5" class:

```
from sklearn.base import BaseEstimator

class Never5Classifier(BaseEstimator):

def fit(self, X, y=None):

pass

def predict(self, X):

return np.zeros((len(X), 1), dtype=bool)
```

What do you reckon the accuracy is?

```
>>> never_5_clf = Never5Classifier()

>>> cross_val_score(never_5_clf, X_train, y_train_5, cv=3,
scoring="accuracy") array([ 0.909 , 0.90715, 0.9128 ])
```

If you guessed over 90% then you were right. Why? Because around 10% of the images in the set contain 5 so, if your model is guessing not-5 all the time, correct predictions will be made around 90% of the time.

This just shows you why accuracy should not be considered the number one measure for classifier performance, especially when your datasets are skewed – by this I mean that some classes are more frequent than others.

Confusion Matrix

There is a better way of evaluating classifier performance: viewing the confusion matrix. The idea is to count how many instances of class A are misclassified as class B. For example, if you wanted to see how many times images of the digit 5 were confused with images of digit 3, you would need to look at row 5, column 3 of the matrix.

Computing the matrix requires a set of predictions – these will be compared with the real targets. Predictions can be made on the test set but, for now, we'll leave that be. The test set really only wants to be used at the end of a project, when you have got the classifier that you want. For this test, then, we are going to use the function called cross_val_predict():

```
from sklearn.model_selection import cross_val_predict

y_train_pred = cross_val_predict(sgd_clf, X_train, y_train_5, cv=3)
```

Much like cross_val_score(), this function also does K-fold cross-validations but, rather than the evaluation scores being returned, we get the predictions that were made on each of the test folds. What this means is every instance in the training dataset gets a clean prediction – by this we mean the prediction comes from a model that did not see the data during the training.

Now we can call the confusion matrix and, to do this, we will use the confusion_matrix() function and we will pass it the target and predicted classes, y_train_5 and y_train_pred respectively.

```
>>> from sklearn.metrics import confusion_matrix

>>> confusion_matrix(y_train_5, y_train_pred)

array([[53272, 1307],

[ 1077, 4344]])
```

The rows in the matrix are representative of real classes while the columns are representative of predicted classes. Row 1 of the matrix looks at the non-5 images – this is the negative class. The number of images correctly classified is 53, 272 (true negatives) and the remainder, 1,307, were incorrectly classified as 5 – these are called False positives. Row 2 looks at digit 5 images (positive class) and the number of correct classifications was 4,344 (true positives) while the remaining 1,077 were incorrectly classified False negatives. An absolute perfect classifier would only contain true negatives and true positives, so the main diagonal of the confusion matrix would display nonzeros.

```
>>> confusion_matrix(y_train_5, y_train_perfect_predictions)

array([[54579, 0],

[ 0, 5421]])
```

You can get a lot of useful information from a confusion matrix, but it may not always be as concise as you want. One measurement you could look at is how accurate the positive predictions are, and this is known as classifier precision.

$$recall = \frac{TP}{TP + FN}$$
$$precision = \frac{TP}{TP + FP}$$

Equation– Precision

TP signifies how many True Positives there are, and FP is for False Positives, while FN, as you probably guessed, is for False Negatives.

Precision and Recall

In scikit-learn you will fund a number of metrics that help you to compute metrics, and that includes precision and recall:

```
>>> from sklearn.metrics import precision_score, recall_score

>>> precision_score(y_train_5, y_pred) # == 4344 / (4344 + 1307)

0.76871350203503808

>>> recall_score(y_train_5, y_train_pred) # == 4344 / (4344 + 1077)

0.79136690647482011
```

Now you can see that your detector isn't looking quite so good – it is only accurately classifying a 5-image 77% of time and is only finding 79% of the 5's in the dataset.

Sometimes you will find it better to combine these into one metric named F1 score, especially if you want a comparison of two classifiers. The F1 score provides the 'harmonic mean' of the two metrics. Values are treated equally with a regular mean but the harmonic mean leans toward to the low values and the only way of getting a high F1 score is if both metrics are high.

If you want to compute the F1 score, all you do is call the relevant function, f1_score():

```
>>> from sklearn.metrics import f1_score

>>> f1_score(y_train_5, y_pred)

0.78468208092485547
```

F1 score tends to prefer the classifiers where precision and recall are much the same, but you won't always want this. Sometimes you will only really want precision, other times you will want recall. You can't always have it both ways. If you increase precision, recall drops off and vice versa; we call this precision/recall tradeoff.

Precision/Recall Tradeoff

To understand how this works, we need to look at the SGDClassifier decisions on classifications. For each individual instance, it will use a decision function to work out the score and if that score is above a preset threshold, the instance is assigned to a positive class; below it and it goes to the negative class.

You can't directly set the threshold in scikit-learn but you can see the decision scores used for the predictions. Rather than the predict() method of the classifier, you call the decision_function() instead and this returns the score and the prediction is made based on the score with any threshold that you want:

```
>>> y_scores = sgd_clf.decision_function([some_digit])

>>> y_scores

array([ 161855.74572176])

>>> threshold = 0

>>> y_some_digit_pred = (y_scores > threshold)

array([ True], dtype=bool)
```

The threshold that SGDClassifier uses is equal to zero so the code written above will return an identical result to using the predict() method. What happens if we up the threshold?

```
>>> threshold = 200000

>>> y_some_digit_pred = (y_scores > threshold)

>>> y_some_digit_pred

array([False], dtype=bool)
```

By raising that threshold, recall is decreased. How do you decide on the threshold that you are going to use? You need the scores for every training dataset instance and you get these using the cross_val_predict() function. However, you must specify that you want decision scores and not predictions:

```
y_scores = cross_val_predict(sgd_clf, X_train, y_train_5, cv=3,

method="decision_function")
```

With the scores precision and recall can now be computer for all thresholds by using a function called precision_recall_curve():

```
from sklearn.metrics import precision_recall_curve

precisions, recalls, thresholds = precision_recall_curve(y_train_5,
y_scores)
```

Finally, you can plot precision and recall as functions of the threshold value using Matplotlib:

```
def plot_precision_recall_vs_threshold(precisions, recalls,
thresholds):

plt.plot(thresholds, precisions[:-1], "b--", label="Precision")

plt.plot(thresholds, recalls[:-1], "g-", label="Recall")

plt.xlabel("Threshold")

plt.legend(loc="upper left")

plt.ylim([0, 1])

plot_precision_recall_vs_threshold(precisions, recalls, thresholds)

plt.show()
```

Note

The reason behind the precision curve looking somewhat less smooth than the recall curve is that, when you raise a threshold, precision might go down, although it usually goes up. All you need to do is choose the threshold values that provide the best tradeoff for the job in hand.

If you were to plot precision against recall, you would see where precision began to drop so you want a tradeoff just before the drop, although that will depend on your project.

Let's say you want a precision of 90%. You would look at plot 1, determine that you need a threshold of around 70,000 and then, instead of calling the predict() method, you simply run the code below:

```
y_train_pred_90 = (y_scores > 70000)
```

Check the resulting precision and recall:

```
>>> precision_score(y_train_5, y_train_pred_90)

0.8998702983138781

>>> recall_score(y_train_5, y_train_pred_90)
```

```
0.63991883416343853
```

Bingo – 90% precision, or near enough. You now have the classifier you want and, as you have seen, it is relatively easy to train a classifier with the precision that you want just by setting the threshold high enough.

ROC Curve

The ROC or Receiver Operating Characteristic curve is another tool commonly used with binary classifiers. It looks much like the precision/recall curve, but it plots TPR (True Positive Rate) against FPR (False Positive Rate). FPR is defined as the ratio of wrongly classified negative instances – those classified as positive in error. It's equal to 1 minus TNR (True Negative Rate), which are the negative instances classified correctly as negative. TNR is often known as specificity, so the curve will plot:

```
Sensitivity (recall) v 1-specificity (TNR)
```

Before you can plot the curve, you need to know what the TPR and FPR are for several thresholds and we do this using roc_curve():

```
from sklearn.metrics import roc_curve

fpr, tpr, thresholds = roc_curve(y_train_5, y_scores)
```

Then you can plot the FPR against the TPR using Matplotlib.

```
def plot_roc_curve(fpr, tpr, label=None):

plt.plot(fpr, tpr, linewidth=2, label=label)

plt.plot([0, 1], [0, 1], 'k--')

plt.axis([0, 1, 0, 1])

plt.xlabel('False Positive Rate')

plt.ylabel('True Positive Rate')

plot_roc_curve(fpr, tpr)

plt.show()
```

Again, we have a tradeoff – a high recall or TPR creates more FPR from the classifier.

You can use AUC to compare classifiers. This means Area Under Curve and the perfect classifier will show a ROC AUC as equal to 1 – a random classifier will be 0.5. There is a function in scikit-learn to help you do this:

```
>>> from sklearn.metrics import roc_auc_score
```

```
>>> roc_auc_score(y_train_5, y_scores)
0.97061072797174941
```

> **Tip**
>
> ROC and PR curves are similar so, when you are more interested in False positives than negatives or when the positive class is rare, use PR (precision/Recall). Otherwise, use ROC.

It's time to put a RandomForestClassifier through training and then we can compare the ROC curve and the ROC AUC score with the SGDClassifier. To start, we need the individual scores for all the instances; however, there is no decision_function() method in RandomForestClassifier (you will learn more about this later in this guide). What you will find is a method called predict_proba(). This method will return an array that has a row for each instance and a column for each class. Each of these will have the probability that the contained instance will belong to the given class:

```
from sklearn.ensemble import RandomForestClassifier

forest_clf = RandomForestClassifier(random_state=42)

y_probas_forest = cross_val_predict(forest_clf, X_train, y_train_5,
cv=3,

method="predict_proba")
```

However, plotting the ROC curve requires scores and not probabilities so the easiest way is to use the probability from the positive class as the score:

```
y_scores_forest = y_probas_forest[:, 1] # score = proba of positive
class

fpr_forest, tpr_forest, thresholds_forest =
roc_curve(y_train_5,y_scores_forest)
```

We can now plot the ROC curve:

```
plt.plot(fpr, tpr, "b:", label="SGD")

plot_roc_curve(fpr_forest, tpr_forest, "Random Forest")

plt.legend(loc="bottom right")

plt.show()
```

The ROC curve for the RandomForestClassifier looks better than that of the SGDClassifier; it is nearer to the top-left corner. That means the AUC score is also much better:

```
>>> roc_auc_score(y_train_5, y_scores_forest)
```

```
0.99312433660038291
```

That's training of binary classifiers completed; you know now how to pick the right metric, use cross-validation to evaluate the classifiers, pick the right PR tradeoff and compare the models using ROC AUC scores and ROC curves. Now we're going to go one step further.

Multiclass

A binary classifier can identify the difference between a pair of classes, but multiclass classifiers can do more. Some of the algorithms can handle a multiclass classifier directly, like the RandomForestClassifier, but others are purely binary classifiers. There are ways to use these binary classifiers to carry out multiclass classification.

You could create a system that classifies the images of the digits 0 through 9 by training up 10 separate binary classifiers. When you want an image classified, you use the decision scores from each of the classifiers for the image to choose the classifier with the highest score output. We call this OvA or One versus All.

You could train one binary classifier for each pair of digits, known as OvO, or One versus One. However, let's say you are using the MNIST dataset; you would need to train up 45 of these classifiers and, when you wanted an image classified, you would need to go through all of them to see which one wins. The advantage of using OvO is that you only need to train a classifier on a specific bit of the training set – the two classes it must tell the difference between.

Some of the algorithms, like the Support Vector Machine classifiers, do not scale well with large datasets so OvO is the preferred method for these – it's much quicker to train a lot of classifiers on smaller sets than it is to train one classifier on a huge dataset. However, OvA is the preferred method for most of the binary classifiers.

Scikit-learn is able to tell when you are attempting to do multiclass classification with binary classifiers; it will run OvA automatically unless the classifier is an SVM, in which case, it will run OvO. We'll have a go with the SGDClassifier:

```
>>> sgd_clf.fit(X_train, y_train) # y_train, not y_train_5

>>> sgd_clf.predict([some_digit])

array([ 5.])
```

Easy enough. Instead of using 5 against all the target classes, that code will train the classifier using 0 to 9, the original targets, and then it makes the prediction. Out of sight, what scikit-learn did was to train up 10 binary classifiers, considered the scores and chose the class that had the highest score.

If you wanted to check this, you could use the method called decision_function(); the return would be 10 scores for 10 classes:

```
>>> some_digit_scores = sgd_clf.decision_function([some_digit])

>>> some_digit_scores

array([[-311402.62954431, -363517.28355739, -446449.5306454 ,

 -183226.61023518, -414337.15339485, 161855.74572176,

-452576.39616343, -471957.14962573, -518542.33997148,

-536774.63961222]])
```

Warning

Be aware that, when you train a classifier, the target class list is stored in the class attribute in order of value. In the example above, the index of the class matched with the class (index 5, class 5) but it won't always be this way.

You can force scikit-learn into using OvO or OvA by using the correct classifier – OneVsOneClassifier for OvO and OneVsRestClassifier for OvA. All you need to do is create the instance and pass the binary classifier to the constructor. In the following example, a multiclass classifier is created using OvA and an SGDClassifier:

```
>>> from sklearn.multiclass import OneVsOneClassifier

>>> ovo_clf = OneVsOneClassifier(SGDClassifier(random_state=42))

>>> ovo_clf.fit(X_train, y_train)

>>> ovo_clf.predict([some_digit])

array([ 5.])

>>> len(ovo_clf.estimators_)

45
```

And it is just as simple to train a RandomForestClassifier:

```
>>> forest_clf.fit(X_train, y_train)

>>> forest_clf.predict([some_digit])

array([ 5.])
```

Neither OvO nor OvA were run this time because, as you know, the RandomForestClassifier can already do multiple classifications. You can get the probabilities list that each instance in each class was assigned by using predict_proba():

```
>>> forest_clf.predict_proba([some_digit])
```

```
array([[ 0.1, 0. , 0. , 0.1, 0. , 0.8, 0. , 0. , 0. , 0. ]])
```

As you can see, the classifier is pretty darned confident it got the prediction right: the 5th index is 0.8 which means an 80% probability.

Next, we evaluate the classifiers using cross_val; we'll start with the accuracy of SGDClassifier using cross_val_score():

```
>>> cross_val_score(sgd_clf, X_train, y_train, cv=3,
scoring="accuracy") array([ 0.84063187, 0.84899245, 0.86652998])
```

The score on all of the test folds is more than 84%; if a random classifier were used, the accuracy would be 10% so, while this is good, we can do better. By using input scaling, we can push the accuracy to more than 90%:

```
>>> from sklearn.preprocessing import StandardScaler
```

```
>>> scaler = StandardScaler()
```

```
>>> X_train_scaled = scaler.fit_transform(X_train.astype(np.float64))
```

```
>>> cross_val_score(sgd_clf, X_train_scaled, y_train, cv=3,
scoring="accuracy") array([ 0.91011798, 0.90874544, 0.906636 ])
```

Error Analysis

If you were doing this for real, you would do so much more – explore the options for data preparation, try several models, choose the best and fine-tune, automate as much as you can. For this though, we will just assume that we have the right model and are just looking to make improvements. A good way of doing this is to analyze the errors and we start with the confusion matrix. We will use cross_val_predict() to make our predictions and then we'll call confusion_matrix():

```
>>> y_train_pred = cross_val_predict(sgd_clf, X_train_scaled,
y_train, cv=3)
```

```
>>> conf_mx = confusion_matrix(y_train, y_train_pred)
```

```
>>> conf_mx
```

```
array([[5725, 3, 24, 9, 10, 49, 50, 10, 39, 4],

[ 2, 6493, 43, 25, 7, 40, 5, 10, 109, 8],

[ 51, 41, 5321, 104, 89, 26, 87, 60, 166, 13],

[ 47, 46, 141, 5342, 1, 231, 40, 50, 141, 92],

[ 19, 29, 41, 10, 5366, 9, 56, 37, 86, 189],
```

```
[ 73,   45,   36,  193,   64, 4582,  111,   30,  193,   94],

[ 29,   34,   44,    2,   42,   85, 5627,   10,   45,    0],

[ 25,   24,   74,   32,   54,   12,    6, 5787,   15,  236],

[ 52,  161,   73,  156,   10,  163,   61,   25, 5027,  123],

[ 43,   35,   26,   92,  178,   28,    2,  223,   82, 5240]])
```

Rather a lot of numbers there! Sometimes, it is better to use the matshow() function in Matplotlib to see an image of the matrix:

```
plt.matshow(conf_mx, cmap=plt.cm.gray)

plt.show()
```

The matrix looks okay because the bulk of the images show up on the main diagonal – this means correct classification. The digit 5 looks a little darker but that could mean one of two things – there aren't many images, or the classifier doesn't work so well on them.

We will now divide each of the values in the matrix by how many images are in the corresponding class, thus comparing the rate of error and not the number of errors (absolute):

```
row_sums = conf_mx.sum(axis=1, keepdims=True)

norm_conf_mx = conf_mx / row_sums
```

So that we keep just the errors, we'll fill up the diagonal with zeros and plot it:

```
np.fill_diagonal(norm_conf_mx, 0)

plt.matshow(norm_conf_mx, cmap=plt.cm.gray)

plt.show()
```

Now it's clear what errors are being made. Keep in mind that rows equal real classes while columns equal predicted classes. The plot shows the 8 and 9 columns as being brighter than the others and this tells you that there are quite a few misclassified images. In the same way, the 8 and 9 rows are brighter, which tells you that the 8 and the 9 are very often mistaken for other digits. On the other hand, some rows are dark, which means that most of the images were correctly classified. One thing you should notice is that there is no symmetry in the errors; more instances of digit 5 are wrongly classified as 8 than the other way around.

By looking at the confusion matrix, you can often see ways that your classifier can be improved. For example, with this matrix, it looks like improvement is needed for classifying the 8 and the 9. You could try to get more data for the digits or you could find new features to assist the classifier. For example, you could devise an algorithm that would count closed loops – a 6 and a 9 each have one while the 8 has two and a 4 has none. You could use Pillow, scikit-Image or OpenCV for preprocessing images; this would make some of the patterns stand out better.

```
cl_a, cl_b = 3, 5

X_aa = X_train[(y_train == cl_a) & (y_train_pred == cl_a)]

X_ab = X_train[(y_train == cl_a) & (y_train_pred == cl_b)]

X_ba = X_train[(y_train == cl_b) & (y_train_pred == cl_a)]

X_bb = X_train[(y_train == cl_b) & (y_train_pred == cl_b)]

plt.figure(figsize=(8,8))

plt.subplot(221); plot_digits(X_aa[:25], images_per_row=5)

plt.subplot(222); plot_digits(X_ab[:25], images_per_row=5)

plt.subplot(223); plot_digits(X_ba[:25], images_per_row=5)

plt.subplot(224); plot_digits(X_bb[:25], images_per_row=5)

plt.show()
```

On the left of the plot, there are two blocks of 5x5 that have been wrongly classified as 3 and the two 5x5 blocks on the right show those images classified as a 5. To be fair to the classifier, many of the images it gets wrong are written so poorly that even the human eye would struggle to read them but, on the surface, most of the misclassification errors look pretty obvious and you might struggle to understand why the classifier couldn't do it. This is why we go for the SGDClassifier model; it is linear and does nothing more than assign one weight in each class to all the pixels. When a new image appears it adds the pixel intensities and provides a score. Because the digits 3 and 5 are only a couple of pixels different in size, the model confuses them. Much of this can be eradicated by preprocessing the images to center them ensuring that the digits are not rotated too much as the classifier is clearly sensitive to rotation and shifting.

Multilabel

So far, we have assigned one instance to one class but sometimes you might want each instance to have an output of several classes. Take face recognition. What would happen if your classifier recognized multiple people in a single image? It should label each of the people. Let's assume that it has been trained on three faces – Simon, Penelope, and Karen. We show the classifier an image of Simon and Penelope and the output should be [1, 1, 0] – Yes, Yes, and No. This type of classification is called 'multilabel classification'. We'll save face recognition until later; for now, here is a simple example:

```
from sklearn.neighbors import KNeighborsClassifier
```

```
y_train_large = (y_train >= 7)

y_train_odd = (y_train % 2 == 1)

y_multilabel = np.c_[y_train_large, y_train_odd]

knn_clf = KNeighborsClassifier()

knn_clf.fit(X_train, y_multilabel)
```

What we have created is an array called y_multilabel and this has got a pair of target labels for each of the digit images. The first label is an indicator of whether the image is a large one (7 upwards) and the second is an indicator of whether the digit is an odd number.

On the next line, we have created a KneighborsClassifier instance – this one has support for multilabel classification – and then we have trained it with the y_multilabel array. You the prediction can be made, and we get an output of two labels:

```
>>> knn_clf.predict([some_digit])

array([[False, True]], dtype=bool)
```

In this case, the prediction is correct – 5 is not a large number and it is an odd so False, True.

There are several ways that you can evaluate these multilabel classifiers and your project will dictate which metrics you use. You could go down the road of measuring the F1 score on each label and then work out the average. The following code will give you the average score across all the labels:

```
>>> y_train_knn_pred = cross_val_predict(knn_clf, X_train, y_train, cv=3)

>>> f1_score(y_train, y_train_knn_pred, average="macro")

0.96845540180280221
```

This is based on the assumption that every label is of equal importance, but that may not be correct. If you have more images of Penelope than you have of Karen or Simon, you might want to give more weight to the classifier score on images of Penelope. A simple way would be to provide a weight to each label, one that matches the support – for example, how many instances there are with that label. Doing this is simple; in the last piece of code where it says "average=", replace 'macro' with 'weighted'.

Multi-output

The final classification type is multi-output-multiclass classification. It is nothing more than the multiclass classification with each label having more than two potential values. To show you how this works, we'll create a system that takes the noise out of images. The input will be a noisy image and the output should be a cleaner image, with a pixel intensity array representing the image. The classifier is a multilabel classifier and each of the labels can have several values. This is a multi-output classification.

Note

Before we carry on with that, it is worth noting that there is a fine line between regression and classification. It could be argued that pixel intensity prediction is more like regression and the multi-output systems don't just do classification – you could create a system that will output several labels for each instance including value and class labels.

Now we are going to create the test and training sets. We add noise to the MNIST images using the randint() function in NumPy and the original images will be the target images:

```
noise = rnd.randint(0, 100, (len(X_train), 784))

noise = rnd.randint(0, 100, (len(X_test), 784))

X_train_mod = X_train + noise

X_test_mod = X_test + noise

y_train_mod = X_train

y_test_mod = X_test
```

Next, the classifier needs to be trained to clean the images:

```
knn_clf.fit(X_train_mod, y_train_mod)

clean_digit = knn_clf.predict([X_test_mod[some_index]])

plot_digit(clean_digit)
```

You should see a cleaned image that looks much like the target image.

That's it for classification, time to move on to the training models.

Chapter 3: The Different Training Models

So, how surprised are you at how much you can do with machine learning without knowing anything about what goes on behind the scenes? To be fair, there are many things you can do with machine learning that don't require you to know anything about the implementation, but this is not a good thing. It is always better to understand at least something about how it all works so you can choose the right model for the task, find the correct training algorithm, and use the right hyperparameters.

Knowing what's going on out of sight will also allow you to effectively debug and analyze errors more efficiently. Most of what you read in this chapter will be essential for the later chapters on neural networks - so pay attention. We are going to begin with a training model called Linear Regression. It is a very simple model and there are two ways to train it:

- Closed-form equation
- Iterative optimization

The closed-form equation is a direct approach that works out the parameters that fit the models and the training set. The second approach, iterative optimization, is also called GD, or Gradient Descent and this is used for tweaking the parameters so that, eventually, they converge with those of the first approach. We'll be discussing a few different variations of GD that we will use later in this book.

We will also be discussing Polynomial Regression. This is somewhat more complex and is used for nonlinear datasets. There are more parameters to this than with Linear Regression and, because of that, overfitting the data tends to happen more often. We'll be using the learning curve to find out whether this has happened or not, along with a number of regularization techniques that can cut down on overfitting. Overfitting is merely overgeneralization of data; in human terms, it would be like you had a bad experience with one taxi driver and then tarred all taxi drivers with the same brush. Machines can do this too.

Lastly, we will look at SoftMax Regression and Logistic Regression, two classification models.

Note

There are lots of equations here and they all use basic calculus and linear algebra notations. You do need to understand what matrices and vectors are; you need to understand transposition; the dot product; matrix inverse and partial derivatives. If you do not understand them, you need to brush up, learn what they are and then come back.

Linear Regression

In general terms, linear models predict by taking the input features, working out a weighted sum and adding a constant. This constant is known as a bias term or an intercept term and you can see this in the equation below:

$$\hat{y} = \theta_0 + \theta_1 x_1 + \theta_2 x_2 + \cdots + \theta_n x_n$$

Equation – Model Prediction – Linear Regression

- The predicted value is $\hat{y}$
- The number of features is n
- The value of the ith feature is x
- The model parameter of the jth model is θ_j and this includes the feature weights (θ_1, θ_2, etc.) and the bias term (θ_0)

As with many equations, we can use a vectorized format to write this one in a more compact way:

$$\hat{y} = h_\theta(\mathbf{x}) = \theta^T \cdot \mathbf{x}$$

Equation – Vectorized Format of The Model Prediction

- The parameter vector for the model is θ and this has the feature weights (θ_1 to θ_n) and the bias term (θ_0)
- Θ has been transposed as θ^T – this means it is now a row vector rather than a column vector
- The feature vector of the instance is x, with x_0 to x_n (x_0 always equals 1)
- θ^T and x has a dot product of $\theta^T \cdot x$
- The hypothesis function is h_θ and uses the parameter of θ

Now, how do we train a Linear Regression model? If you remember, we need to set the parameters of a model before we can train it – this is to make sure that the model and the training set are a good fit. To do this, we need to measure how well or otherwise the model fits and the commonest measure of the performance of a regression model is RMSE – Root Mean Square Error:

$$\text{RMSE}(\mathbf{X}, h) = \sqrt{\frac{1}{m} \sum_{i=1}^{m} (h(\mathbf{x}^{(i)}) - y^{(i)})^2}$$

$$\mathbf{x}^{(1)} = \begin{pmatrix} -118.29 \\ 33.91 \\ 1,416 \\ 38,372 \end{pmatrix}$$

$$y^{(1)} = 156,400$$

Equation –Root Mean Square Error

To train the model, we need to find out what value of θ will minimize RMSE. In practical terms, it is far easier to minimize MSE that it is RMSE and the result is the same – any value that can minimize a function will also minimize the square root of the function.

The next equation is what we use to calculate the MSE of the hypothesis hθ using a training set called x:

$$\text{MSE}\,(\mathbf{X}\ h_\theta) = \frac{1}{m}\sum_{i=1}^{m}(\theta^T \cdot \mathbf{x}^{(i)} - y^{(i)})^2$$

Equation – Linear Regression Model MSE Cost Function

In these equations, note that we used hθ to indicate the model is vectorized. From now on, we will drop the h and use MSE(θ) rather than MSE(X, hθ).

Closed-Form Solution – Normal Equation

If we want to find the θ value that will minimize the cost function, we can use a closed-form solution. This is an equation that directly provides the result and is called a Normal Equation:

$$\hat{\theta} = (\mathbf{X}^T \cdot \mathbf{X})^{-1} \cdot \mathbf{X}^T \cdot \mathbf{y}$$

Equation - Normal Equation

- The cost function is minimized with value θ
- The target value y contains y(1) to y(m)

Time to test the equation by generating a bit of data:

```
import numpy as np

X = 2 * np.random.rand(100, 1)

y = 4 + 3 * X + np.random.randn(100, 1)
```

Now we need to work out the Norma Equation and we'll do this using a function called inv() that can be found in the NumPy Linear Algebra module. This will work out the matrix inverse, and we will use the dot(o method for the purposes of matrix multiplication:

```
X_b = np.c_[np.ones((100, 1)), X] # add x0 = 1 to each instance

theta_best = np.linalg.inv(X_b.T.dot(X_b)).dot(X_b.T).dot(y)
```

The result of that equation:

```
>>> theta_best

array([[ 4.21509616],

[ 2.77011339]])
```

Because of the noise, although the result was close, it wasn't close enough because the noise smothered the exact parameters in the original function.

You could use the following to make predictions:

```
>>> X_new = np.array([[0], [2]])

>>> X_new_b = np.c_[np.ones((2, 1)), X_new] # add x0 = 1 to each
instance

>>> y_predict = X_new_b.dot(theta_best)

>>> y_predict

array([[ 4.21509616],

[ 9.75532293]])
```

Plotting the predictions would look like this:

```
plt.plot(X_new, y_predict, "r-")

plt.plot(X, y, "b.")
```

```
plt.axis([0, 2, 0, 15])

plt.show()
```

The code in scikit-learn would look like this:

```
>>> from sklearn.linear_model import LinearRegression

>>> lin_reg = LinearRegression()

>>> lin_reg.fit(X, y)

>>> lin_reg.intercept_, lin_reg.coef_

(array([ 4.21509616]), array([[ 2.77011339]]))

>>> lin_reg.predict(X_new)

array([[ 4.21509616],

[ 9.75532293]])
```

Computational Complexity

With the Normal Equation, we can take X T. X and work out its inverse. This is an n x n matrix and the computational complexity involved in inverting a matrix like this is about O(n 2.4) to O(n 3), although that will depend on the implementation. Put simply, double the number of features and the computation time is multiplied by approximately 22.4 = 5.3 to 23 =8.

If you have too many features, the Normal Equation slows down but, on the upside, the Normal Equation is linear in terms of how many instances there are in the training set. Because of that, it can easily handle larger training sets with good efficiency as long as they fit in the memory. When the Linear Regression model has been trained, it will be quick at making predictions. Computational complexity refers to both the number of features and how many instances there are for predictions to be made. Simply, it will take twice as much time to make predictions on twice the number of features.

Let's look at another way of training Linear Regression models, a way that is better used on problems where there are a significant number of features or there are too many instances and they won't fit in the memory.

Gradient Descent

This is one of the generic algorithms used to find the optimal solution for a broad range of tasks. The idea behind it is that it will iteratively tweak parameters to change the minimized cost function. It does this by looking at the error function, measuring the local gradient, using θ, which is the parameter vector, and it heads the same way that the gradient is descending in. Once it reaches zero, you are at the minimum.

We start by putting a load of random values into θ, a practice known as random initialization. Then slowly we improve it, one small step at a time, each time trying to minimize the cost function. Eventually, the algorithm will converge to the minimum.

One of the most important parameters is how the steps are sized and the learning rate parameter is what determines this. Too small and the algorithm needs to go through multiple iterations – very time-consuming. Too high and you could end up in a higher position than when you started. The algorithm could end up diverging with the values getting increasingly bigger and still not finding the right solution.

Lastly, cost functions don't all look the same and convergence isn't always very easy. Thankfully, with the Linear Regression model, the MSE cost function is a convex function – choose two points, anywhere you like, on the curve and the joining line segment will not cross the curve. By this, we can deduce that there aren't any local minima, simply one global minimum. We also have a continuous function whose slope does not ever abruptly change. There is a consequence to this – one guarantee with Gradient Descent is that it will approach very close to the global minimum, so long as you are prepared to wait, and you don't have a high learning rate.

The shape of the cost function can be likened to a bowl but not necessarily a standard bowl – if none of the features have the same scales, it could be elongated. Let's say that we use the Gradient Descent on two training sets – one where features a and b have the same scale and one contains smaller values than b. On the first set, the algorithm would go straight to the global minimum and get there very quickly whereas, on the second set, the direction would be almost a right angle to the global minimum direction and it would finish with a long descent down to the flat. It will get to the global minimum but it won't be very quick.

Note

When you use Gradient Descent, all the features should have scales that are much the same or convergence time will take much longer.

When it comes to training the model, you also need to find the right combination of parameters that will minimize the cost function. You are searching in the parameter space of the model and, the more parameters there are, the more dimensions in this space; this results in a harder search. Luckily, in the Linear Regression model, we have a convex cost function, and this makes the search easier.

Batch Gradient Descent

Implementing Gradient Descent requires you to work out what the cost function gradient regarding each parameter θj. Put another way, if we change θj even a little, we need to work out how the cost function will change and by how much. We call this partial derivative and the equation below shows the cost function partial derivative in relation to the θj parameter.

$$\frac{\partial}{\partial \theta_j} \text{MSE}(\theta) = \frac{2}{m} \sum_{i=1}^{m} (\theta^T \cdot x^{(i)} - y^{(i)}) x_j^{(i)}$$

$$\nabla_\theta \text{MSE}(\theta) = \begin{pmatrix} \frac{\partial}{\partial \theta_0} \text{MSE}(\theta) \\ \frac{\partial}{\partial \theta_1} \text{MSE}(\theta) \\ \vdots \\ \frac{\partial}{\partial \theta_n} \text{MSE}(\theta) \end{pmatrix} = \frac{2}{m} X^T \cdot (X \cdot \theta - y)$$

However, instead of doing them one at a time, you could do them all together:

The gradient vector ($\nabla_\theta \text{MSE}(\theta)$) has got all the cost function partial derivatives - one for each of the parameters.

Note

This formula is making calculations over the entire set at every step of the Gradient Descent. This is why it is called Batch Gradient Descent because the entire batch of data is used at every step. This makes it very slow on large datasets, but it does scale well with the numbers of features. It is much faster to train a Linear Regression model on thousands of features with Gradient Descent than it is to use Normal Equation.

When we have the vector, which you will find is pointing uphill, all you do is go in the opposite direction. To do this, we subtract $\nabla_\theta \text{MSE}(\theta)$ from θ, using the learning rate of η. Take the gradient vector and work out what size the downhill step should be:

$$\theta^{(\text{next step})} = \theta - \eta \nabla_\theta \text{MSE}(\theta)$$

Here's how this algorithm is implemented:

```
eta = 0.1 # learning rate

n_iterations = 1000

m = 100

theta = np.random.randn(2,1) # random initialization

for iteration in range(n_iterations):

gradients = 2/m * X_b.T.dot(X_b.dot(theta) - y)

theta = theta - eta * gradients
```

The theta that results from this is:

```
>>> theta

array([[ 4.21509616],

[ 2.77011339]])
```

This is the exact same result that we got with Normal Equation.

To find the best learning rate, a grid search can be used but you might want to think about limiting how many iterations there are – the grid search needs to get rid of those models that take a long time to converge. But how do we set how many iterations we need? Too low and you won't be anywhere near the best solution when the algorithm comes to a stop; too high and we waste a lot of time while there are no more changes being made to the parameters. The easiest solution is to set a high iteration number but have the algorithm interrupted when the gradient vector norm reaches a number that is smaller than tiny – this will happen when the Gradient Descent is almost at the minimum.

Stochastic Gradient Descent

Batch Gradient Descent has one problem – it uses the entire training data at every step to work out the gradients and this slows it down considerably with large datasets. Stochastic Gradient Descent is the opposite end of the spectrum – it takes one instance, completely random, from each instance at each step and the gradients are worked out using that random instance. This does speed up the algorithm because there isn't much data to be manipulated at each iteration and it also means it is possible to use it on large datasets because there only needs to be a single instance in memory for each iteration.

However, the stochastic, or random, nature of the algorithm means that it is not as regular as the Batch Gradient Descent; rather than descending in gentle steps until the minimum is reached, we get a bouncing cost function that only decreases on average. Yes, it will get to near the cost minimum, but it will take time and it will carry on bouncing when it gets there; it won't settle. So, when the algorithm has stopped, the values of the parameters are ok but not great.

Having an irregular function can be helpful in getting the algorithm out of the local minima. In this case, Stochastic Gradient Descent is better for finding global minimums than Batch Gradient Descent.

So being random can help to get out of local optima but not good because the algorithm never settles. There is a solution and it's called simulated annealing. This reduces the learning rate slowly, so we start with large steps, thus speeding things up, and end with smaller steps so the algorithm can settle. It's called annealing because it is very much like the metallurgy process of annealing – when molten metal cools slowly.

The learning schedule function is used for determining the learning rate for every iteration; reduce it too fast and you could get stuck at the local minimum or halfway to it; too slow and you end up bouncing around and the result is a less than optimal solution.

The following code uses a simple learning schedule function to implement Stochastic Gradient Descent:

```
n_epochs = 50

t0, t1 = 5, 50 # learning schedule hyperparameters

def learning_schedule(t):

return t0 / (t + t1)

theta = np.random.randn(2,1) # random initialization

for epoch in range(n_epochs):

for i in range(m):

random_index = np.random.randint(m)

xi = X_b[random_index:random_index+1]

yi = y[random_index:random_index+1]

gradients = 2 * xi.T.dot(xi.dot(theta) - yi)

eta = learning_schedule(epoch * m + i)

theta = theta - eta * gradients
```

Convention dictates that rounds of m iterations, each one called an epoch, are done. The Batch Gradient Descent code went through 1,000 iterations of the dataset but this one only does 50 iterations and we still arrive at a decent solution:

```
>>> theta

array([[ 4.21076011],

[ 2.74856079]])
```

Be aware that, because the instances are randomly chosen, some may be chosen multiple times while others won't be chosen at all. If you want to be sure that the algorithm is iterating through all instances at every epoch, you need to shuffle the data and then iterate one instance at a time; shuffle and repeat. This results in slower convergence, however.

If you wanted to use SGD and scikit-learn to do the Linear Regression, you would use a class called SGDRegressor. This will default to providing an error cost function squared. The next piece of code will iterate 50 times or do 50 epochs, beginning with (eta0=0.1)learning rate and using the default class learning schedule. O regularization is used either:

```
from sklearn.linear_model import SGDRegressor

sgd_reg = SGDRegressor(n_iter=50, penalty=None, eta0=0.1)

sgd_reg.fit(X, y.ravel())
```

Again, we get an answer that is much like the solution Normal Equation returns:

```
>>> sgd_reg.intercept_, sgd_reg.coef_

(array([ 4.18380366]), array([ 2.74205299]))
```

Mini-batch Gradient Descent

This is the final Gradient Descent algorithm and it is easy to grasp once you understand the Batch and the Stochastic Gradients. Simply put, rather than using the entire training set or a single instance, mini-batch will work out the gradients using mini-batches of random instances. It will do this at each step and the biggest advantage is for those who use their GPUs for machine learning – you get a boost in performance through hard optimization when doing matrix operations.

The algorithm is also less erratic when it progresses through parameter space and it does get a bit closer to the minimum. However, it might not be able to get out of local minima quite so easily.

Polynomial Regression

What if you were using more complex data and not just a straight line? You might be surprised to learn that you can fit nonlinear data to a linear model and the easiest way to do this is to take the powers of each feature, add them as new features, and then train up a linear model on the extended features. We call this Polynomial Regression.

Before we go any further, we'll generate data. It is nonlinear data based on a quadratic equation with a little noise added for good measure.

```
m = 100

X = 6 * np.random.rand(m, 1) - 3

y = 0.5 * X**2 + X + 2 + np.random.randn(m, 1)
```

There is no way that a straight line is going to fit this, so we'll use the PolynomialFeatures class in scikit-learn. This will transform the data and add the 2nd-degree polynomial (the square) of each of the features as a new feature:

```
>>> from sklearn.preprocessing import PolynomialFeatures

>>> poly_features = PolynomialFeatures(degree=2, include_bias=False)

>>> X_poly = poly_features.fit_transform(X)

>>> X[0]

array([-0.75275929])

>>> X_poly[0]

array([-0.75275929, 0.56664654])
```

As you can see, X-Poly has now got the original X feature and the square of it; the result is a Linear Regression model that will now fit the data:

```
>>> lin_reg = LinearRegression()

>>> lin_reg.fit(X_poly, y)

>>> lin_reg.intercept_, lin_reg.coef_

(array([ 1.78134581]), array([[ 0.93366893, 0.56456263]]))
```

Note

We only had the one feature here but, when multiple features are used, Polynomial Regression can seek out any relationships between the features – a normal Linear Regression model cannot do this. Polynomial Regression can do it because the PolynomialFeatures class will add every combination of the features up to the degree provided. For example, if you have 2 features called a and b and you set PolynomialFeatures with degree=3, the class will add a2, b2, a3, and b3 but it will also add in the other combinations of ab, ab 2 and a2b.

Learning Curves

If you use Polynomial Regression with a high degree, the data will fit better than it would with standard Linear Regression. Let's say that you use the preceding training data and apply a polynomial model with a 300-degree to it. Do the same with a linear model and with a quadratic model and compare the results. You would see that the polynomial model moves around quite a bit to get as close as it can to the instances in the training set.

However, the model overfits the data quite badly but the linear model underfits it, so in this example, the quadratic model would be better. This does make sense because a quadratic model was used to generate the training data but, generally, you will not know what function was used – unless you generate your own dataset, of course – so how are you supposed to know whether your model fits the data properly, whether it is too simple or too complex?

Earlier, we used cross-validation to estimate the generalization performance of a model. If a model performs as it should on training data but doesn't generalize very well as per the metrics from the cross-validation, your model is overfitting the data. If it doesn't perform well on either, it is underfitting the data. This is just one way of knowing whether your model is too complex or too simple.

You could also take a look at the learning curves. A learning curve is a plot that shows the performance of a model, as function of the dataset size, on training data and the validation data. Generating these plots is easy; all you do is train up the model multiple times on data subsets that are all different sizes. The next example will define the function used for plotting these learning curves – this is for a model that has been provided with some data:

```python
from sklearn.metrics import mean_squared_error

from sklearn.model_selection import train_test_split

def plot_learning_curves(model, X, y):

X_train, X_val, y_train, y_val = train_test_split(X, y,
test_size=0.2)

train_errors, val_errors = [], []

for m in range(1, len(X_train)):

model.fit(X_train[:m], y_train[:m])

y_train_predict = model.predict(X_train[:m])

y_val_predict = model.predict(X_val)

train_errors.append(mean_squared_error(y_train_predict, y_train[:m]))

val_errors.append(mean_squared_error(y_val_predict, y_val))
```

```
plt.plot(np.sqrt(train_errors), "r-+", linewidth=2, label="train")

plt.plot(np.sqrt(val_errors), "b-", linewidth=3, label="val")
```

Using a Linear Regression model, the learning curves would be:

```
lin_reg = LinearRegression()

plot_learning_curves(lin_reg, X, y)
```

You probably want an explanation of this. Look at the model's performance on the training dataset – if there are only a couple of instances there, the model fits them like a glove, hence the curve beginning at zero. Add some new instances and things get noisy and stops the model from fitting the data properly – not only is it noisy, it isn't linear. The error shown on the training set will continue rising until it gets to a plateau – at this point, new instances won't affect the average error.

If you look at the way the model performs on the validation data, you will see that, with a few instances, the model can't generalize correctly so the initial validation error is large. Give it more examples and it will begin to learn, gradually reducing the error average. Again, we cannot use a straight line for data modeling, so we still reach that plateau.

Both of these curves show underfitting – both reach a plateau, fairly high up and close together. However, it should be noted that when a model underfits, adding more examples isn't going to help. You either need better features or another model.

The following code produces the learning curves for a polynomial model using the date data but with a 10th-degree:

```
from sklearn.pipeline import Pipeline

polynomial_regression = Pipeline((

("poly_features", PolynomialFeatures(degree=10, include_bias=False)),

("sgd_reg", LinearRegression()),

))

plot_learning_curves(polynomial_regression, X, y)
```

These curves look a little like the last ones but note two differences:

The training data error is lower than the Linear Regression error.

Note the gap in between the curves. This show that the model is performing much better on training than it is on validation. What does this show? The model is overfitting. Use a bigger training dataset and the curves would move nearer to one another.

You could improve the model by providing more data until the validation and training errors are level.

Tradeoffs – Bias/Variance

One vital theoretical statistical result of machine learning is that the generalization error of a model is expressed as a sum of three errors, each very different:

Bias

This is down to incorrect assumptions, like assuming that you are using linear data when it is quadratic. Models with a high bias are the most likely candidates for underfitting

Variance

This is down to excess sensitivity to minor data variations. A model that has a lot of freedom, like the high-degree polynomials, will tend to have a high-level of variance and most likely to overfit the data.

Irreducible Error

This is down to noisy data and the only way the error can be reduced is by cleaning the data – fixing broken sensors, removing outliers, etc.

The more complex a model is, the higher the variance, and the lower the bias. On the other hand, if you reduce the complexity, you increase bias and reduce variance and that is why we call it a tradeoff.

Regularized Linear Models

We know that one way to cut down on overfitting is by regularizing or constraining a model – the less freedom it has, the less chance of overfitting. With the polynomial model, for example, you would simply cut down on the number of degrees.

With linear models, we tend to regularize them by curbing the model's weights. There are three ways that we can do this:

- Ridge Regression
- Lasso Regression
- Elastic Net

We'll look at each of them in turn.

Ridge Regression

Also known as Tikhonov Regularization, Ridge Regression is a version of Linear Regression that has been regularized. To do this, we simply add a regularization term to the cost function.

The algorithm is forced to fit the data while maintaining weights that are as small as possible. This term should only be added for training purposes and not for validation.

The cost function is quite often different between the training and validation models. Not only is this for regularization, it is important that cost functions are easy to optimize in the training set but as near to the end objective as possible in the validation set. An example of this would be a classifier that has been trained using a log loss function and evaluated with Precision/Recall.

The hyperparameter called a is used for determining how the model is regularized, for example, where a = 0, the Ridge Regression is purely a Linear but if a = a large number, the weights would be all be near to zero and you would have a flat line through the mean of the data.

$$J(\theta) = \text{MSE}(\theta) + \alpha \frac{1}{2} \sum_{i=1}^{n} \theta_i^2$$

Equation – Ridge Regression

Ridge Regression can be done using Gradient Descent or closed-for equation. Both are the same and the following equation shows you the closed-form version:

$$\hat{\theta} = (X^T \cdot X + \alpha A)^{-1} \cdot X^T \cdot y$$

Equation – Closed-Form Ridge Regression

Now we look at how to use scikit-learn to do the Ridge Regression, using a variation of the closed-form equation:

```
>>> from sklearn.linear_model import Ridge
>>> ridge_reg = Ridge(alpha=1, solver="cholesky")
>>> ridge_reg.fit(X, y)
>>> ridge_reg.predict([[1.5]])
array([[ 1.55071465]])
```

And again with Stochastic Gradient Descent:

```
>>> sgd_reg = SGDRegressor(penalty="l2")

>>> sgd_reg.fit(X, y.ravel())

>>> sgd_reg.predict([[1.5]])

array([[ 1.13500145]])
```

Lasso Regression

Lasso stands for Least Aggressive Shrinkage and Selection Operator and this kind of regression is just another regularized Linear Regression. A regularization term is added to the cost function but, instead of using half the l2 norm squared, it uses the weight vector's l1 norm as you can see in the following equation:

$$J(\theta) = \text{MSE}(\theta) + \alpha \sum_{i=1}^{n} | \theta_i |$$

Equation - Lasso Regression Cost Function

Lasso Regression will remove all the weights from the features that are the least important by setting them to zero. In short, it carries out feature selection automatically and outputs what is known as a sparse model.

It is worth noting that the BGD path of the Lasso cost function bounces around to the end because there is an abrupt change in the slope at $\theta_2=0$. To ensure that convergence happens at the global minimum, the learning rate must be gradually reduced.

When you use $\theta_i=0$ (for i = 1, 2, 3, ...n) the cost function is not differentiable. However, if you use the g15 subgradient vector when $\theta_i=0$, Gradient Descent will work. The next equation shows an example of this:

$$g(\theta, J) = \nabla_\theta \text{MSE}(\theta) + \alpha \begin{pmatrix} \text{sign}(\theta_1) \\ \text{sign}(\theta_2) \\ \vdots \\ \text{sign}(\theta_n) \end{pmatrix} \quad \text{where} \quad \text{sign}(\theta_i) = \begin{cases} -1 & \text{if } \theta_i < 0 \\ 0 & \text{if } \theta_i = 0 \\ +1 & \text{if } \theta_i > 0 \end{cases}$$

Here is an example that uses the Lasso class from scikit-learn:

```
>>> from sklearn.linear_model import Lasso
```

```
>>> lasso_reg = Lasso(alpha=0.1)

>>> lasso_reg.fit(X, y)

>>> lasso_reg.predict([[1.5]])

array([ 1.53788174])
```

Elastic Net

The Elastic Net regularization term is a combination of both Ridge and Lasso Regression terms and the mix ratio can be better controlled. When r=0, Elastic Net is the same as Ridge Regression and when r=1 it is the same as Lasso. The next equation is the Elastic Net Cost Function:

$$J(\theta) = \text{MSE}(\theta) + r\alpha \sum_{i=1}^{n} |\theta_i| + \frac{1-r}{2}\alpha \sum_{i=1}^{n} \theta_i^2$$

Equation – Elastic Net Cost Function

So now the question arises – when do you use each of these? Mostly, some regularization is preferable so Linear Regression shouldn't be used in those cases. Ridge Regression is perhaps the best unless you think that there are only a handful of useful features, in which case you would choose Elastic or Lasso – both reduce the weights of useless features to zero. Elastic Net is better than Lasso because the latter may not behave when there are more features than training instances or there is a correlation between several features.

This next example shows ElasticNet from scikit-learn:

```
>>> from sklearn.linear_model import ElasticNet

>>> elastic_net = ElasticNet(alpha=0.1, l1_ratio=0.5)

>>> elastic_net.fit(X, y)

>>> elastic_net.predict([[1.5]])

array([ 1.54333232])
```

Early Stopping

If you wanted to regularize an iterative algorithm, like Gradient Descent, a good way is to cease training the minute the validation error is at a minimum. We call this Early Stopping. If you think about Batch Gradient Descent, after each epoch, the algorithm learns a little more and the prediction error starts to decrease on both training and validation sets. However, the validation error will stop going down and begin rising again, an indicator that overfitting is happening. Using Early Stopping, the training is stopped when the error gets to the minimum.

Do note that the curves are less smooth with mini-batch and Stochastic Gradient Descent and it might not be so easy to determine when the minimum is reached. You could stop when the validation error has been over the minimum for a while because you know the model won't improve and then roll the parameters back to where the minimum was reached.

Let's look at a simple Early Stopping implementation:

```python
from sklearn.base import clone

sgd_reg = SGDRegressor(n_iter=1, warm_start=True, penalty=None,

learning_rate="constant", eta0=0.0005)

minimum_val_error = float("inf")

best_epoch = None

best_model = None

for epoch in range(1000):

sgd_reg.fit(X_train_poly_scaled, y_train) # continues where it left off

y_val_predict = sgd_reg.predict(X_val_poly_scaled)

val_error = mean_squared_error(y_val_predict, y_val)

if val_error < minimum_val_error:

minimum_val_error = val_error

best_epoch = epoch

best_model = clone(sgd_reg)
```

Logistic Regression

We can use regression algorithms for the purpose of classification and classification algorithms for regression. One of the commonly used is Logistic Regression, used for estimating how probable it is that a specific instance should be in a specific class. If the estimation is more than 50% the prediction is made that the instance should be in that class; less than 50% and it should be in that class. Look familiar? Logistic Regression is a binary classifier.

Probability Estimation

In much the same way that the Linear Regression works, the Logistic Regression works out a sum weighted from the input features with a bias term added. Rather than a direct output of the result though, we get the logistic result instead - see the next equation:

$$\hat{p} = h_\theta(\mathbf{x}) = \sigma(\theta^T \cdot \mathbf{x})$$

Equation – Vectorized Form of Logistic Regression Model Estimated Probability

The Logistic is a Sigmoid function, shaped like an S and the output is a number from 0 to 1. You can see the definition of this in the next equation, showing the logistic function:

$$\sigma(t) = \frac{1}{1 + \exp(-t)}$$

Equation - Logistic Function

And the next one shows the model prediction of Logistic Regression:

$$\hat{y} = \begin{cases} 0 & \text{if } \hat{p} < 0.5, \\ 1 & \text{if } \hat{p} \geq 0.5. \end{cases}$$

Equation - Logistic Regression Model Prediction

Training and Cost Function

So, we know how the probability estimation is done and how the Logistic Regression model makes its predictions but what about training it? When you train a model, the objective is to set the θ parameter vector in such a way that high probabilities are estimated for the positive instances and low ones for the negative. The next equation shows this idea for one training instance:

$$c(\theta) = \begin{cases} -\log(\hat{p}) & \text{if } y = 1, \\ -\log(1 - \hat{p}) & \text{if } y = 0. \end{cases}$$

Equation - Cost Function for One Training Instance

Now, this makes sense. When t gets close to 0, the -log(t) will get big; the result is a large cost if the model has given a probability estimation for a positive instance near to 0. It will also be big if near to 1 is estimated for the negative instance. However, when t is near to 1, -log(t) is near to 0 which means the cost will be near to 0 should the probability be near to 0 for negative or near to 1 for positive – this is exactly what we are looking for.

The cost function for the training set is nothing more than the average cost over all instances and it can be defined in one expression known as log loss, as the next equation shows you:

$$J(\theta) = -\frac{1}{m} \sum_{i=1}^{m} [y^{(i)} \log(\hat{p}^{(i)}) + (1 - y^{(i)}) \log(1 - \hat{p}^{(i)})]$$

Equation – Log Loss

However, we do not have a closed-form equation to work out the θ value to minimize the function. But, as this is a convex cost function, we can use an optimization algorithm, such as Gradient Descent, to locate the global minimum – so long as you don't have a large learning curve and you have time to kill. The next equation shows the partial derivative regarding the jth parameter of the cost function:

$$\frac{\partial}{\partial \theta_j} J(\theta) = \frac{1}{m} \sum_{i=1}^{m} (\sigma(\theta^T \cdot x^{(i)}) - y^{(i)}) x_j^{(i)}$$

Equation - Logistic Cost Function Partial Derivatives

As you can see, a prediction error is computed for each instance and then multiplied by the feature value for the jth parameter. The average over all the instances is then computed. When the gradient vector has all the partial derivatives in it, it can be used in the algorithm for Batch Gradient Descent.

Decision Boundaries

To show you Logistic Regression, we'll take the world-famous Iris dataset and build a classifier that will detect one of the three types of iris species based on the width of the petals. The dataset contains details of three different species – Setosa, Virginica and Versicolor, along with the length and width of the sepals and petals of more than 150 varieties. We're going to detect Virginica and we start by loading the data:

```
>>> from sklearn import datasets

>>> iris = datasets.load_iris()

>>> list(iris.keys())

['data', 'target_names', 'feature_names', 'target', 'DESCR']

>>> X = iris["data"][:, 3:] # petal width

>>> y = (iris["target"] == 2).astype(np.int) # 1 if Iris-Virginica,
else 0
```

Now let's train a Logistic Regression model:

```
from sklearn.linear_model import LogisticRegression

log_reg = LogisticRegression()

log_reg.fit(X, y)
```

The probabilities estimated for those flowers that have a petal width between 0 and 3cm:

```
X_new = np.linspace(0, 3, 1000).reshape(-1, 1)

y_proba = log_reg.predict_proba(X_new)

plt.plot(X_new, y_proba[:, 1], "g-", label="Iris-Virginica")

plt.plot(X_new, y_proba[:, 0], "b--", label="Not Iris-Virginica")

# + a bit more Matplotlib code to make the image look nicer
```

So, the petal width of the Virginica species is between 1.4cm and 2.5cm' the other two species have smaller petals. Above the size of 2cm the classifier is very confident that the flower is the Virginica species, and under 1cm the classifier is confident it isn't that species. In between 1 and 2 cm, the classifier isn't too confident, but if you use the predict() method and not the predict_proba() method, the predictions will return as the most likely class. What this tells us is that, at about 1.6cm, we have a decision boundary – both of the probabilities are even. If the width is 1.6cm or over, we get a prediction of Virginica; below that and we get a prediction that it isn't Virginica, albeit not a confident prediction:

```
>>> log_reg.predict([[1.7], [1.5]])

array([1, 0])
```

You can use the l1 and l2 penalties to regularize the models for Logistic Regression although, by default, the l2 penalty is added by scikit-learn.

SoftMax Regression

We can generalize the Logistic Regression model so it directly supports multiple classes without the need to train it and combine several binary classifiers. This is known as SoftMax Regression or sometimes known as Multinomial Logistic Regression. It really is quite simple – give the SoftMax model an instance and it will work out a score for each of the classes before applying the SoftMax function to each score to estimate a probability for each class. The equation below should look familiar as it is similar to that of Linear Regression Prediction:

$$s_k(\mathbf{x}) = \theta_k^T \cdot \mathbf{x}$$

Equation - Softmax Score for Class K

Each of the classes has its own θk parameter vector and these are all stored in a parameter matrix in rows. Once the score has been worked out for each class for the given instance, the probability exponentials can be estimated.

Have a look at the next equation, which shows you the exponential of each score being computer and then normalized through the division of the sum of the exponentials:

$$\hat{p}_k = \sigma(\mathbf{s}(\mathbf{x}))_k = \frac{\exp\left(s_k(\mathbf{x})\right)}{\sum_{j=1}^{K} \exp\left(s_j(\mathbf{x})\right)}$$

Equation - Softmax Function

Breaking this equation down:

- The number of classes is indicated by k
- The vector, s(x) has got all the scores of all the classes for the given instance, x

- The estimated probability of x belonging to k, given the individual class scores for the instance is σ(s(x)) k

Similar to the classifier for Logistic Regression, the SoftMax classifier will make a prediction of the class that has the highest score, as you will see in the next equation:

$$\hat{y} = \underset{k}{argmax}\ \sigma(s(x))_k = \underset{k}{argmax}\ s_k(x) = \underset{k}{argmax}\ \left(\theta_k^T \cdot x\right)$$

Equation - Softmax Regression Classifier Prediction

The value returned by the argmax operator is that of a variable that will maximize a function.

The classifier for the SoftMax Regression will only predict a single class at a time – it is, after all, not a multi-output classifier. As such, you should only use it with classes that are mutually exclusive, for example, different plant types, and not for identifying several people in an image.

Now we know how probabilities are estimated and predictions made, we'll have a look at training briefly. The objective of the training is to come up with a model that will estimate low probabilities for all classes except the target class, which will be high-probability. The next equation shows you the Cost Entropy cost function and this should achieve the objective we want because the model is penalized when a low probability is offered for a target class.

$$J(\Theta) = -\frac{1}{m}\sum_{i=1}^{m}\sum_{k=1}^{K} y_k^{(i)} \log\left(\hat{p}_k^{(i)}\right)$$

Equation - Cross Entropy Cost Function

Provided the ith instance of the target class is k, then y_k is the same as 1. If not, it is the same as 0. Where k has two classes, the above cost function would be equivalent to the log loss cost function for Logistic Regression.

Cross Entropy

To see where cross entropy originated, you would need to look at information theory. Let's suppose that you wanted an efficient way of transmitting weather information every day. You have eight options, such as rainy, sunny, thunderstorms, snow, etc. and each of the options could be encoded using 3 bits – 23 is equal to 8. However, if you thought that the weather would be sunny almost every day, a more efficient way of coding it would be to have the 'sunny' option on a single bit of 0 and the rest of the options would be 4 bits, beginning at 1. With cross entropy, the average number of bits that are sent per option can be measured. If you make the correct assumption about what the weather will be, cross entropy will be equal to the weather entropy, i.e. the fact that it is not predictable. But if you get it wrong, cross entropy will be bigger by a number called the Kullback-Leibler Divergence.

Taking p and q and probability distributions, we can see the definition of the cross entropy between them as:

```
H(p, q) = - Σxp(x) log q(x)
```

The next equation shows the gradient vector of the function in respect of Θk:

$$\nabla_{\theta_k} J(\Theta) = \frac{1}{m} \sum_{i=1}^{m} (\hat{p}_k^{(i)} - y_k^{(i)}) x^{(i)}$$

Equation - Cross Entropy Gradient Vector For Class K

Now that you know how to work out the gradient vector of every class, you can locate the parameter matrix, Θ by using an optimization algorithm like Gradient Descent.

To end this chapter, we'll classify the Iris dataset into the three classes using SoftMax Regression. Logistic Regression defaults to OvA when it is trained on two or more classes but the hyperparameter multi_class can easily be set to multinomial, so it changes to SoftMax Regression.

It is also important that the solver specified has support for SoftMax Regression, something like 'lbfgs' solver. It will also apply, by default, l2 regularization and this is controlled using the C hyperparameter.

```
X = iris["data"][:, (2, 3)] # petal length, petal width

y = iris["target"]

softmax_reg =
LogisticRegression(multi_class="multinomial",solver="lbfgs", C=10)

softmax_reg.fit(X, y)
```

Chapter 4: Support Vector Machines

The SVM or Support Vector Machine is one of the most powerful of all the Machine Learning models as well as being the most versatile. With an SVM, you can do linear classification, nonlinear, regression and you can even do outlier detection. It is an incredibly popular model and if you are genuinely interested in learning about Machine Learning, you need to know how to use it. Generally, SM is used for small to medium complex datasets and in this chapter, we will look at how to use the core concepts of the SVM.

SVM – Linear Classification

An SVM classifier can be used to fit the widest possible track in between classes and we call this a large margin classification. This is useful when other linear classifiers cannot separate the classes, or the decision boundaries are not clearly marked, and the models can't perform as they should do. SVM classifiers separate the classes while staying as far from the nearest training instance as it can.

If you were to add more training instances, the decision boundary would not be affected in the slightest – the decision is made using the instances that are located to the edge of the track and these are called Support Vectors.

Soft Margin Classification

If we were to impose a strict rule that all the instances should be to the right side of the plot and off the track, it would be called Hard Margin Classification, but this has two issues. The first is that it will work only on linearly separable data and the second is that it is very sensitive to the outliers. Generally, you would struggle to find a hard margin if outliers are present and the decision boundary will not be what you expect it to be.

Avoiding these issues is a case of using a model that is a little more flexible. What you want to achieve is a balance between keeping that track as big as possible and keeping margin violations to a minimum – these are the instances that wind up on the wrong side of the track or in the middle of it. That model is called Soft Margin Classification.

Scikit-learn has its own SVM classes and in these, you can use the C hyperparameter to control the balance. A c value that is smaller will lead to a wider track, but you will get more margin violations. With a high c value, you get fewer of the margin violations, but you also get a much smaller margin. The smaller c value is likely to generalize much better and make fewer errors in prediction. So, if you find your SVM model starts overfitting, reduce the C hyperparameter to try to regularize it.

In the following code from scikit-learn, we are loading the Iris dataset, then we will scale the features and train up a linear SVM model. We'll do this with LinearSVC class where C = 0.1 and we will use the hinge loss function, which we will talk about later, to try to detect the Virginica species:

```python
import numpy as np

from sklearn import datasets

from sklearn.pipeline import Pipeline

from sklearn.preprocessing import StandardScaler

from sklearn.svm import LinearSVC

iris = datasets.load_iris()

X = iris["data"][:, (2, 3)] # petal length, petal width

y = (iris["target"] == 2).astype(np.float64) # Iris-Virginica

svm_clf = Pipeline((

("scaler", StandardScaler()),

("linear_svc", LinearSVC(C=1, loss="hinge")),

))

svm_clf.fit(X_scaled, y)
```

That model can then be used for making predictions:

```python
>>> svm_clf.predict([[5.5, 1.7]])

array([ 1.])
```

Be aware that SVM classifier will not output probabilities for each individual class like the Logistic Regression Classifiers do.

You could, if you wanted, make use of the SVC class, with SVC(kernel='linear', C=1) but this will be significantly slower, especially where you are using large datasets for training, so it really isn't recommended. There is another option – the SGDClassifier class, using SGDClassifier(loss= "hinge", alpha=1/(m*C)). This will train a linear SVM classifier using Stochastic Gradient Descent, but convergence doesn't happen as quickly as the LinearSVC class. However, this method can be useful for when you need to handle massive datasets that won't fit in the memory or when you have an online classification that needs handling.

Nonlinear SVM Classification

Linear SVM classifiers work very well for many tasks and they are quite efficient. However, not all datasets are anywhere near to being linearly separable; so, where you have nonlinear datasets, you can add extra features, like polynomials. Sometimes, the result will be a database that is linearly separable. For example, if you have a dataset that has a single feature it isn't linearly separable; add another and it is.

To do this in scikit-learn, we use pipelines. We need to create one that has a Polynomial Features transformer, a standard scaler and then a linear SVC. We'll test this on another dataset called Moons:

```
from sklearn.datasets import make_moons

from sklearn.pipeline import Pipeline

from sklearn.preprocessing import PolynomialFeatures

polynomial_svm_clf = Pipeline((

("poly_features", PolynomialFeatures(degree=3)),

("scaler", StandardScaler()),

("svm_clf", LinearSVC(C=10, loss="hinge"))

))

polynomial_svm_clf.fit(X, y)
```

Polynomial Kernel

It is very easy to implement the addition of polynomial features and this works very well with many different algorithms. However, at a low degree, it will not work well with datasets that are complex and, at a high degree, you get a vast amount of features which just slows the model down.

Thankfully, when we use an SVM, we can apply a kernel trick, a magical mathematical technique. This kernel trick allows you to get the exact same result as you would get if you added multiple polynomial features, even if they were high-degree features without needing to actually add them. This way you don't get the feature explosion. We use the SVC class to implement this trick and we're going to try it on the Moons dataset:

```
from sklearn.svm import SVC

poly_kernel_svm_clf = Pipeline((

("scaler", StandardScaler()),

("svm_clf", SVC(kernel="poly", degree=3, coef0=1, C=5))

))

poly_kernel_svm_clf.fit(X, y)
```

This piece of code will use a third-degree polynomial kernel to train the SVM classifier. If you find your model is overfitting, you can try reducing the degree and, if it is underfitting, increase the degree. The coefo hyperparameter will control the level of influence of high degree against low-degree polynomials.

One of the commonest ways to find the correct hyperparameter values is through a grid search. The fastest way is to start with a coarse search and then refine it using the best of the values that you find with the first search. It's also a good idea to learn what each of the parameters does so that you like in the correct hyperparameter space.

Similarity Features

Another way of attacking the nonlinear problems is to use a similarity function to compute new features which can then be added. The similarity function will measure the resemblance between each of the instances and a landmark. For example, if you added a pair of landmarks to a one-dimensional dataset, adding them at x 1 = 1 and x 1 = -2, you could then define a similarity function as the Gaussian RBF (Radial Basis Function) using y = 0.3, as shown in the equation below:

$$\phi\gamma(\mathbf{x}, \ell) = \exp\left(-\gamma\|\mathbf{x} - \ell\|^2\right)$$

Equation – Gaussian RBF

The function is bell-shaped with a variance of 0, which is the furthest from the landmark to 1, which is right at the landmark. Next, the new features can be computed. So, let's take x = 1 -1 – this would be a distance of 1 from the nearest landmark and a distance of 2 from the next one. This means the new features would be:

x 2 = exp (−0.3 x 12) ≈ 0.74

x 3 = exp (−0.3 x 22) ≈ 0.30

If you were to see this on a plot, you would see that it is linearly separable.

You might ask how you would choose the landmarks and the easiest way would be to create one where each instance is located in the dataset. What this does is creates multiple dimensions and the result of this is an increase in the chance that training set we transformed will now be linearly separable. There is a downside; if the training set has n features and m instances, it will be transformed into a training set the same, assuming that the original features have been dropped. If the training set is a big one, you will end with many features.

The Gaussian RBF Kernel

In the same way as the method using polynomial features, the similarity features method can be used with most algorithms but if you have a large dataset and many additional features, in computation terms it can work out to be expensive. However, this is where the SVM kernel trick comes into its own; using the trick, you get the same result without having to add all the features. Let's see how the FRB kernel works on the SVC class:

```
rbf_kernel_svm_clf = Pipeline((

("scaler", StandardScaler()),

("svm_clf", SVC(kernel="rbf", gamma=5, C=0.001))

))

rbf_kernel_svm_clf.fit(X, y)
```

If you increase the gamma hyperparameter, the bell curve of the plot is narrower, and this means that the influence range of each instance is much smaller; this is because the decision boundary becomes a lot less regular and wriggles around the instances. On the other hand, if you had a smaller gamma the bell shape would be wider, and each instance would have a much bigger influence range; the result of this would be smoother decision boundaries. The gamma hyperparameter, y, is more like a parameter for regularization; if the model overfits, reduce y and, if it underfits, increase it much like you do with the C hyperparameter.

There are other kernels, but they are not used as much. For example, some data structures have specialized kernels, i.e. when you classify DNA sequences or text documents, you would use one based on the Levenshtein distance or a string subsequence kernel.

The problem is, how do you know which kernel to use when there are so many of them? Generally, you should choose the linear kernel in the first instance – keep in mind that LinearSVC is significantly faster than the alternative, SVC(kernel="linear")), especially when you are using a large dataset or one that has a lot of features. If your training set is not too large, you could try the Gaussian RBF; it works very well for most algorithms. Then, if you have time, and you have the computing power, try experimenting with other kernels using grid search and cross-validation. In particular, use those kernels that are specifically for your type of dataset structure.

Computational Complexity

The liblinear library, on which the LinearSVC class is based, implements an algorithm which is fully optimized on linear SVMs. There is no support included for the kernel trick but using a training time complexity of approximately $O(m \times n)$, it can scale pretty linearly with the number of features and instances.

If you need high precision, the algorithm will take longer because it is controlled by something called tol in scikit-learn -the tolerance hyperparameter of ϵ. For most of your classification tasks, you will find that the default tolerance works just fine.

By contrast, the algorithm implemented by the libsvm class, on which the SVC class is based, does have support for the kernel trick. It has a training complexity of around $O(m \cdot 2 \times n)$ and $O($

m 3 x n) but it is quite a bit slower when there are multiple training instances – we are talking hundreds of thousands). This is a great algorithm if you have a complex training set that isn't too large. It does scale quite well with the number of features, particularly the sparse features, or those that have some nonzero features. In this case, the algorithm scaling is roughly in line with the average amount of nonzero features in each instance.

SVM Regression

So, we know that the SVM algorithm is pretty versatile, supporting nonlinear and linear classification as well as nonlinear and Linear Regression. The trick with SVM is to turn the objective around; rather than attempting to fit the largest track possible between a pair of classes while keeping margin violations to a minimum, SVM regression fits as many of the instances as it can onto the track while keeping the margin violations down. Hyperparameter ϵ controls the track width.

If you put more instances into the margin, you will not affect the predictions of the model at all and, as such, the model is termed ϵ-insensitive.

The LinearSVC class in scikit-learn can be used to perform Linear Regression; try the following code and see what the plot looks like (ensuring that the data is first scaled and then centered.):

```
from sklearn.svm import LinearSVR

svm_reg = LinearSVR(epsilon=1.5)

svm_reg.fit(X, y)
```

A kernelized SVM model can be used for nonlinear regression. For example, if you have a random quadratic set and you perform SVM regression with a second-degree polynomial kernel, the plot would show very little regularization on one side and more on the other, i.e. small and large C values.

The next piece of code shows the SVR class from scikit-learn producing the left-hand model from the last plot. SVR is the regression counterpart to SVC class and LinearSVC is the regression counterpart to LinearSVC. LinearSVC will scale in a linear fashion with the size of the dataset while SVR class slows right down when you have a large dataset:

```
from sklearn.svm import SVR

svm_poly_reg = SVR(kernel="poly", degree=2, C=100, epsilon=0.1)

svm_poly_reg.fit(X, y)
```

Behind the Scenes

In this section, we are going to look at how the SVM makes its predictions and the way in which their algorithms work, and we will start with the SVM classifiers. First, we need to mention notations. You may have noticed that in some places we put every model parameter into a single vector, θ, and that includes the input feature weights of θ1 to θn and the θ0 bias term and then added the x 0 = 1 bias input to every instance. For this chapter, we are going to look at a different notation, one that is more convenient for SVMs. We will use b for the bias term and w for the feature weights vector. We will not be adding any bias features to the vectors for the input features.

Decision Function and Predictions

With the linear SVM classifier, we can predict what class instance x is simply by computing this decision function – w T . x + b = w 1 x 1 + ... + wn xn +b. If we get a positive result then ŷ, the predicted class will be the positive class; if negative then the predicted o class will be the negative class, as shown in the equation below:

$$\hat{y} = \begin{cases} 0 & \text{if } \mathbf{w}^T \cdot \mathbf{x} + b < 0, \\ 1 & \text{if } \mathbf{w}^T \cdot \mathbf{x} + b \geq 0 \end{cases}$$

Equation - Linear SVM Classifier Prediction

The dashed lines on the plot are representative of the parts where the decision equation equals -1 or 1. These lines run parallel and are an equal distance from the decision boundary, thus producing a margin. When you train the SVM classifier, you are trying to find the value s of b and w that widen the margin as much as possible while either limiting or steering clear of margin violations.

$$\underset{\mathbf{w},b}{\text{minimize}} \quad \frac{1}{2}\mathbf{w}^T \cdot \mathbf{w}$$

$$\text{subject to} \quad t^{(i)}(\mathbf{w}^T \cdot \mathbf{x}^{(i)} + b) \geq 1 \quad \text{for } i = 1, 2, \cdots, m$$

Equation – Hard Margin Linear Classification Objective

The Objective of Training

Think about the decision function slope and the fact that it equals the norm of the ‖ w ‖ weight vector. If that slope were to be divided by two, where the decision function equals ±1 will be two times further from the decision boundary. In other words, if you divide the slope you multiply the margin.

So, to get the large margin, we minimize ‖ w ‖ but we also don't want any hard margins or margin violation. In this case, we want the decision function to be more than 1 for every one of the positive instances and less than -1 for the negatives. Let's say that we define the negative instances of (if y(i) = 0 as t(i) = -1 and the positive instances of (if y(i) = 1) as t (i) = 1, then the constraint can be expressed as t(i)(w T . x (i) + b) ≥ 1 for every instance.

Note

Instead of minimizing ‖ w ‖, we have minimized w T . w, which is the same as ‖ w ‖2. Why? Because we get the same result (the b and w values are used to minimize a value will also minimize half of the value's square as well). However, ‖ w ‖2 has a much simpler derivative, just w, while ‖ w ‖ will not differentiate at w = 0 The optimization algorithms always work more efficiently on the functions that are differentiable.

In order to get the objective for the soft margin, we will need to add in a slack variable of ζ(i) ≥ 0 for every instance: ζ(i) ½ will measure the level to which the ith instance can violate the soft margin. Now we have a conflict in our objectives; we need to ensure the slack variables are small enough that the margin violations are minimized, and we also need to make w T . w small enough that the margin is increased. Now we need to use the C hyperparameter so that we can get the tradeoff between the objectives defined. The net equation shows you the constrained optimization problem:

$$\underset{w,b,\zeta}{\text{minimize}} \quad \frac{1}{2}w^T \cdot w + C \sum_{i=1}^{m} \zeta^{(i)}$$

$$\text{subject to} \quad t^{(i)}(w^T \cdot x^{(i)} + b) \geq 1 - \zeta^{(i)} \quad \text{and} \quad \zeta^{(i)} \geq 0 \quad \text{for } i = 1, 2, \cdots, m$$

Equation - Soft Margin Linear SVM Classifier Objective

Quadratic Programming

The problems of the soft and the hard margins are known as convex quadratic optimization problems with constraints that are linear, otherwise known as QP, or Quadratic Programming problems. There are quite a few existing solvers that can help us with these problems and a number of techniques that do not fall into the scope of the guide, but you can see the general formula in the next equation:

Minimize $\quad \frac{1}{2}p^T \cdot Hp \; + \; f^T \cdot p$

subject to $\quad A \cdot p \le b$

where
$$\begin{cases} p & \text{is an } n_p\text{-dimensional vector } (n_p = \text{number of parameters}), \\ H & \text{is an } n_p \times n_p \text{ matrix}, \\ f & \text{is an } n_p\text{-dimensional vector}, \\ A & \text{is an } n_c \times n_p \text{ matrix } (n_c = \text{number of constraints}), \\ b & \text{is an } n_c\text{-dimensional vector}. \end{cases}$$

Equation – Quadratic Programming Problem

$A \cdot p \le b$ is the expression used to define the nc constraints, i.e. $p^T \cdot a(i) \le b(i)$ for $i = 1, 2, \cdots,$ nc, - the vector $a(i)$ has the elements from the ith row in A and the vector $b(i)$ is the ith element in b. If you use the following method to set the QP parameters, you can check to see that the result is the SVM classifier objective with the hard margin:

- np = n + 1 (the number of features is n and +1 is the bias term)
- nc = m (the number of instances is m)
- The np x np identity matrix is H with zero in the top -left, so that the bias term is ignored
- f = 0 (a vector with np dimensions and full of zeros)
- b = 1 (a vector with nc dimensions and full of ones)
- a(i) = -t(i)
- – (i) equals x and has an additional bias feature
- 0 = 1

You could easily train the hard margin classifier by passing the preceding parameters to a standard QP solver. The vector that results, p, has the bias term b = p0 and it also contains wi = pi for i = 1, 2 ... , m, which are the feature weights. In the same way, you could also use a QP solver for solving soft margin problems but we're going to be using the kernel trick by looking at another constrained optimization problem.

Dual Problems

Constrained optimization problems are called primal problems and, given one of these, we can express a problem that is related yet different – the dual problem. Dual problem solutions tend to give lower bounds to the primal problem solutions but can, in some cases, have the exact same solution. The SVM problem meets all the conditions so you make the decision – solve the dual or primal problem; the solution will be the same.

In the next equation you can see the linear SVM objective in its dual form:

$$\underset{\alpha}{\text{minimize}}\frac{1}{2}\sum_{i=1}^{m}\sum_{j=1}^{m}\alpha^{(i)}\alpha^{(j)}t^{(i)}t^{(j)}\mathbf{x}^{(i)T}\cdot\mathbf{x}^{(j)} - \sum_{i=1}^{m}\alpha^{(i)}$$

$$\text{subject to}\quad \alpha^{(i)} \geq 0 \quad \text{for } i = 1, 2, \cdots, m$$

Equation – Linear SVM Objective – Dual Form

Using a QP solver, you can find the vector that will minimize the equation and then compute it, minimizing the primal problem as shown in the next equation:

$$\mathbf{w} = \sum_{i=1}^{m}\hat{\alpha}^{(i)}t^{(i)}\mathbf{x}^{(i)}$$

$$\hat{b} = \frac{1}{n_s}\sum_{\substack{i=1 \\ \hat{\alpha}^{(i)}>0}}^{m}(1 - t^{(i)}(\mathbf{w}^T\cdot\mathbf{x}^{(i)}))$$

Equation – Dual to Primal Solution

It is quicker to solve the dual problem when there are fewer training instances than there are features but, even more importantly, the kernel trick can be used; it can't be with the primal problem.

What is this kernel trick?

Kernelized SVM

Let's say that you have a two-dimensional training set and you want a second-degree polynomial transformation applied to it; you then want a linear SVM classifier trained on the newly transformed set. The next equation shows the second-degree polynomial mapping function that you are going to apply:

$$\phi(\mathbf{x}) = \phi\left(\begin{pmatrix} x_1 \\ x_2 \end{pmatrix}\right) = \begin{pmatrix} x_1^2 \\ \sqrt{2}\, x_1 x_2 \\ x_2^2 \end{pmatrix}$$

Equation – Second-Degree Polynomial Mapping Function

Did you spot that the newly transformed vector is actually three-dimensional, not two? Now, what would happen to a and b, both two-dimensional if were to apply the polynomial mapping and then try to work out what the dot product of the vectors we transformed is? Look at this equation:

$$\phi(\mathbf{a})^T \cdot \phi(\mathbf{b}) \quad = \begin{pmatrix} a_1^2 \\ \sqrt{2}\, a_1 a_2 \\ a_2^2 \end{pmatrix}^T \cdot \begin{pmatrix} b_1^2 \\ \sqrt{2}\, b_1 b_2 \\ b_2^2 \end{pmatrix} = a_1^2 b_1^2 + 2 a_1 b_1 a_2 b_2 + a_2^2 b_2^2$$

$$= (a_1 b_1 + a_2 b_2)^2 = \left(\begin{pmatrix} a_1 \\ a_2 \end{pmatrix}^T \cdot \begin{pmatrix} b_1 \\ b_2 \end{pmatrix} \right)^2 = (\mathbf{a}^T \cdot \mathbf{b})^2$$

Equation – Kernel Trick for the Second-Degree Polynomial Mapping

Well, will you look at that! The dot product that we get from the transformed vectors is the same as the square of the original vectors' dot product – Ø(a) T . Ø(b) = (a T . b)2

Now, if you were to apply Ø to ever training instance, the dual problem will have the $\phi(x\,(i))\,T \cdot \phi(x\,(j))$ dot product. However, if Ø were the earlier defined second-degree polynomial then the dot product of the transformed vectors could be replaced by (x(i)T.x(j))2. In this case, there is no need to make any transformation to the instances – just put the square of the dot product in place of the dot product. The result would be exactly the same as if you transformed the set and fitted the linear SVM algorithm; using the kernel trick, it's much more efficient.

So, K(a, b) = (a T .b)2 is the second-degree polynomial kernel. Kernels are functions that can compute the dot product $\phi(a)\,T \cdot \phi(b)$ using the original a and b vectors. It doesn't need to compute or have knowledge of the transformation function Ø to do this. The equation below shows you some of the more common kernels:

$$\text{Linear:} \qquad K(a, b) = a^T \cdot b$$

$$\text{Polynomial:} \qquad K(a, b) = (\gamma a^T \cdot b + r)^d$$

$$\text{Gaussian RBF:} \qquad K(a, b) = \exp(-\gamma \| a - b \|^2)$$

$$\text{Sigmoid:} \qquad K(a, b) = \tanh(\gamma a^T \cdot b + r)$$

Commonly Used Kernels

Mercer's Theorem

Mercer's Theorem states that, if some mathematical conditions are respected by the function K(a, b), conditions that state that the arguments of K are to be continuous and symmetrical, i.e. K(a, b) = K(b, a), then function Ø can map a and b to an alternative space, maybe with a higher dimension, in such a way that K(a, b) = Ø(a) T. Ø(b). K can be used as a kernel because you know that Ø actually exists even if you are not aware of what it is. Where the Gaussian RBF Kernel is concerned, you can show that Ø will map every instance to a space of infinite dimensions – it is probably good that you don't need to manually do the mapping!

Be aware that most of the common kernels, although they work well, do not always respect Mercer's Conditions.

We're not done yet though; we saw the equation that took us from a dual to a primal solution with linear SVM classification but, if you were to use the kernel trick, the equations would include Ø(x(i)). In actual fact, w^ has got to match ϕ(x(i)) in terms of how many dimensions it has and this could be an infinite number, so large that it can't be computed. So, how do we make predictions when we don't what w^ is?

There is good news; the w^ formula from the earlier equation for the dual to primal solutions can be added to the decision function to create a new instance of x(n) and the resulting equation contains dot products in between vectors; because of this, we can use that kernel trick, as shown in the next equation:

$$h_{\mathbf{w},\hat{b}}(\phi(\mathbf{x}^{(n)})) = \mathbf{w}^T \cdot \phi(\mathbf{x}^{(n)}) + \hat{b} = \left(\sum_{i=1}^{m} \hat{\alpha}^{(i)} t^{(i)} \phi(\mathbf{x}^{(i)})\right)^T \cdot \phi(\mathbf{x}^{(n)}) + \hat{b}$$

$$= \sum_{i=1}^{m} \hat{\alpha}^{(i)} t^{(i)} \left(\phi(\mathbf{x}^{(i)})^T \cdot \phi(\mathbf{x}^{(n)})\right) + \hat{b}$$

$$= \sum_{\substack{i=1 \\ \hat{\alpha}^{(i)}>0}}^{m} \hat{\alpha}^{(i)} t^{(i)} K(\mathbf{x}^{(i)}, \mathbf{x}^{(n)}) + \hat{b}$$

Equation - Making Predictions With A Kernelized SVM

Because $\alpha(i) \neq 0$ is only used for support vectors, predictions can only be made through the computation of the input vector dot product using the support vectors only, none of the instances. Obviously, you will need to compute $b^\wedge$, which is the bias term, using the same kernel trick, as the next equation shows:

$$\hat{b} = \frac{1}{n_s} \sum_{\substack{i=1 \\ \hat{\alpha}^{(i)}>0}}^{m} (1 - t^{(i)} \mathbf{w}^T \cdot \phi(\mathbf{x}^{(i)})) = \frac{1}{n_s} \sum_{\substack{i=1 \\ \hat{\alpha}^{(i)}>0}}^{m} \left(1 - t^{(i)} \left(\sum_{j=1}^{m} \hat{\alpha}^{(j)} t^{(j)} \phi(\mathbf{x}^{(j)})\right)^T \cdot \phi(\mathbf{x}^{(i)})\right)$$

$$= \frac{1}{n_s} \sum_{\substack{i=1 \\ \hat{\alpha}^{(i)}>0}}^{m} \left(1 - t^{(i)} \sum_{\substack{j=1 \\ \hat{\alpha}^{(j)}>0}}^{m} \hat{\alpha}^{(j)} t^{(j)} K(\mathbf{x}^{(i)}, \mathbf{x}^{(j)})\right)$$

Equation – Using the Kernel Trick to Compute the Bias

Online SVMs

Before we come to the end of this chapter, we'll look very quickly at the online SVM classifiers – online learning means learning as and when new instances appear. For the linear SVM classifier, we can minimize the cost function by using Gradient Descent and this is a derivation of the primal problem. The only problem is that convergence is incredibly slow, more so than any of the QP-based methods:

$$J(w, b) = \frac{1}{2}w^T \cdot w \quad + \quad C\sum_{i=1}^{m} max(0, 1 - t^{(i)}(w^T \cdot x^{(i)} + b))$$

Equation - Linear SVM Classifier Cost Function

The first cost function sum gives a small weight vector to the model which results in a larger margin. Sum two computes the total of all of the violations. If a violation is found off the track but on the right side, it is equal to 0 or is proportionate to how far it is to the right side of the track. If you minimize the term, you are ensuring that the margin violations are as small as they can be and few and far between.

Hinge Loss

The hinge loss function is the function called $max(0, 1 - t)$. When $t \geq 1$, the hinge loss is equal to 0 and, if $t < 1$, the derivative is equal to -1, 0 f t >> 1. The hinge loss function is not differentiable at $t = 1$ but, similar to Lasso Regression, Gradient Descent can be used with any sub-derivative or value that is between -1 and 0.

Chapter 5: Decision Tree Algorithms

Much like the SVMs, the Decision Tree is also a powerful and versatile algorithm for machine learning. It can do regression, classification, multi-output tasks, and are ideal for fitting the more complex datasets. Decision Trees are also a vital part of the Random Forests, which we will be talking more about later – Random Forests are one of the most powerful of all the algorithms in use today.

In this section, we are going to look at training Decision Trees, then visualizing and making predictions. We will then look at the CART algorithm that scikit-learn uses and regularization of the trees and how to use them in regression. We'll finish by talking about some of the limitations of the Decision Trees.

Train and Visualize a Decision Tree

The best way to understand a Decision Tree is to simply build one and then look at the way it makes its predictions. This next code will take the Iris dataset and train a DecisionTreeClassifier:

```
from sklearn.datasets import load_iris

from sklearn.tree import DecisionTreeClassifier

iris = load_iris()

X = iris.data[:, 2:] # petal length and width

y = iris.target

tree_clf = DecisionTreeClassifier(max_depth=2)

tree_clf.fit(X, y)
```

To visualize the tree once trained, we use the export_graphviz() method – this outputs a file called iris_tree.dot, which is a graph definition:

```
from sklearn.tree import export_graphviz

export_graphviz(

tree_clf,

out_file=image_path("iris_tree.dot"),

feature_names=iris.feature_names[2:],

class_names=iris.target_names,

rounded=True,
```

```
filled=True
)
```

Now, this .dot file can be converted into several different formats, like PNG, or PDF and this is done with the dot command-line tool that is found in the Graphviz package. You can use this to convert a .dot file into a .png file:

```
$ dot -Tpng iris_tree.dot -o iris_tree.png
```

Using Decision Trees to Make Predictions

We have our tree and now we want to make some predictions with it. Let's say that you want to classify an iris flower that you found. The starting point is the root node, at the top at depth 0. The node will want to know if the length of the petal is less than 2.45 cm. If yes, we move on to the left child node of the root, on the left at depth 1. If it is a leaf node, it won't have any child nodes so there won't be any questions asked; all you would do is view the class that predicted for the node and the Decision Tree will make the prediction that you have a Setosa variety of iris.

Now let's say that you have another flower but the length of the petal is more than 2.45 cm. This time, we need to go down the right of the child node on the root, which is at depth 1. This is not a leaf node so another question gets asked – is the width of the petal-less than 1.75 cm? If the answer is yes, then the flower is likely to be classified as a Versicolor species, to the left at depth 2 whereas, if the answer is no, it is likely to be classified as a Virginica species, to the right at depth 2. That is how simple it is.

It is worth noting that the Decision Trees have a very useful quality – they do not need much in the way of data preparation and they don't need any centering or scaling at all.

The samples attribute of a node will count the number of training instances the attribute applies to. For example, we have a set of 100 training instances where the length of the petal is more than 2.45 cm. Of those 100, the width of the petal of 54 instances is less than 1.75 cm. The value attribute of the node will tell you the number of instances in each class that the node applies to. An example of this would be the node at the bottom right, applying the value attribute as follows:

- 0 – Iris-Setosa
- 1 – Iris-Versicolor
- 45 – Iris-Virginica

Lastly, the impurity is measured by the Gini attribute of the node – if all of the instances that the node applies to belong to one class, the node is considered pure, i.e. gini=0. For example, the left node, depth 1 is applicable to the Setosa instances and that makes it pure with gini=0.

The next equation demonstrates the training algorithm for computing the Gini score, Gi of the ith node. For example, the left node, depth 2 has a score of gini=1 - 0/54)2 − (49/54)2 − (5/54)2 ≈ 0.168. Shortly, we will be looking at another impurity measure:

$$G_i = 1 - \sum_{k=1}^{n} p_{i,k}^{2}$$

Equation – Gini Impurity

Note

In scikit-learn we have the CART algorithm, used for the production of binary trees; the non-leaf nodes will always have two children and the questions will always have either a yes or a no answer. However, there are other algorithms that can produce Decision Trees with more than two children, like the ID3 algorithm.

Interpreting Models: White vs. Black Boxes

Decision Trees are pretty intuitive and we can easily interpret the decisions they make. Models like this tend to be known as white box models. However, as you will see later in the guide, neural networks, or Random Forests tend to be known as black box models. These make really good predictions and the calculations they use to make their predictions can easily be checked. That said, it isn't easy to use simple terms to explain why a particular prediction was made.

Let's say that you have a neural network that indicates a specific person shows up in an image; it isn't easy to determine why this prediction was made – was it the eyes, the nose, or the mouth? Was it something in the background? On the other hand, a Decision Tree will provide simple rules for classification that we can manually apply if we need to.

Class Probability Estimation

We can also use a Decision Tree for estimating what the probability is of a specific instance belonging to a specific class k. To do this, it will go through the tree looking for the leaf node for the instance; next, the Tree determines how many training instances of that class are in the node. Let's assume that you have a flower with 5 cm long petals that are 1.5 cm wide. The leaf node that corresponds to this is a left node at depth 2 so the Tree should, in theory, output these probabilities:

```
0% - Iris-Setosa (0/54)

90.7% - Iris-Versicolor (49/54)

9.3% - Iris-Virginica (5/54)
```

And, if you wanted a prediction of the class, the output would be class 1, Iris-Versicolor, as this has got the largest probability. We can check it like this:

```
>>> tree_clf.predict_proba([[5, 1.5]])

array([[ 0. , 0.90740741, 0.09259259]])

>>> tree_clf.predict([[5, 1.5]])

array([1])
```

Training Algorithms – CART

Scikit-learn makes use of the CART algorithm for training Decision Trees (also known as growing the tree). CART stands for Classification and Regression Tree and the idea behind it is simple: First, CART will divide the training dataset into a pair of subsets. This is done using a threshold of tk and a single feature of k. How does it decide on these? It will look for the pair, k, tk, from which the purest subsets are produced and this is determined by weighting and size. The next equation shows you the cost function that the CART algorithm is attempting to minimize:

$$J(k, t_k) = \frac{m_{\text{left}}}{m} G_{\text{left}} + \frac{m_{\text{right}}}{m} G_{\text{right}}$$

$$\text{where} \begin{cases} G_{\text{left/right}} \text{ measures the impurity of the left/right subset,} \\ m_{\text{left/right}} \text{ is the number of instances in the left/right subset.} \end{cases}$$

Equation - CART Cost Function For Classification

When the division into two has been successful, the algorithm will then use the exact same logic to divide the subsets, followed by the sub-subsets, all the way through, recursively. When it gets to the maximum depth, re-cursing stops – this depth is defined by the hyperparameter max_depth. It will also stop if a split can't be found that reduces the impurity. There are other hyperparameters that can be used for controlling extra conditions for stopping, such as:

- min_samples_split
- min_samples_leaf
- min_weight_fraction_leaf
- max_leaf_nodes

Warning

You might have spotted that the CART algorithm is somewhat greedy; first, it searches greedily for the best divide at the top and then repeats for each level. What it doesn't do is look to see if the division leads to a low impurity in lower levels. While algorithms like this do tend to produce solutions that are okay, it isn't guaranteed to be the best solution. The optimal tree is an NC-Complete Problem and that means it needs O(exp(m)) time and this leads to the problem being intractable, even when you only have a small training dataset – for this reason, we tend to settle for a result that okay.

Computational Complexity

To make a prediction, we must go through the Decision Tree, starting at the root and ending at a leaf. The Decision Trees tend to be balanced approximately so going through it will require going through approximately O(log 2) m)) nodes. Each node only needs one feature value to be checked, the complexity in terms of predictions is just O(log 2(m)), independently of how many features there are. This makes the predictions fast, even on large datasets.

That said, the algorithm does compare all of the features on all of the samples at every node unless you set max_features. The result of this is a complexity of O(n x m log(m)). If the dataset is small, i.e. a few thousand instances or lower, the training can be sped up by scikit-learn; it does this by sorting the data – you need to set preset=true, but if you have a large dataset, the training will be significantly slower.

Gini Impurity or Entropy?

The Gini impurity measure is the one used by default but you do have the option of choosing the entropy impurity measure. To do this, we just set entropy as the criterion hyperparameter. The entropy concept originally came from thermodynamics, where it was used as a molecular disorder measure – when the molecules are in a good order and are still, entropy is near to zero. Later, it spread to many other domains, one of which was Shannon's Information Theory where it was used as a measurement of the average contents of a message – when all the messages are the same, entropy is zero. With machine learning, we use entropy as one of the impurity measures – the entropy of a set is zero when there are only instances from just one class. The next equation demonstrates the entropy of the ith node:

$$H_i = -\sum_{\substack{k=1 \\ p_{i,k}\neq 0}}^{n} p_{i,k} \log(p_{i,k})$$

Equation - Entropy

So which do you use – impurity or entropy? To be honest, it really doesn't matter which one you use most of the time because they both result in trees that are very similar. Gini impurity tends to be a little faster in terms of computation so it is probably a good one to default to but, when there is a difference, Gini impurity will isolate the class that appears most frequently on its own branch while, with entropy, the trees tend to be a bit more balanced.

Hyperparameters for Regularization

Where a linear model will assume that the training data is linear, a Decision Tree doesn't go down the route of making assumptions. If you leave a Decision Tree unconstrained, the structure will eventually adapt to the data; it will fit the data closely, more often than not, overfitting. We call these nonparametric models. This is nothing to do with it having no parameters; on the contrary, it will often have many parameters. Rather, it is because there is no determination of the number of parameters before training starts so a nonparametric model can stay close to the data. Conversely, a parametric model, like the linear models, will already have the number of parameters determined beforehand so it doesn't have the same freedom; this cuts the overfitting risk but increases the underfitting risk.

To stop the model overfitting, we need to curtail the amount of freedom that the Decision Tree has during training. We call this, as you already know, regularization. The hyperparameters for the regularization will depend on which algorithm is in use but, usually, restriction of the maximum depth is possible. In scikit-learn, the max-depth hyperparameter is used – it has a default of None so it is not limited. If you reduce max_depth, the model is regularized and overfitting is limited.

There are a few more parameters in the DecisionTreeClassifier class that also restrict how the Decision Tree is shaped:

- min_samples_split – specifies the minimum samples a node needs before it can be divided
- min_samples_leaf – specifies the minimum samples in a leaf node
- min_weight_fraction_leaf – as above but a fraction is used to express how many weighted instances there are
- max_leaf_nodes – specifies the maximum leaf nodes

- max_features – specifies the maximum features that will be evaluated when each node is divided

To regularize the model, you can increase the min hyperparameters and decrease the max hyperparameters.

Note

Most other algorithms will work by training the Tree with no restrictions before deleting the nodes that are not necessary, known as pruning. If all the children of a node are leaf nodes, the node is not necessary if it can't provide a purity improvement that is significant in statistical terms.

We can use a standard statistical test, like the X 2 test, for estimating the probability that the purity improvement was by chance, known as a null hypothesis. The probability is called the p-value and if it is more than the specified threshold (usually 5% and controlled with a hyperparameter) the node is seen as not necessary; all its children will be pruned and this continues until such time that all the unnecessary nodes have been removed.

Regression

You can also do regression tasks with a Decision Tree. Using the following code, we will use the DecisionTreeRegressor class from scikit-learn to build the regression tree and then train it on a quadratic dataset that has a lot of noise and a max_depth=2:

```
from sklearn.tree import DecisionTreeRegressor

tree_reg = DecisionTreeRegressor(max_depth=2)

tree_reg.fit(X, y)
```

This looks a lot like the classification tree from earlier but there is a big difference – rather than a class prediction in every node, a value is predicted instead. For example, let's say that we have a new instance that has x 1 = 0.6 and we want to make a prediction on it. We go through the tree, beginning at the root, and, at some point, we will come to the leaf node that predicts the value of value=0.1106. All this prediction is doing is giving us the average target value of all the training instances (110 in total) that have an association with the leaf node. The result will be an MSE or Mean Squared Error that equals 0.0151 over 110 instances.

The CART algorithm works much the same way as it did earlier but, instead of attempting to divide the dataset so as to minimize impurity, it will attempt to divide the set to minimize MSE. The next equation shows the CART cost function for minimization:

$$J(k, t_k) = \frac{m_{\text{left}}}{m}\text{MSE}_{\text{left}} + \frac{m_{\text{right}}}{m}\text{MSE}_{\text{right}} \quad \text{where} \begin{cases} \text{MSE}_{\text{node}} = \sum_{i \in \text{node}}\left(\hat{y}_{\text{node}} - y^{(i)}\right)^2 \\ \hat{y}_{\text{node}} = \frac{1}{m_{\text{node}}}\sum_{i \in \text{node}} y^{(i)} \end{cases}$$

Equation – CART Cost Function for Regression

As with classification, overfitting is common with Decision Trees for regression. When we don't regularize them by using the correct hyperparameter, the predictions will come out on the left, showing poor overfitting. All you need to do is set the hyperparameter min_samples_leaf=110 and you get a much better model.

Decision Tree Limitations

By now, you should be of the opinion that Decision Trees are useful – we can understand them easily and we can interpret them. They are powerful, they are versatile, and they are easy to use. What's not to like? Unfortunately, Decision Trees do have certain limitations. For a start, you may already have spotted that they prefer orthogonal decision boundaries, which means that all the divisions are going to be perpendicular to an axis. This makes them very sensitive when it comes to rotating the training dataset.

The biggest issue is that they are incredibly sensitive to even the smallest variations in the dataset. For example, if we were to take out the Versicolor species from the Iris dataset, and then train up a new Tree, the new Tree will look very different from the one we produced with all species present and correct. The scikit-learn algorithm is stochastic so you are likely to get varying models from the same dataset – a way around this is to set the hyperparameter called random_state.

One way of limiting the instability is to average the predictions over multiple Decision Trees and we do this with Random Forests, which leads us nicely to the next chapter.

Chapter 6: Random Forest and Ensemble Learning

Let's suppose that you canvass thousands of people and ask each of them a complex question, and then you aggregate all the answers. Most of the time, the aggregated answer will be much better than any answer from an expert and this is known as the wisdom of the crowd. In the same way, if you were aggregate all the predictions from a group of classifiers or regressors, the overall prediction will usually be a lot better than what you would get with the top individual predictor. We call a group of predictors an ensemble and the techniques is known as Ensemble Learning; that means the algorithm used by this technique is an Ensemble Method.

For example, you could take a group of Decision Tree classifiers and train them, each one on a random and different subset of the main training set. For the predictions to be made, all you need to do is get the predictions of each tree and then make a prediction on which class is voted on the most. An ensemble of Decision Trees like this is known as Random Forest and, although it is very simple, it is also an incredibly powerful algorithm; one of the most powerful in machine learning.

You will use these ensemble methods most often toward the end of your project, once a handful of good predictors have already been built and you can combine them to make one excellent predictor. We'll be talking about the more popular of the Ensemble methods in this chapter including boosting, bagging, and stacking, as well as looking at Random Forests.

Voting Classifier

Let's say that we have a few classifiers trained up and each one has about 80% accuracy. You could have an SVM classifier, a K-Nearest Neighbors, a Random Forest, and a Logistic Regression classifier, along with a handful of others. The easiest way to create one excellent classifier is to take the predictions from each of the classifiers and aggregate them to predict which class will have the majority of the votes. We call the majority vote classifier a hard-voting classifier.

It's quite surprising to find that a hard-voting classifier will, more often than not, achieve a much higher level of accuracy that the very best classifier from the entire ensemble. In fact, even if every one of the classifiers was a weak learner and only does a little better than just random guesses, you can still have a strong learner ensemble, in as much as there need to be enough weak learners with enough diversity.

How can this be?

Let's have a look at an analogy that might clear this up:

Let's say that you have a coin that is a little biased; with it, you have a 49% chance of tails and 51% of heads. Toss the coin 1000 times and you should get more heads than tails, approximately 510 to 490. Do the math and you will see that there is approximately 75% probability of getting more heads than tails after tossing the coin 1000 times. The more times you toss the coin, the higher the probability. If you tossed the coin 10,000 times, for example, that probability would be approximately 97%. This is down to something called the Law of Large Numbers. The more the coin is tossed, the closer the ratio gets to the probability of heads coming up.

In much the same way, let's say that an ensemble is built that contains 1000 classifiers; each is right only 51% of the time individually, again not much better than making a random guess. If you were to predict what would be the most voted-for class, you could expect around 75% accuracy. However, this is only going to be true if all of the classifiers are completely independent. This means that they are capable of making errors that are not correlated and this cannot be the case because each has been trained using the same training data. They are more likely to have similar error types so there will be quite a few majority votes for an incorrect class and this considerably reduces the accuracy of the ensemble.

Tip

It is worth noting that ensemble methods will work better when you have independent predictors or at least have those that are as independent as they possibly can be. If you want diverse classifiers, you need to train them with algorithms that are different; thus, the chance of them making different error types is increased and the accuracy of the ensemble is improved.

The next piece of code is going to create a voting classifier in scikit-learn and then train it. The classifier will be made up of three classifiers, each diverse and we are using the Moons dataset:

```
from sklearn.ensemble import RandomForestClassifier

from sklearn.ensemble import VotingClassifier

from sklearn.linear_model import LogisticRegression

from sklearn.svm import SVC

log_clf = LogisticRegression()

rnd_clf = RandomForestClassifier()

svm_clf = SVC()

voting_clf = VotingClassifier(

estimators=[('lr', log_clf), ('rf', rnd_clf), ('svc', svm_clf)],

voting='hard'

)

voting_clf.fit(X_train, y_train)
```

Now we need to look at the accuracy of each classifier on the test dataset:

```
>>> from sklearn.metrics import accuracy_score
>>> for clf in (log_clf, rnd_clf, svm_clf, voting_clf):
>>>    clf.fit(X_train, y_train)
>>>    y_pred = clf.predict(X_test)
>>>    print(clf.__class__.__name__, accuracy_score(y_test, y_pred))
LogisticRegression 0.864
RandomForestClassifier 0.872
SVC 0.888
VotingClassifier 0.896
```

That's it, the voting classifier outperformed the individual ones just a little.

If class probabilities could be estimated by all classifiers, for example, if they all had the predict_proba() method, you could then tell scikit-learn that you want the prediction to be the class that has the highest class probability and this is to be averaged over all the classifiers together. We call this soft voting and we often get much better performance than the hard voting because votes that are more confident are given more weight. All that is required is to use voting="hard" with voting="soft" and then make sure that every classifier you are using has the ability to estimate the class probabilities.

However, by default, this doesn't happen with the SVC class. Therefore, you would need to change the hyperparameter for probability so it is True and then the SVC class can make use of cross-validation techniques to estimate the probabilities. This will slow the training and it will add in the predict_proba() method. If the code we used last was modified so it used soft voting, you would get more than 91% accuracy from the voting classifier.

Bagging and Pasting

There is a way that you can get a set of diverse classifiers and that is to use different algorithms for training, as we mentioned earlier. Another way would be to use the exact same algorithm on every individual predictor but train each one on a random and different subset. When we perform sampling with replacement, it is called the bagging method, which is actually short for bootstrap aggregating. When we perform the sampling without replacement, it is known as pasting. In both cases, we can sample training instances multiple times over multiple predictors but you can only sample instances multiple times on one predictor with bagging.

Once the predictors have all been trained, the ensemble will make the prediction for the new instance and it does this through aggregation of all the predictions from all the predictors. The function for aggregation tends to be the statistical mode, or, in the same way as the hard-voting classifier, the prediction that happens most frequently, for classification or, in the case of regression, it will be the average. The bias for each predictor is higher than if the original training set was used, but aggregation will reduce variance and bias. In general, the result is that the ensemble will have a similar bias to an individual predictor that has been trained using the original set, but it will have a lower variance.

You can train all the predictors in parallel, using different servers or CPU cores and, in much the same way the predictions can also be made in parallel. This is one of the main reasons why methods like bagging and pasting have proven so popular, simply because they are highly scalable.

Bagging and Pasting Using Scikit-Learn

There is a very simple API in scikit-learn that is useful for both bagging and pasting – BaggingClassifier class or BaggingRegressor. The next piece of code will train an ensemble containing 500 Decision Tree classifiers. Groups of five classifiers have been trained on 100 randomly sampled training instances from the training dataset using replacement. The parameter called n_jobs informs scikit-learn how many CPU cores are to be used for the training and the predictions, in this case -1, which is all the cores available should be used:

```
from sklearn.ensemble import BaggingClassifier

from sklearn.tree import DecisionTreeClassifier

bag_clf = BaggingClassifier(

DecisionTreeClassifier(), n_estimators=500,

max_samples=100, bootstrap=True, n_jobs=-1

)

bag_clf.fit(X_train, y_train)

y_pred = bag_clf.predict(X_test)
```

Note

The BaggingClassifier will carry out soft voting automatically, not hard voting, should it be found that the base classifier has the ability to estimate the class probabilities – for this, it must have the predict_proba() method and this is normally the case where Decision Tree classifiers are concerned.

If you were to look at and compare the decision boundaries for a single Tree and an ensemble containing 500 trees, both of which have been trained using the Moons dataset, you would see that the predictions from the ensemble are much better generalized than those of the single tree predictions. The ensemble's bias is comparable but the variance is smaller, which means that it will make almost the same amount of errors but with a more regular decision boundary.

With bootstrapping, there is more diversity in the subsets that the individual predictors are trained on so bagging shows higher bias compared to pasting. However, this also means that there is less correlation between the predictors and the overall variance is reduced. You do tend to get better models from bagging, which is why it tends to be the preferred method. However, if you have the time available and some spare CPU power, you could evaluate bagging and pasting by using cross-validation to see which is the best.

Out-of-Bag (oob) Evaluation

You can sample several instances multiple times with bagging for any chosen predictor but there are other instances that can't be sampled. The BaggingClassifier will, by default, sample m instances using a replacement – set bootstrap=True (m indicates how big the training set is). This means is that around 63% of all instances are sampled for each of the predictors – this is an average. The remainder of the instances that are not sampled, around 37%, are known as oob instances, or out-of-bag. Note that those will not be the same 37% on each of the predictors.

During training, a predictor will not see any of the oob instances, so the evaluation can happen without needing a separate cross-validation or validation set. The ensemble can be evaluated by itself – simply get the average of all the oob evaluations from each individual predictor.

When you create a BaggingClassifier in scikit-learn, oob_score=True can be set so that oob evaluation happens automatically when the training is complete. You can see this in the next piece of code and the evaluation score that results from this can be obtained through the variable called oob_score_:

```
>>> bag_clf = BaggingClassifier(

>>>   DecisionTreeClassifier(), n_estimators=500,

>>>   bootstrap=True, n_jobs=-1, oob_score=True)

>>> bag_clf.fit(X_train, y_train)

>>> bag_clf.oob_score_

0.9306666666666664
```

The oob evaluation will tell us that an accuracy of just over 93% will be achieved on the test set by the BaggingClassifier. We can verify like this:

```
>>> from sklearn.metrics import accuracy_score

>>> y_pred = bag_clf.predict(X_test)
```

```
>>> accuracy_score(y_test, y_pred)
```

```
0.9360000000000005
```

An accuracy of 93.6% is close enough.

You can also use the variable called oob_decision_function to get the function for each individual training instance. Because the base estimator contains the predict_proba() method, we get the class probabilities returned for each of the training instances. For example, an estimate of 60.6% probability is given by the oob evaluation for the second instance – this means that there is a 60.6% chance that it belongs to the positive class:

```
>>> bag_clf.oob_decision_function_
```

```
array([[ 0. , 1. ],
```

```
[ 0.60588235, 0.39411765],
```

```
[ 1. , 0. ],
```

```
...
```

```
[ 1. , 0. ],
```

```
[ 0. , 1. ],
```

```
[ 0.48958333, 0.51041667]])
```

Random Patches and Subspaces

The BaggingClassifier also has support for feature sampling and there are two hyperparameters that control this – max_features and bootstrap_features. These both work in a similar way to max_samples and bootstrap but, rather than instance sampling, they are for feature sampling. As such, we train each predictor on a random subset taken from the input features.

This is very useful when you have inputs that are high-dimensional, like images. To sample training features and training instances we use a method called Random Patches. If you keep the training instances, for example, max_samples=1.0 and bootstrap=false and sampling the features that are below 1.0, such as max_features or bootstrap_features=True, it is a method known as Random Subspaces. When you sample features you get even more diversity in the predictors and gain a little extra bias but paying for it with lower variance.

Random Forests

Random Forests are ensembles made up of multiple Decision Trees. These are usually trained using the Bagging method or, on rare occasions, pasting but usually with the max_samples set as the training set size.

Rather than constructing a BaggingClassifier and then passing a DecisionTreeClassifier to it, we could use the class called RandomForestClassifier. This is optimized and much more convenient for Decision Trees and there is also a DecisionTreeRegressor for cases of regression.

The next code is going to take a Random Forest Classifier that has 500 trees and train it. Each tree has a limit of 16 nodes and the training is done using all the CPU cores available:

```
from sklearn.ensemble import RandomForestClassifier

rnd_clf = RandomForestClassifier(n_estimators=500, max_leaf_nodes=16,
n_jobs=-1)

rnd_clf.fit(X_train, y_train)

y_pred_rf = rnd_clf.predict(X_test)
```

RandomForestClassifiers contain the same hyperparameters that a DecisionTreeClassifier has, with a couple of exceptions. These are used for controlling the way the trees grow and, for controlling the ensemble, there are also the same hyperparameters as the BaggingClassifier.

The algorithm for the Random Forest provides an extra degree of randomness for growing the trees; rather than looking for the top features when the nodes are being split, the algorithm looks in a random features subset for the best features. The result of this is more diversity in the trees, once again gaining higher bias at the cost of lower variance but, overall, the model is generally much better. The BaggingClassifier below is much the same as the RandomForestClassifier we just produced:

```
bag_clf = BaggingClassifier(

DecisionTreeClassifier(splitter="random", max_leaf_nodes=16),

n_estimators=500, max_samples=1.0, bootstrap=True, n_jobs=-1

)
```

Extra-Trees

When a tree is grown in a Random Forest, only a subset of the features is chosen for the division at each node and that subset is random. You can use random thresholds to make things even more random (used on each feature) instead of looking for the best threshold as you do with a regular Decision Tree.

A forest full of random trees is known as an Extremely Randomized Trees ensemble, shortened to Extra-Trees for ease of use. Again, we trade higher bias for a lower variance with this and this makes it faster to train Extra-Trees than it does the regular Random Forest. This is because looking for the best threshold for every feature at every single node is an incredibly time-consuming part of tree growing.

Using the ExtraTreesClassifier class in scikit-learn we can create, as you would expect, an Extra-Trees classifier. The API for this classifier is the same as the RandomForestClassifier class and, in the same way, the API for the ExtraTreesRegressor is the same as the RandomForestRegressor class.

Tip

You can't tell very easily which will perform better – the RandomForestClassifier or the ExtraTreesClassifier. The only way to know is to use them and then compare them with cross-validation and use a grid search to tweak the hyperparameters.

Feature Importance

Finally, you will see on a single Decision Tree that the important features tend to be nearer to the root while those that are not important either don't show up at all or are nearer to the leaves. We can estimate how important a feature is by determining the average of the depths that it appears on all the forest trees. This is done automatically by scikit-learn for each feature once training has finished and you can use the variable called feature_importances_ to get to the result. For example, in the next code, we will train a RandomForestClassifier using the Iris dataset. We will then output the importance of each feature. With this dataset, the features considered important are the length and the width of the petals while the length and width of the sepals are not considered important:

```
>>> from sklearn.datasets import load_iris

>>> iris = load_iris()

>>> rnd_clf = RandomForestClassifier(n_estimators=500, n_jobs=-1)

>>> rnd_clf.fit(iris["data"], iris["target"])

>>> for name, score in zip(iris["feature_names"],
rnd_clf.feature_importances_):

>>>   print(name, score)

sepal length (cm) 0.112492250999

sepal width (cm) 0.0231192882825

petal length (cm) 0.441030464364

petal width (cm) 0.423357996355
```

Simply put, the Random Forests are very useful for when you want a quick idea of what features are important, especially where feature selection is required.

Boosting

The full name is Hypothesis Boosting and this refers to an Ensemble Method that has the ability to take a few weak learners and transform them into strong learners. Generally, the idea behind using boosting is to use sequential methods for training predictors with each one attempting to correct the one that came before it. There are a few boosting methods that you can use but there are two popular ones – Adaptive Boosting (AdaBoost) and Gradient Boosting.

AdaBoost

One of the best ways for a predictor to correct the predictor that preceded it is to look more closely at the underfitted instances. The result of this will be that the new predictor focuses on harder cases and this is what happens with AdaBoost.

If you wanted to build an AdaBoost classifier, you would need to create a first-base classifier, like a Decision Tree, train it, and then use it on the training set to make predictions. You would then increase the weight on the misclassified instances before training another classifier on the new weights; again, the training set is used for making predictions, the weights get updated and so it goes on.

When all of the predictors have been trained, the predictions made by the ensemble are similar to pasting or bagging with one exception – the predictors all have different weights and these depend on how accurate the predictors are on the weighted training dataset.

Warning

Sequential learning can be useful but there is a downside to it; parallelization is not possible because each predictor can be trained only when the previous one has undergone training and evaluation. This means it doesn't scale very well, at least not quite as well as pasting and bagging do.

Let's look at the algorithm used by AdaBoost. The instance weights are denoted by w(i) and each is set, to begin with, to 1/π. The first predictor gets trained and r 1, which is the rate of the weighted error, is computed using the training dataset. The next equation shows this:

$$r_j = \frac{\displaystyle\sum_{\substack{i=1 \\ \hat{y}_j^{(i)} \neq y^{(i)}}}^{m} w^{(i)}}{\displaystyle\sum_{i=1}^{m} w^{(i)}} \qquad \text{where } \hat{y}_j^{(i)} \text{ is the } j^{th} \text{ predictor's prediction for the } i^{th} \text{ instance.}$$

Equation - Weighted Error Rate Of The jth Predictor

The weight for the predictor is aj and this computed using the equation that you see below (predicted weight). In this equation, the learning rate hyperparameter is n and it will default to 1. The accuracy of the predictor will dictate its weight – the more accurate, the higher the weight. It takes random guesses that the weight will be nearer to zero, but if it is wrong more than it is right, the weight will be a negative weight.

$$\alpha_j = \eta \log \frac{1 - r_j}{r_j}$$

Equation - Predictor Weight

Then, the next equation is used to update the weights and any instances that were misclassified will be boosted:

$$\text{for } i = 1, 2, \cdots, m$$

$$w^{(i)} \leftarrow \begin{cases} w^{(i)} & \text{if } \hat{y}_j^{(i)} = y^{(i)} \\ w^{(i)} \exp(\alpha_j) & \text{if } \hat{y}_j^{(i)} \neq y^{(i)} \end{cases}$$

Equation - Weight Update Rule

The weights are then divided by v\$\sum^m_{i=1}w(i)$ to normalize them. Lastly, another predictor gets trained on the updated weights and we start over, repeating the process. The algorithm will continue like this until the perfect predictor is located or it reaches the requisite number of predictors.

AdaBoost makes predictions by computing all the predictions made across all the predictors and then uses aj, the predictor weight, to weigh the predictions. The class predicted is the one that gets the most weighted votes as the next equation shows:

$$\hat{y}(\mathbf{x}) = \underset{k}{\operatorname{argmax}} \sum_{\substack{j=1 \\ \hat{y}_j(\mathbf{x})=k}}^{N} \alpha_j \qquad \text{where } N \text{ is the number of predictors.}$$

Equation - AdaBoost Predictions

Scikit-learn makes use of SAMME, a multiclass flavor of AdaBoost that stands for Stagewise Additive Modeling using a Multiclass Exponential Loss Function. SAMME is the same as AdaBoost when you have two classes and, provided the predictors have the predict_proba() method and estimate the class probabilities, a variant called SAMME-R can be used (the R is for Real). SAMME.R doesn't rely on predictions, but rather on class probabilities and it works quite a bit better.

With the next code, we use a set of Decision Stumps (200 in total) to train the AdaBoost classifier using the AdaBoostClassifier class from scikit-learn. What is a Decision Stump? It is a tree that is made up of one decision node and a pair of leaf nodes with a max_depth=1. This base estimator is the default for the AdaBoostClassifier class:

```
from sklearn.ensemble import AdaBoostClassifier

ada_clf = AdaBoostClassifier(

DecisionTreeClassifier(max_depth=1), n_estimators=200,

algorithm="SAMME.R", learning_rate=0.5

)

ada_clf.fit(X_train, y_train)
```

> **Tip**
>
> If you find that the ensemble overfits the dataset, reduce the estimators or do some stronger regularization on the base estimator.

Gradient Boosting

Gradient Boosting is another of the popular algorithms for boosting. Much like AdaBoost, it uses a sequential technique adding the predictors to the ensemble, each making corrections to its predecessor. However, it doesn't tweak the instance weights with every iteration. Instead, it attempts to take the residual errors from the previous predictor and fit the new predictor to them. We'll look at a regression example with the base predictors being Decision Trees. Gradient Boosting works well with regression and is known as Gradient Tree Boosting, sometimes as GBRT – Gradient Boosted Regression Trees. The first thing to do is fit the DecisionTreeRegressor to a very noisy quadratic training dataset:

```
from sklearn.tree import DecisionTreeRegressor

tree_reg1 = DecisionTreeRegressor(max_depth=2)

tree_reg1.fit(X, y)
```

Next, we take the residual errors and train another DecisionTreeRegressor:

```
y2 = y - tree_reg1.predict(X)

tree_reg2 = DecisionTreeRegressor(max_depth=2)

tree_reg2.fit(X, y2)
```

Lastly, the residual errors from this predictor are used to train the third one:

```
y3 = y2 - tree_reg2.predict(X)

tree_reg3 = DecisionTreeRegressor(max_depth=2)

tree_reg3.fit(X, y3)
```

What we have now is an ensemble that has three trees in it and predictions can be made on new instances just by adding the predictions from the three trees:

```
y_pred = sum(tree.predict(X_new) for tree in (tree_reg1, tree_reg2,
tree_reg3))
```

Perhaps an easier way of training GBRT ensembles would be to use the GradientBoostingRegressor class from scikit-learn. In a similar way to the RandomForestRegressor class, this one also contains the hyperparameters needed for controlling how the Decision Trees grow, i.e. min_samples_leaf, max_depth, etc. It also has the hyperparameters needed for controlling the training of the ensemble, for example, n_estimators, which is the number of the trees.

The next code will create an identical ensemble to the one you just created:

```
from sklearn.ensemble import GradientBoostingRegressor

gbrt = GradientBoostingRegressor(max_depth=2, n_estimators=3,
learning_rate=1.0)

gbrt.fit(X, y)
```

The hyperparameter called learning_rate will take the contributions of each of the trees and scale them. If a low value, such as 0.1, is set, the ensemble needs more trees if it is to fit the dataset but you get better generalization on the predictions. This technique is called shrinkage and it is used for regularization.

Early Stopping could be used as a way of finding the optimal tree number and the best implementation method is the method called staged_predict(). This method will take the predictions that the ensemble makes at each training stage and returns an iterator over them.

The next code shows a GBRT ensemble being trained – the ensemble contains 120 trees. The validation error is then measured for each training stage so that the optimal number can be found and then another GBRT ensemble is trained using that number:

```
import numpy as np

from sklearn.model_selection import train_test_split

from sklearn.metrics import mean_squared_error

X_train, X_val, y_train, y_val = train_test_split(X, y)

gbrt = GradientBoostingRegressor(max_depth=2, n_estimators=120)

gbrt.fit(X_train, y_train)

errors = [mean_squared_error(y_val, y_pred)

for y_pred in gbrt.staged_predict(X_val)]

bst_n_estimators = np.argmin(errors)

gbrt_best =
GradientBoostingRegressor(max_depth=2,n_estimators=bst_n_estimators)

gbrt_best.fit(X_train, y_train)
```

Another implementation method for Early Stopping is to simply halt the training early and not train loads of trees first before looking for the optimal number. To do this, warm_Start=True is set and this will make scikit-learn retain the existing trees whenever fit() is called – this allows for training to be done in increments.

This next code will stop the training when there is no improvement in the validation error for a sequence of five concurrent iterations:

```
gbrt = GradientBoostingRegressor(max_depth=2, warm_start=True)

min_val_error = float("inf")

error_going_up = 0

for n_estimators in range(1, 120):

gbrt.n_estimators = n_estimators

gbrt.fit(X_train, y_train)
```

```
y_pred = gbrt.predict(X_val)

val_error = mean_squared_error(y_val, y_pred)

if val_error < min_val_error:

min_val_error = val_error

error_going_up = 0

else:

error_going_up += 1

if error_going_up == 5:

break # early stopping
```

A subsample hyperparameter is used to specify the training instances required for each tree to be trained (specified as a fraction) and is also supported in the GradientBoostingRegressor class. For example, let's say that the subsample=0.25 – this would mean that 25% of training instances are used for training each tree and these are randomly selected. As you might guess, you get a higher bias traded off for a lower variance. You also get faster training and this is known as Stochastic Gradient Boosting.

Stacking

The final method we are going to look at briefly is called stacking, which is the shortened version of stacked generalization. It's quite simple to understand – rather than aggregating the predictions from all the predictors in the ensemble using hard voting or another trivial function, we can simply train a model that will do the aggregation for us. Each of the predictions is taken and a blender, which is another type of predictor, takes them as inputs and comes up with one last prediction.

Training the blender requires a hold-out set; the training dataset is divided into a pair of subsets. The first one trains the first layer predictors which then go on to produce predictions for the second set, known as a held-out set. This way we know that we have clean predictions because the instances were never seen by the predictors during training. Each of the instances in the hold-out set has three predicted values and we can use these values as the input features making the training set into a three-dimensional set. This also retains the target values. We then train the blender on the new set; in this way, it will learn to take the predictions from the first layer to predict the target value.

You could train multiple blenders like this so you get a layer of different ones. The trick is in dividing the training set into three subsets rather than two – the first is for training layer one, the second creates the set needed for training layer two (using the predictions from layer one) and the third does the same for layer three using the predictions from layer two. When you have done this, you can go through the three layers in sequence to predict a new instance.

Chapter 7: What is Dimensionality Reduction?

A high proportion of the problems we use machine learning to involve hundreds of thousands, in some cases millions of features for every individual training instance. This does two things – it slows the training significantly and it makes finding a good solution very difficult, as you are going to see. We often hear this called the Curse of Dimensionality.

Thankfully, when it comes to real-world issues, we can, on many occasions, make a significant reduction to the number of features making what seemed to be an unmanageable problem into one that is much easier to manage. For example, take the images from the MNIST dataset; on pretty much every image, the pixels that border them are usually white so you could lose these pixels from the dataset without losing any real information – these pixels are not important in terms of classification. Not only that, there is often a high correlation between the pair of neighboring pixels; merge them into a single pixel and you lose very little information.

Warning

When you reduce dimensionality, you will lose some information. Think of when you compress an image down to JPEG format; the quality is degraded because some information has been lost. Reducing dimensionality is much the same. It may speed up the training but it may also make performance a little bit worse. Your pipelines will be more complex and that will make maintaining them harder to do. So, before you even think about reducing the dimensionality in cases of slow training, you should make every attempt to train the system using the original data. In short, exhaust every avenue before you go to dimensionality reduction. There are cases where reducing the training data dimensionality can remove some of the noise and some details that are not required and this, in turn, can raise the performance – although generally, all it will do is speed the training.

As well as speeding the training, dimensionality is also good for the purpose of data visualization. When we cut the dimensions down to just two or three, plotting a high-dimension set is made possible and you can often see patterns, like clusters, a lot easier.

In this chapter, we will be looking at the Curse of Dimensionality and take a peek at what happens in high-dimensional space. After that, we will look at the two most common approaches to reducing dimensionality – Manifold Learning and Projection – and then a look at the three most popular techniques – PCA, Kernel PCA, and LLE.

The Curse of Dimensionality

Because we are conditioned to living in three-dimensional space, when we attempt to imagine high-dimensional spaces, our intuition tends to let us down. It is even hard to visualize a 4D hypercube, a basic structure, let alone trying to visualize an ellipsoid with 200 dimensions and bent in a space of 1,000 dimensions!

As it turns out, there are a lot of things that behave in very different ways when they are in high-dimensional space. Let's say you take a 1 x 1 unit square and choose any random point. That point will have a 0.4% chance of being within 0.001 of a border. What this means is that a random point is not likely to be "extreme" on any dimension. But, let's say that 1 x 1 square is now a hypercube of 10,000-dimensional units – basically, a cube of 1 x 1 x ... x 1 with a total of 10,000 1s. Picking a random point from a hypercube of that size would give you a probability that is more than 99.999999% - in other words, most high-dimensional hypercube points are extremely close to the border.

Let's make it a bit more difficult: take a unit square and choose two random points. The distance from one point to the next will be about 0.52. If you had a 3D unit cube and chose two random points, the distance would be about 0.66. But what if you chose those random points from a hypercube of 1,000,000 dimensions. The distance would average out at approximately 408.25 x sqrt(1,000,000/6).

This is, as you can probably see, somewhat counterintuitive. How is it possible for there to be so much distance between two points in the same hypercube? The implication is that high-dimensional datasets run a high risk of being sparse, which means that most of the instances will be a long way from one another. This also means that new instances are also going to be a long way from the training instances and that makes predictions unreliable in the lower dimensions. This is because the extrapolations they are based on are considerably larger. Basically, the more dimensions that a training dataset has, the higher the risk there is of overfitting.

There is a theoretical solution to this Curse of Dimensionality; increasing the training set size so it can reach a sufficient training instance density. In practice, this rarely works because, to reach that density, the number of training instances that you require will grow aggressively depending on how many dimensions there are. If you just had 100 features, which is significantly less than the MNIST issues, the number of training instances required for each instance to be no more than 0.1 apart would number more than the number of atoms there are in the observable universe. And that is assuming that all your training instances are uniformly spread across every dimension.

Dimensionality Reduction – The Main Approaches

Before we start looking into the algorithms that are specific to dimensionality reduction, we'll look at Projection and Manifold Learning, the main approach used to reduce dimensionality.

Projection

When it comes to real-world problems, the training instances are not going to be evenly spread over all the dimensions. Most features will be constant and others will be highly correlated. The result of this is that a high percentage of the training instances will be close to or even within a subspace of the high-dimensional space, a subspace of much lower dimensions. This all sounds a little hypothetical so we need to look at it in a different way.

Let's say that you have a 3D dataset that is represented by circles on a graph. All of the instances are very close to one of the planes and this is the 2D low-dimension subspace of the 3D high-dimension space. If every one of the training instances were to be perpendicularly projected onto the subspace, you would get a brand new 2D dataset. As such, we have reduced the dimensionality of the dataset from 3D down to 2D.

All that being said, projection really isn't the right solution for all cases of dimensionality reduction. In many cases, the subspace is likely to turn and twist quite a bit, much like a Swiss Roll dataset. If you were to project onto the plane, the layers of the Swiss Roll would all be squashed in together. Whereas, what you really want is the layers unrolled so that you can get to the 2D dataset.

Manifold Learning

The Swiss Roll is one example of the 2D manifold. In simple terms, 2D manifolds are 2D shapes that can be twisted and bent to make high-dimensional spaces. In general terms, a manifold of d-dimensions is a part of the n-dimensional space that looks, locally, much like a hyperplane of d-dimensions. With the Swiss Roll, where d = 2 and n = 3, it looks like a 2D plane but is rolled in 3D (the third dimension).

For many of the algorithms for dimensionality reduction to work, the manifold where the instances lie needs to be modeled and we call this Manifold Learning. The Manifold Assumption, sometimes known as the Manifold Hypothesis, on which Manifold Learning relies, holds that the high-dimensional datasets in real-world problems are, in actual fact, nearer to a low-dimension manifold.

Let's take the MNIST dataset again. All of the images are handwritten and they all share some similarity. Each is constructed of lines that are connected; each has a white border; all are pretty much centered, and so on. If you were to generate a random set of images, there would be such a small percentage, a fraction really, that would actually look like they were handwritten digits. What I really mean is, if you were to try creating a digit image, the degree of freedom that you would have would be significantly lower than the freedom you would have if you could generate any image that you wanted.

All these constraints do is push the given dataset down into a manifold with lower dimensions. Often, an additional implicit assumption accompanies the Manifold Assumption and that assumption is that the task you are doing, be it regression or classification, would be much easier if it were expressed in that lower dimension. However, this isn't always the case. Let's say that you have a decision boundary at $x_1 = 5$ and, while it may look like a simple decision boundary in the 3D space, look at it in the unrolled manifold and it looks much more complex.

Simply put, if your training set is reduced in dimensionality before you use it to train a model, the training will be faster but it doesn't necessarily follow that the solution is better; that will depend entirely on the dataset.

By now you should have, at the very least, a basic idea of the Curse of Dimensionality and specific algorithms can help, particularly when the Manifold Assumption is true. For the remainder of this chapter, we will explain the most popular of those dimensionality reduction algorithms.

PCA

PCA or Principal Component Analysis is the most popular of the algorithms for dimensionality reduction. It first finds the hyperplane that is nearest to the data and then it projects that data onto the hyperplane.

Variance Preservation

Before the training set can be projected onto the hyperplane, you need to make sure you have the correct hyperplane. Let's say that you have a 2D dataset and three separate axes, all 1D hyperplanes. If you were to project the data onto each of these hyperplanes, you would see which one preserves the variance the most and which one preserves it the least. It would not be unreasonable to choose the one with the maximum variance preservation because it is less likely to lose information. You could justify your choice by saying that this hyperplane takes the mean squared distance between the original and the projected datasets and minimizes it. That is a simplified idea of PCA.

Principal Components

PCA will find the axis or hyperplane that shows the majority of the variance but it will also find the orthogonal second axis that accounts for the majority of the left-over variance. Should the dataset be higher-dimensional, then PCA would find the third orthogonal axis, and a fourth, and so on, for as many as there are in the dataset.

The ith axis is defined by a unit vector that this called ith PC or ith Principal Component.

The principal component direction is not terribly stable. If you upset the training set even a little, and then run PCA again, you will likely find that some PCs point opposite to the originals but they will tend to be on the exact same axis as the original. Sometimes pairs of PCs can swap or rotate but they will tend to define the same plane they did originally.

How do we go about finding what the training set principal components are? There is a way and it's a technique for standard matrix factorization known as SVD or Singular Value Decomposition. SVD has the ability to take the training set matrix x and break it down so we have the dot product of matrices $U \cdot \Sigma \cdot V$ T. VT and all the PCs that we need as you can see in the following equation:

$$V^T = \begin{pmatrix} | & | & & | \\ c_1 & c_2 & \cdots & c_n \\ | & | & & | \end{pmatrix}$$

Equation - Principal Components Matrix

The next piece of code in Python makes use of the svd() function in NumPy to get the PCs of the set and will then extract PCs one and two:

```
X_centered = X - X.mean(axis=0)

U, s, V = np.linalg.svd(X_centered)

c1 = V.T[:, 0]

c2 = V.T[:, 1]
```

Warning

PCA will always conclude that the dataset will be centered on the origin and the PCA classes in scikit-learn take care of this for you. But, if you manually implement PCA, or you make use of alternative libraries, you must center the data yourself.

Projecting Down to d-Dimensions

When the principal components have all been identified, the dataset dimensionality can be reduced down to d dimension and this is done by projecting it to the hyperplane that the initial d PCs defined.

When you choose this hyperplane, you make sure that the maximum amount of variance is preserved by the projection. Let's say that you have a 3D dataset that you project down to the 2D plane. The first two PCs define the 2D plane and, at the same time, they preserve the maximum amount of the dataset variance. The result of this is that the projection onto the 2D plane looks very similar to the 3D dataset.

Projection of the training set is quite simple – we just take matrix (the training set) and work out the dot product by matrix Wd – this is the matrix that has the first d PCs, or the first columns in VT, as you can see in the next equation:

$$X_{d\text{-proj}} = X \cdot W_d$$

Equation – Training Set Projection Down To D-Dimensions

This next Python code will project the set to the plane that the first PCs defined:

```
W2 = V.T[:, :2]

X2D = X_centered.dot(W2)
```

That's all there is to it - reducing the dimensionality of any given dataset down to whatever number of dimensions you want while preserving the maximum variance.

Using Scikit-Learn

The PCA class in scikit-learn will use SVD decomposition to implement PCA. The next piece of code will reduce the dataset dimensionality to 2D by applying PCA – it will center the data automatically:

```
from sklearn.decomposition import PCA

pca = PCA(n_components = 2)

X2D = pca.fit_transform(X)
```

Once the PCA transformer has been fitted to the dataset, we can use the variable called components_ to get to the principal components – note that horizontal vectors represent the PCs in the variable. For example, the first PC would be equal to pca.components_.T[:,0]).

Explained Variance Ratio

Explained Variance Ratio is incredibly useful and it relates to each of the principal components. We can get this from the variable called explained_variance_ratio_ and this will give you an indication of the variance that is along each PCs axis.

```
>>> print(pca.explained_variance_ratio_)

array([ 0.84248607, 0.14631839])
```

What this tells us is that the percentage of variance on axis 1 is 84.2%, with 14.6% on axis 2. The remainder lies on axis 3 so it wouldn't be unreasonable to assume that axis 3 has very little information.

How to Choose the Correct Number of Dimensions

Rather than quickly picking how many dimensions are to be reduced, the better way is to pick the dimensions that make up a considerable amount of the variance, for example, 95%. Of course, if the dimensionality reduction is for the purpose of data visualization, you would want the dimensionality down to 2D or 3D at the most.

This next code is going to compute the PCA without any dimensionality reduction. Then, it will compute the lowest number of dimensions needed for preserving 95% of the variance of the training set:

```
pca = PCA()

pca.fit(X)

cumsum = np.cumsum(pca.explained_variance_ratio_)

d = np.argmax(cumsum >= 0.95) + 1
```

After setting n_components=d, you would then run PCA again. But there is a better way. Rather than specifying how many of the principal components you want to be preserved, you could set n_components as a float, somewhere between 0.0 and 1.0, thus indicating what Variance Ratio you want to be preserved:

```
pca = PCA(n_components=0.95)

X_reduced = pca.fit_transform(X)
```

You could do it another way. Take the explained variance and plot it as a function of the dimensions for preservation. Usually, you will see the curve with an elbow in it; this is where the explained variance ceases growing. This could be seen as intrinsic dataset dimensionality and you can see that, by reducing dimensionality to around 100 dimensions, you won't lose much of the explained variance.

PCA for Compression

Once you have done some dimensionality reduction, you will find that the training set doesn't take up so much space. For example, take the MNIST dataset and preserve 95% of the variance while you apply PCA. What you should see is that each individual instance will have a little more than 150 features; before, it would have had 784. While you have preserved the maximum amount of variance, the dataset has been reduced to less than 20% of the size it was originally. This compression ratio is quite reasonable and it's easy to see how this could be used to significantly speed up classification algorithms, like the SVM classifier.

You could also carry out decompression, taking the dataset back to its original 784 dimensions. To do that, we take the PCA projection and apply inverse transformation to it. What this won't do is provide you with the data that was in the set originally because, during the projection, we lost some information – remember, we preserved 95% variance but 5% was dropped. However, it will be as near to the original as we can get it. Between the compressed data (original) and decompressed data (reconstructed), the mean square distance is known as the Reconstruction Error. For example, in the next code, we will take the MNIST dataset and compress it to 154 dimensions. Then the inverse_transformation() method will decompress it so it is back to 784 dimensions. There will be a slight loss of image quality but most of it will be intact:

```
pca = PCA(n_components = 154)

X_mnist_reduced = pca.fit_transform(X_mnist)

X_mnist_recovered = pca.inverse_transform(X_mnist_reduced)
```

Have a look at the next equation, which will show the inverse transformation:

$$X_{recovered} = X_{d\text{-proj}} \cdot W_d^T$$

Equation - PCA Inverse Transformation

Incremental PCA

There is a problem with the PCA implementation we just did; for the SVD algorithm to run correctly, the entire training dataset has got to fit into memory. We do have a solution though, IPCA algorithms. These are Incremental PCA algorithms and we use them by dividing the dataset into smaller batches and feed each batch an IPCA algorithm, one batch at a time. This works very well when you have a large dataset and you can also use it for online applications of PCA, i.e. applying it as each new instance arrives.

With the next code, we are dividing the MNIST dataset into a total of 100 smaller batches. We use the array_split() function from NumPy to do this and then we feed each batch, one at a time, with the IncrementalPCA class from scikit-learn. This reduces the MNIST dataset dimensionality to 154 dimensions. Note that, instead of calling the fit() method on the entire set, we call partial_fit() on each batch:

```
from sklearn.decomposition import IncrementalPCA

n_batches = 100

inc_pca = IncrementalPCA(n_components=154)

for X_batch in np.array_split(X_mnist, n_batches):

inc_pca.partial_fit(X_batch)

X_mnist_reduced = inc_pca.transform(X_mnist)
```

You could also use the memmap class in NumPy. This will let you take a large array that has been stored on disk in a binary file, just as if it were in memory, and manipulate it. The class will only load what data is needed in memory and it will only load that data when it needs it.

Because IncrementalPCA will only use a small bit of the array at any one time, we can retain control over the memory usage. Using this, we can call the fit() method and you will see this demonstrated in the next piece of code:

```
X_mm = np.memmap(filename, dtype="float32", mode="readonly",
shape=(m, n))

batch_size = m // n_batches

inc_pca = IncrementalPCA(n_components=154, batch_size=batch_size)

inc_pca.fit(X_mm)
```

Randomized PCA

There is one more option in scikit-learn to perform PCA. It's called Randomized PCA and it is a stochastic algorithm that is used to locate a resemblance of the initial d PCs. The complexity of Randomized PCA in computational terms is o(m x d 2) + o(d 3) and not, as you might expect, o(m x n 2) + o(n 3). This makes it considerably faster, where d is significantly smaller than n, than the other algorithms.

```
rnd_pca = PCA(n_components=154, svd_solver="randomized")

X_reduced = rnd_pca.fit_transform(X_mnist)
```

Kernel PCA

A little earlier in this guide, we talked about the kernel trick. This is a technique that maps instances implicitly into a feature space (or a space that is very high-dimensional). This enables us to do nonlinear regression and classification using an SVM. If you remember, linear decision boundaries that are in this feature space will correspond directly to nonlinear decision boundaries that are in the original space.

As it happens, we can apply this to PCA as well and that will make it entirely possible for us to perform a nonlinear projection for the purpose of dimensionality reduction. This is known as kPCA or kernel PCA and it is very useful for when you want clusters of instances to be preserved after projection or for unrolling any datasets that are close to a manifold that is twisted.

The following piece of code performs kPCA using the KernelPCA class in scikit-learn. It uses an RBF kernel to do this:

```
from sklearn.decomposition import KernelPCA

rbf_pca = KernelPCA(n_components = 2, kernel="rbf", gamma=0.04)

X_reduced = rbf_pca.fit_transform(X)
```

Choosing a Kernel and Fine-tuning the Hyperparameters

kPCA comes under unsupervised learning so we don't have any obvious measures for performance that would help you choose the right kernel and the right hyperparameter values. But, with dimensionality reduction, we are usually making preparations for supervised learning tasks like classification. What you could do is use grid search to choose your kernel and the hyperparameters that will provide the best possible performance of the given task.

An example can be seen in the next code. We are going to create a pipeline (two-step) by using dimensionality reduction. We use kPCA to bring dimensionality down to 2D and then we use Logistic Regression for the classification. GridSearchCV is then used to find the best possible kernel and the kPCA gamma value so that we can have the best accuracy in terms of classification when the pipeline ends:

```
from sklearn.model_selection import GridSearchCV

from sklearn.linear_model import LogisticRegression

from sklearn.pipeline import Pipeline

clf = Pipeline([

("kpca", KernelPCA(n_components=2)),

("log_reg", LogisticRegression())

])

param_grid = [{

"kpca__gamma": np.linspace(0.03, 0.05, 10),

"kpca__kernel": ["rbf", "sigmoid"]

}]

grid_search = GridSearchCV(clf, param_grid, cv=3)

grid_search.fit(X, y)
```

You will find that kernel and the hyperparameters in the variable called best_params_:

```
>>> print(grid_search.best_params_)

{'kpca__gamma': 0.043333333333333335, 'kpca__kernel': 'rbf'}
```

We could use an unsupervised approach; we would choose the kernel and the right hyperparameters to provide the lowest reconstruction error. But it isn't easy to do reconstruction with linear PCA and here's why.

Let's say that we have a Swiss Roll dataset (3D) and, after we apply kPCA with the RBF kernel, we have a 2D dataset. By using the kernel trick, we have produced the mathematical equivalent of using φ, which is the feature map to map the whole set to a feature space of infinite dimensions and then using projection with linear PCA to bring the new training set down to a 2D set.

Note that, if the linear PCA step could be inverted for any given instance inside the reduced space, the reconstruction would be in the feature space and not the original. Because features space has an infinite number of dimensions, the reconstructed point cannot be computed and that means the true reconstruction error also cannot be computed. Thankfully, we can find the point inside the original space that would be near to the reconstruction point. We call this reconstruction pre-image and, once we have this, the squared distance can be measured to the original instance. Then, the kernel and the hyperparameters can be selected and the pre-image error can be minimized.

So how do we do this reconstruction? One way would be to take a supervised regression model and train it – the training set would be the projected instances and the target would be the original instances. This is done automatically in scikit-learn by setting fit_inverse_transform=True, as you can see in the next code:

```
rbf_pca = KernelPCA(n_components = 2, kernel="rbf", gamma=0.0433,

fit_inverse_transform=True)

X_reduced = rbf_pca.fit_transform(X)

X_preimage = rbf_pca.inverse_transform(X_reduced)
```

Note

By default, neither KernalPCA nor fit_inverse_transform=False has got the inverse_transform() method; this will only be created when fit_inverse_transform=True is set.

You can then compute the reconstruction pre-image error:

```
>>> from sklearn.metrics import mean_squared_error

>>> mean_squared_error(X, X_preimage)

32.786308795766132
```

Now grid search and cross-validation may be used to find the kernel and the hyperparameters that will minimize the error.

LLE

LLE, or Locally Linearly Embedding is an NLDR technique that is incredibly powerful. NLDR is nonlinear dimensionality reduction and it is a Manifold Learning technique that doesn't need projections to work, unlike the last algorithms. Put simply, LLE uses measurements to determine how close linearly each instance relates to its nearest neighbors. It will then look for the best representation that shows the best preservation of the local relationships. This makes LLE very good for unrolling manifolds that are twisted, especially those that are not too noisy.

The following code shows how the LocallyLinearEmbedding class from scikit-learn unrolls the Swiss Roll. The distances that are shown between each of the instances are well reserved in local terms but, on a larger scale, they are not.

```
from sklearn.manifold import LocallyLinearEmbedding

lle = LocallyLinearEmbedding(n_components=2, n_neighbors=10)

X_reduced = lle.fit_transform(X)
```

So, how does LLE work? First, for each of the training instances, x (i), LLE will work out the k closest neighbors (k = 10 in the code above). It will then attempt to reconstruct x (i) so it is a linear function of the neighbors. In more specific terms, it will find wi,j, which are the weights, in a way that the squared distance from x (i) to $\sum_{i=1}^{m}$wijx(j) is as small as it can be, making the assumption that wi,j = 0 provided x (j) is not a k closest neighbor of x(i).

As such, LLE's first step is shown in the following equation as a constrained optimization problem. The weight matrix is W and it has all the wi,j weights in it. The weights for each of the training instances x (i) are normalized by the second constraint:

$$W = \underset{W}{\arg\min} \sum_{i=1}^{m} \left\| x^{(i)} - \sum_{j=1}^{m} w_{i,j} x^{(j)} \right\|^2$$

$$\text{subject to} \begin{cases} w_{i,j} = 0 & \text{if } x^{(j)} \text{ is not one of the } k \text{ c.n. of } x^{(i)} \\ \sum_{j=1}^{m} w_{i,j} = 1 & \text{for } i = 1, 2, \cdots, m \end{cases}$$

Equation - LLE Step 1: Linearly Modeling Local Relationships

Next, the weight matrix will encode the LLE relationships between each training instance. Step two is mapping the instances to a d-dimensional space while preserving as much of the relationships as possible. Let's say that, while in the d-dimensional space, z (i) is an image of x (i)'; in this case, the squared distances from z (i) to $\sum_{i=1}^{m}$w ijx(j) should be as small as possible. This leads to what was seen in the unconstrained optimization problem equation. It looks much like step 1 but, rather than the instances being kept fixed and looking for the optimal weights, we do the reverse – the weights are kept fixed and we'll look in the low-dimensional space for the optimal position of the images.

$$\mathbf{Z} = \arg\min_{\mathbf{Z}} \sum_{i=1}^{m} \| z^{(i)} - \sum_{j=1}^{m} \hat{w}_{i,j} z^{(j)} \|^2$$

Equation - LLE Step 2: Reducing Dimensionality While Preserving Relationships

The LLE implementation in scikit-learn displays this complexity in computational terms:

- o(m) n log(k) – to find the k closest neighbors
- o(mnk 3) – to optimize the weights
- o(dm 2) – to construct the representations in the low-dimensions

The m2 that you see in the final computation doesn't make this algorithm scale very well when you have large datasets.

Chapter 8: Introducing TensorFlow

TensorFlow is one of the most powerful numerical computation libraries. It is open-source and it is very well suited to machine learning on a large scale. The basic idea behind TensorFlow is very simple – you define a computation graph in Python and TensorFlow will take that graph and use C++ code that has been fully optimized to run it.

Perhaps even more important is that TensorFlow can take that graph and break it down into multiple pieces and then run them parallel to one another across multiple GPUs and/or CPUs. TensorFlow also has support for distributed computing giving you the tools to train massive neural networks on massive training sets in a reasonable period of time. How? By dividing the computations over multiple servers, and we're talking hundreds. TensorFlow is able to train a network that has many millions of parameters using a training dataset that has many billions of instances, each with many millions of features – you can see the extent it goes to. In all honesty, this shouldn't cause any surprise because TensorFlow comes from the Google Brain Team and is used on most of the larger scale services that Google offers, such as Photos, Search, and Cloud Speech.

With TensorFlow, you will find TF.Learn, a Python API that is fully compatible with scikit-learn. You will see throughout this chapter that you can use this API (tensorflow.contrib.learn) to train numerous different types of neural networks using the minimum amount of code. There is also one more very simple API, TF-slim (tensorflow.contrib.slim) that is used for the simplification of building neural networks, train them and then evaluate them. Other high-level APIs have been developed independently on TensorFlow, like Pretty Tensor and Keras.

The fundamental Python API provides a high-level of flexibility with a higher level of complexity providing the tools to create all manner of different computations. In short, it handles any architecture related to neural networks that you could possibly think of. In TensorFlow are a number of highly capable C++ implementations that relate to multiple machine learning operations, in particular, those operations that relate to the neural networks. And you can define your own operations using the C++ API.

TensorFlow has a number of highly progressive optimization nodes that help with cost function minimization by finding the requisite parameters. These are incredibly simple to use because TensorFlow will work out the gradients automatically for any function that you define and this is known as Automatic Differentiating or autodiff for short.

TensorBoard is a visualization tool included to give you the ability to browse through a graph, look at the learning curves and much, much more. And, it might interest you to know that Google Cloud has recently launched its own cloud service for running the TensorFlow graphs.

For the rest of this chapter, we are going to delve into TensorFlow, learn how it works, how to create graphs, run them, save them, and visualize them. We'll start with the installation procedure. Master the basics of TensorFlow and you will be on the first rung of the ladder needed to build your own neural network.

Installing TensorFlow

Time to get into TensorFlow and we need to start by installing it. You should already have scikit-learn and Jupyter installed making TensorFlow installation simple. Just use pip to install it.

If you want GPU support, instead of using pip tensorflow, you will need to use pip tensorflow gpu.

Now it's time to test that TensorFlow is installed correctly. At the command prompt, type in this command – you should see the installed version of TensorFlow as the output:

```
$ python3 -c 'import tensorflow; print(tensorflow.__version__)'
```

Let's Create a Graph and Run It

Input the following code to produce the graph:

```
import tensorflow as tf

x = tf.Variable(3, name="x")

y = tf.Variable(4, name="y")

f = x*x*y + y + 2
```

That's all there is to do. What is important is that the code will not carry out any computations although at first glance you would be mistaken for thinking it does. All it does is create the computation graph. We haven't even initialized the variables yet!

Evaluating the graph requires a TensorFlow session to be opened; then it can be used to initialize the variables and evaluate f. The session will place and run all the operations onto devices like GPUs and CPUs automatically and it will also retain the values for all the variables.

The next code will create the TensorFlow session and then it will initialize all the variables and evaluate f before closing the session to free up the resources:

```
>>> sess = tf.Session()

>>> sess.run(x.initializer)

>>> sess.run(y.initializer)

>>> result = sess.run(f)

>>> print(result)

42

>>> sess.close()
```

Now, it all looks a bit much, having to repeat sess.run() over and again, but there is a more efficient way:

```
with tf.Session() as sess:

x.initializer.run()

y.initializer.run()

result = f.eval()
```

You can see that, in the with block, we've set the default session. X.initializer.run(o is the same as calling the much longer tf.get_default_session().run(x.initializer) and f.eval() is the same as tf.get_default_session().run(f) – much easier to read and a far more efficient use of resources.

Even better, the session gets automatically closed when the block ends. Rather than having to manually run the initializer for each individual variable, the function called global_variables_initializer() can be used, but you should note that initialization will not be done immediately; instead, a node is created in the graph where all the variables will be initialized when it runs:

```
init = tf.global_variables_initializer() # prepare an init node

with tf.Session() as sess:

init.run() # initialize all the variables

result = f.eval()
```

You could create an InteractiveSession in a Python shell or in Jupyter if you want – the difference between that and a regular session is that an InteractiveSession will automatically set itself as a default session upon creation. That means you do not need to use the with block but you will need to manually close the session when you are finished:

```
>>> sess = tf.InteractiveSession()

>>> init.run()

>>> result = f.eval()

>>> print(result)

42

>>> sess.close()
```

TensorFlow programs are usually divided in two – part one is to build the graph and is known as the Construction Phase, while part two runs the graph and is known as the Execution Phase. Usually, the construction phase will build a graph that represents the machine learning model and all the computations needed to train that model. The Execution phase will run a loop that repeatedly evaluates a step in the training and will make gradual improvements to the parameters of the given model.

Graph Management

Whenever you create a node, it is added to the default graph automatically:

```
>>> x1 = tf.Variable(1)

>>> x1.graph is tf.get_default_graph()

True
```

Most of the time this will be just fine but there will be occasions when you have several independent graphs and you want to manage them. To do this, you would create another graph and give it a temporary status as the default graph using the with block, as in the example below:

```
>>> graph = tf.Graph()

>>> with graph.as_default():

...    x2 = tf.Variable(2)

...

>>> x2.graph is graph

True

>>> x2.graph is tf.get_default_graph()

False
```

Tip

In a Python shell or Jupyter, you can run the same commands multiple times while you experiment. The result of this may be a default graph that has several duplicated nodes on it. A solution would be to start the Python shell or Jupyter again, but a better way would be to run tf.reset_default_graph() and reset the graph.

Node Value Lifecycle

When a node is evaluated, TensorFlow will determine the nodes set that the given node depends on automatically and these nodes will be evaluated first. For example, look at the next code

```
w = tf.constant(3)

x = w + 2

y = x + 5

z = x * 3

with tf.Session() as sess:

print(y.eval()) # 10

print(z.eval()) # 15
```

All we have done here is defined as a simple graph. A session is then started and the graph is run so that y can be evaluated. We can see that y is dependent on w, which is dependent on x and Tensorflow will detect this automatically. It will evaluate w first, then x and lastly y, and return the y value. Lastly, the graph is run so z can be evaluated. Again, TensorFlow knows that it will need to evaluate w first and then x. Be aware that TensorFlow will NOT make use of the first w and x evaluation which means that the previous code will be run twice.

In between each graph run, all the node values are dropped with the exception of the variable values – the session will maintain these values across every graph run. The variable begins its life when the initializer that goes with it is run and its life will end when the session closes.

For efficient evaluation of y and z, rather than doing what we did previously and running two evaluations of w and x, you need to ask TensorFlow to do a single graph run to evaluate y and z, like the example below:

```
with tf.Session() as sess:

y_val, z_val = sess.run([y, z])

print(y_val) # 10

print(z_val) # 15
```

Note

When you use single-process TensorFlow, as in the above example, no state is shared by the multiple sessions, regardless of whether the same graph is used or not. Each of the sessions will have a copy of the variables. In distributed TensorFlow, which we will talk about in a later chapter, the sessions do not store the variable states; this is done on servers and that means variables can be shared by multiple sessions.

Using TensorFlow for Linear Regression

TensorFlow operations are also known by their shortened name of ops and they can take multiple inputs and produce multiple outputs. An example would be the ops for multiplication and addition – each can take a pair of inputs and produce a single output. Variables and constants are source ops and will not take any input.

Inputs and outputs are in the form of multi-dimensional arrays and these are called tensors. Similar to arrays in NumPy, the tensor arrays have a shape and they have a type. In fact, it is NumPy ndarrays that represent the tensors in the Python API. Usually, they will have floats but they can be used for carrying strings as well.

In the examples we have used, the tensors have had just a single scalable value. However, it is possible to carry out computations on any array of any shape. The next piece of code is going to perform Linear Regression by manipulating 2D arrays and we are going to use a dataset called the California Housing dataset. First, we get the dataset, then we add an additional bias input feature of x0 = 1 to each individual training instance – this is done with NumPy so it will run immediately. That is followed by a pair of constant nodes called X and y being created in TensorFlow so that the data and the targets can be held. Theta is defined using matrix operations from Tensorflow, namely transpose(), matrix_inverse() and matmul(), all of which are self-explanatory – what they don't do is immediately perform the computations. The nodes are created in the graphs and the computations are performed when the graph runs.

```
import numpy as np

from sklearn.datasets import fetch_california_housing

housing = fetch_california_housing()

m, n = housing.data.shape

housing_data_plus_bias = np.c_[np.ones((m, 1)), housing.data]

X = tf.constant(housing_data_plus_bias, dtype=tf.float32, name="X")

y = tf.constant(housing.target.reshape(-1, 1), dtype=tf.float32,
name="y")

XT = tf.transpose(X)

theta = tf.matmul(tf.matmul(tf.matrix_inverse(tf.matmul(XT, X)), XT),
y)

with tf.Session() as sess:

theta_value = theta.eval()
```

There is a huge benefit to using this rather than using NumPy to compute the Normal Equation – if you have a GPU card and you installed tensorflow gpu, this will automatically be run on your card by TensorFlow.

Gradient Descent Implementation

First, we'll try Batch Gradient Descent rather than Normal Equation. We do this by manual computation of the gradients first and then using autodiff in TensorFlow to automatically compute them. Lastly, we will make use of some of the built-in optimizers in TensorFlow.

Keep in mind that when you use Gradient Descent the input vector features must be normalized first or you will find that the training is considerably slower. This can be done in a number of ways – with TensorFlow, StandardScaler in scikit-learn, NumPy or any other way. The code below will assume that the normalization has been done.

Manual Computation of the Gradients

The code example we'll look at it should be self-explanatory with the exception of a couple of new elements:

- random_uniform() function – this will create a node that generates a tensor. This tensor has random values and is similar to the rand() function in NumPy assign() function and will create a node that assigns a variable with a new value. In the case of this code, a Batch Gradient Descent step is implemented – that step is θ(next step) = $\theta - \eta\nabla\theta$ MSE(θ).
- The main loop takes the training step and executes it repeatedly (n_epochs times). After it has iterated 100 times, the MSE (Mean Squared Error) is printed out and further 100 iterations is done. This is repeated and the MSE should reduce every time.

```
n_epochs = 1000

learning_rate = 0.01

X = tf.constant(scaled_housing_data_plus_bias, dtype=tf.float32,
name="X")

y = tf.constant(housing.target.reshape(-1, 1), dtype=tf.float32,
name="y")

theta = tf.Variable(tf.random_uniform([n + 1, 1], -1.0, 1.0),
name="theta")

y_pred = tf.matmul(X, theta, name="predictions")

error = y_pred - y

mse = tf.reduce_mean(tf.square(error), name="mse")

gradients = 2/m * tf.matmul(tf.transpose(X), error)
```

```
training_op = tf.assign(theta, theta - learning_rate * gradients)

init = tf.global_variables_initializer()

with tf.Session() as sess:

sess.run(init)

for epoch in range(n_epochs):

if epoch % 100 == 0:

print("Epoch", epoch, "MSE =", mse.eval())

sess.run(training_op)

best_theta = theta.eval()
```

Using Autodiff

The code works okay but the gradients need to be mathematically derived from the MSE or cost function. With Linear Regression, it is quite easy, but if you tried this on any deep neural network you would end up with quite a headache! Not only would it be extremely tedious, it would also be full of errors. You could try to find the equations of the partial derivatives by using symbolic differentiation but the code that results would not be terribly efficient.

In order to understand why that would be the case, you need to think about this function - $f(x)= exp(exp(exp(x)))$. If you are familiar with calculus, you can work out what the derivative is - $f'(x) = exp(x) \times exp(exp(x)) \times exp(exp(exp(x)))$. If $f(x)$ and $f'(x)$ were coded separately and exactly as they are, the resulting code would be inefficient to say the least. A better solution is writing a function that will compute $exp(x)$ first, then it will compute exp exp(x)), followed by $exp(exp(exp(x)))$. All three are then returned. What this does is directly provide you with the third term, $f(x)$; if you need to know what the derivative is, simply multiply all three of the terms. If you had used the naïve approach, the exp function would have needed calling nine times and using this one, it's just three times.

It doesn't get any better when the arbitrary code is used to define the function. Could you find the code or the equation needed for computation of the following functions' partial derivative? Shall I give you a hint? Don't even bother trying!

```
def my_func(a, b):

z = 0

for i in range(100):

z = a * np.cos(z + i) + z * np.sin(b - i)

return z
```

Fortunately, the autodiff feature in TensorFlow saves the day by computing your gradients for you, efficiently and automatically. All you need to do is replace the = ... gradients line in the previous Gradient Descent code with the line below and it will work perfectly:

```
gradients = tf.gradients(mse, [theta])[0]
```

The gradients() function will take an operation and a whole list of variables – in our case, for now, it is just taking the MSE op and the theta variable. It will create an ops list – one op for each variable, and will then compute what the gradients are of each op to its variable. In our case, the MSE gradient vector will be computed by the gradients node with respect to the theta variable.

For automatic gradient computation, we have four main approaches:

- Numerical Differentiation – low accuracy with arbitrary code support and trivial implementation
- Symbolic Differentiation – high accuracy with no support for arbitrary code; a different graph is built
- Forward-Mode autodiff – high accuracy with support for arbitrary code; makes use of dual numbers
- Reverse-Mode autodiff – high accuracy, supports arbiter code and implementation is through TensorFlow

As you can see, reverse-mode autodiff is used by TensorFlow and this is both accurate and efficient for cases when we have a lot more inputs than we do outputs – you often find this with neural networks. All the partial derivatives are computed in respect of the inputs and it is down with n number of inputs and one traversal of the graph.

Using Optimizers

While TensorFlow does all the gradient computation for you, it gets better because it also has several built-in optimizers and one of those is Gradient Descent optimizer. All the gradients in the last code on the training_op= and = ... lines with the code below and, again, it all works as it should:

```
optimizer =
tf.train.GradientDescentOptimizer(learning_rate=learning_rate)

training_op = optimizer.minimize(mse)
```

There are other types of optimizers and to use one you only need to change a single line in the code. Let's say that you want a momentum optimizer – convergence is much quicker with these than it is with Gradient Descent (more on this later); you would define that optimizer in this way:

```
optimizer = tf.train.MomentumOptimizer(learning_rate=learning_rate,
```

```
momentum=0.9)
```

Feeding the Training Algorithm Some Data

Let's take the previous piece of code and modify it so that Mini-Batch Gradient Descent can be implemented. To do this, for each iteration, X and y needs to be replaced with the new mini-batch and the easiest way to do this is with placeholder nodes. These are kind of special – they don't do any computing; all they do is output whatever data you tell them to when it comes to runtime. Usually, we use these for passing TensorFlow the training data in training. If a value is not specified for the placeholder at runtime, an exception will occur.

Creating a placeholder node requires calling the placeholder() function and specifying the data type of the output tensor. You could also specify the shape if you wanted to enforce it. If None is specified for a dimension, it means it can be any size. For example, the code below will create a placeholder node called A and a node called B = A + 5. When B is evaluated, a feed_dict is passed to the method called aval() – this method specifies what A's value is. Note that A has a rank of 2 – it has to be two-dimensional – and, while it can have any amount of rows, it must have three columns:

```
>>> A = tf.placeholder(tf.float32, shape=(None, 3))

>>> B = A + 5

>>> with tf.Session() as sess:

...    B_val_1 = B.eval(feed_dict={A: [[1, 2, 3]]})

...    B_val_2 = B.eval(feed_dict={A: [[4, 5, 6], [7, 8, 9]]})

...

>>> print(B_val_1)

[[ 6.  7.  8.]]

>>> print(B_val_2)

[[ 9.  10.  11.]

 [ 12.  13.  14.]]
```

> **Note**
>
> You are not limited to feeding the output of placeholders; you do it with any type of operation. TensorFlow will not make any attempt to evaluate them; it just uses those values that it is fed.

Implementation of Mini-Batch Gradient Descent requires a tweak to our code, but only a small one. The X and y definitions need to be changed in the construction phase so that they become placeholder nodes:

```
X = tf.placeholder(tf.float32, shape=(None, n + 1), name="X")

y = tf.placeholder(tf.float32, shape=(None, 1), name="y")
```

Next the batch size is defined and a computation made of how many batches there will be in total:

```
batch_size = 100

n_batches = int(np.ceil(m / batch_size))
```

Lastly, the mini-batches are fetched one at a time in the Execution phase; if you are evaluating a node that is dependent on X or y, you need to use feed_dict() to provide the X and y values:

```
def fetch_batch(epoch, batch_index, batch_size):

  [...] # load the data from disk

return X_batch, y_batch

with tf.Session() as sess:

sess.run(init)

for epoch in range(n_epochs):

for batch_index in range(n_batches):

X_batch, y_batch = fetch_batch(epoch, batch_index, batch_size)

sess.run(training_op, feed_dict={X: X_batch, y: y_batch})

best_theta = theta.eval()
```

It is worth noting that the values of X and y do not need to be passed when theta is being evaluated because it is not dependent on either.

Saving Models and Restoring Them

Once your model has been trained, its parameters need to be saved to disk – that way, when you need to use it again, you can come back to it. You can use the model in any other program. You can use it for comparison against other models and so on. You will also want to get into the habit of making regular saves at checkpoints throughout the training. If you don't and your computer was to crash while training was ongoing, you would need to start over; save it and you can pick up right where you left off.

It's very easy to save models and restore them with TensorFlow. A Saver must be created at the end of construction once the creation of all variable nodes is complete. When it comes to execution, you just call the save() method whenever you want the model saved. That method must be passed on both the checkpoint file's session and path.

```
[...]

theta = tf.Variable(tf.random_uniform([n + 1, 1], -1.0, 1.0),
name="theta")

[...]

init = tf.global_variables_initializer()

saver = tf.train.Saver()

with tf.Session() as sess:

sess.run(init)

for epoch in range(n_epochs):

if epoch % 100 == 0: # checkpoint every 100 epochs

save_path = saver.save(sess, "/tmp/my_model.ckpt")

sess.run(training_op)

best_theta = theta.eval()

save_path = saver.save(sess, "/tmp/my_model_final.ckpt")
```

It is also easy to restore a model; simply create a Saver at the end of construction, as you did before, but, when execution starts, rather than using the init node to initialize the variables, you simply call the Saver objects restore() method:

```
with tf.Session() as sess:

saver.restore(sess, "/tmp/my_model_final.ckpt")

[...]
```

The Saver will, by default, both save and restore every variable under its own name. You can have more control if you want if you can specify the variables that you want to be saved or restored and you can specify the names if you want as well. For example, the Saver below saves or restores the theta variable with the name of weights:

```
saver = tf.train.Saver({"weights": theta})
```

Using TensorBoard for Graph Visualization and Curve Training

What we have now is a computation graph that will use Mini-Batch Gradient Descent to train a Linear Regression model. We are also making regular saves along the way. Doesn't this sound rather sophisticated? The problem is, we still need to use the print() function if want to visualize your training progress. However, there is a much better way – we can use TensorBoard. If you give TensorBoard a few training stats it will give you some attractive visualizations in your web browser of the same stats. You could also give it the definition of the graph and it will give you the perfect interface for browsing it. This can be extremely useful for the identification of graph errors to see where there are any bottlenecks, and more.

The first thing we need to do is tweak the program a little; we need to get it to write the definition of the graph and a few training stats, like the MSE training error. These are written to a log directory that TensorBoard will read – a different directory is needed whenever the program is run otherwise the stats from each run are merged and that's not what we want because the visualizations will be confused. The easiest way to solve this is to add a timestamp to the name of the log directory. The following code needs to be added at the start of your program:

```
from datetime import datetime

now = datetime.utcnow().strftime("%Y%m%d%H%M%S")

root_logdir = "tf_logs"

logdir = "{}/run-{}/".format(root_logdir, now)
```

Now the following code should be added to the construction phase, at the end:

```
mse_summary = tf.summary.scalar('MSE', mse)

file_writer = tf.summary.FileWriter(logdir, tf.get_default_graph())
```

In line one, the node is created in the graph. This node evaluates the value of the MSE and then writes it to a summary, which is a binary log string compatible with TensorBoard. The FileWriter that we need to write the summary files to the log directory logfiles is create in line one. We indicate the log directory path with parameter one. The second parameter is optional and it is the graph that you want to be visualized. If it isn't already in existence, the log directory is created by FileWriter along with any required parent directories and the graph definitions are written in the events file, which is a binary logfile.

Next, the Execution phase needs to be updates so that evaluation of the mse_summary node can be done on a regular basis throughout training. The output is a summary that can be written to the events file with file_writer. This is the new code:

```
[...]
```

```
for batch_index in range(n_batches):

X_batch, y_batch = fetch_batch(epoch, batch_index, batch_size)

if batch_index % 10 == 0:

summary_str = mse_summary.eval(feed_dict={X: X_batch, y: y_batch})

step = epoch * n_batches + batch_index

file_writer.add_summary(summary_str, step)

sess.run(training_op, feed_dict={X: X_batch, y: y_batch})

[...]
```

Warning

Do not log your training stats at each individual step or you will find the training considerably slower.

The last thing to do is close FileWriter at the very end:

```
file_writer.close()
```

Now you can run the program and you will see that the log directory is created and an events file written in the log directory. This has the definition of the graph and values of the MSE. Open a Python shell and then go to the working directory. At the command prompt, type in ls -l tf_logs/run* - you will now see the log directory contents listed:

```
$ cd $ML_PATH # Your ML working directory (e.g., $HOME/ml)

$ ls -l tf_logs/run*

total 40

-rw-r--r-- 1 ageron staff 18620 Sep 6 11:10
events.out.tfevents.1472553182.mymac
```

Run the program again and another directory will appear in the tf_logs/ directory:

```
$ ls -l tf_logs/

total 0

drwxr-xr-x 3 ageron staff 102 Sep 6 10:07 run-20160906091959

drwxr-xr-x 3 ageron staff 102 Sep 6 10:22 run-20160906092202
```

Now we can open up the TensorBoard server. If you created a virtual environment, you will need to activate virtualenv and then you can run the TensorBoard command so the server starts. You need to point the command to the root log directory; the TensorBoard web server will start and it will listen in port number 6006 – turn that upside down and it reads 'goog'.

```
$ source env/bin/activate

$ tensorboard --logdir tf_logs/
```

Starting Tensorboard on Port 6006

The next step is to open your web browser and type one of the following into the search bar:

http://0.0.0.0:6006, or

http://localhost:6006/

Look for the Events tab and click it. On the right, you will see MSE. Click that and a plot will show up – this is the MSE during the training, both runs. Here, you can check runs that you want to see, uncheck those you don't, zoom in, zoom out, get some details of the curve by hovering over it and more.

Next, click the tab that says Graphs and a graph will appear. To keep the clutter to a minimum, the multi-edged nodes, those that have connections to others, are separated from the rest and you will see them on the right. Nodes can be moved between the auxiliary and the main graph just by right-clicking the one you want to move. You will also see that parts of the graph have been collapsed by default. Try hovering your mouse over the node for gradients and then click the ⊕ icon; this expands the subgraph. Now, inside the subgraph, attempt to expand another subgraph called mse_grad.

Name Scopes

When you have models that are somewhat more complex, like the neural networks, it is very easy for hundreds or thousands of nodes to clutter up the graph. You can get around this by grouping related nodes together in name scopes. For example, taking our previous code, we could modify it so it creates a name scope called "loss" and then defines mse ops and the error inside that name scope:

```
with tf.name_scope("loss") as scope:

error = y_pred - y

mse = tf.reduce_mean(tf.square(error), name="mse")
```

The name of each operation defined within the scope is prefixed with "loss/":

```
>>> print(error.op.name)
```

```
loss/sub
```

```
>>> print(mse.op.name)
```

```
loss/mse
```

The error node and the mse node will now be inside the namespace called loss in TensorBoard; notice that the namespace looks to have collapsed.

Modularity

Let's say that you want a graph that will add up the output from a pair of ReLU – Rectified Linear Units. The ReLU will take the inputs and compute the linear function, outputting the results if the function is positive; if it is negative, a 0 is output, as you can see in the equation below:

$$h_{wb}(X) = \max(X \cdot w + b, 0)$$

Equation - Rectified Linear Unit

The code below will do the job but it is somewhat repetitive:

```
n_features = 3

X = tf.placeholder(tf.float32, shape=(None, n_features), name="X")

w1 = tf.Variable(tf.random_normal((n_features, 1)), name="weights1")

w2 = tf.Variable(tf.random_normal((n_features, 1)), name="weights2")

b1 = tf.Variable(0.0, name="bias1")

b2 = tf.Variable(0.0, name="bias2")

z1 = tf.add(tf.matmul(X, w1), b1, name="z1")

z2 = tf.add(tf.matmul(X, w2), b2, name="z2")

relu1 = tf.maximum(z1, 0., name="relu1")

relu2 = tf.maximum(z1, 0., name="relu2")

output = tf.add(relu1, relu2, name="output")
```

This kind of repetitive code can't be easily maintained and is prone to errors. A little test for you – did you spot the cut and paste error in the code? If you wanted to add some more ReLUs things would get even worse. Thankfully, TensorFlow has a little function called DRY – Don't Repeat Yourself. All you do is create a function that builds the ReLU. The next piece of code will create five of these ReLUs and the sum is output. Note – add_n() will create the operation that takes a list of tensors and computes the sum:

```
def relu(X):

w_shape = (int(X.get_shape()[1]), 1)

w = tf.Variable(tf.random_normal(w_shape), name="weights")

b = tf.Variable(0.0, name="bias")

z = tf.add(tf.matmul(X, w), b, name="z")

return tf.maximum(z, 0., name="relu")

n_features = 3

X = tf.placeholder(tf.float32, shape=(None, n_features), name="X")

relus = [relu(X) for i in range(5)]

output = tf.add_n(relus, name="output")
```

When a node is created, TensorFlow will check to see if the name you gave it is already in existence; if it is, an underscore and an index are appended so the name is made unique. So, our first ReLU has nodes with the names of "bias", "weights", "relu", "z" and many more that have their own default names, such as "MatMul". Our second ReLU has nodes with the same names but appended with an underscore and the number one, while the third has the same names appended with the underscore and the number three, and so on for as many ReLUs you have. TensorBoard will identify series like these and collapse them and bring them together so there is less clutter.

With name scopes, graphs can be made cleaner – just put whatever is in the relu() function into a name scope.

```
def relu(X):

with tf.name_scope("relu"):

[...]
```

Sharing Variables

Let's say that you had a variable that you wanted to share between several of your graph components. An easy way would be to create that variable first and then pass it to the functions as a parameter. For example, the ReLU threshold is hard-coded to 0 and you want to use a shared threshold variable for all the ReLUs to control the threshold. You could create the variable and then pass it to relu():

```
def relu(X, threshold):

with tf.name_scope("relu"):

[...]

return tf.maximum(z, threshold, name="max")

threshold = tf.Variable(0.0, name="threshold")

X = tf.placeholder(tf.float32, shape=(None, n_features), name="X")

relus = [relu(X, threshold) for i in range(5)]

output = tf.add_n(relus, name="output")
```

This works okay; the threshold for all of the ReLUs can now be controlled with the threshold variable. But if you have multiple parameters that are shared, like this one, passing them around all the time as parameters is going to hurt. Many programmers put all their model variables into a custom Python dictionary and this then is passed to each function. Other programmers create individual classes for each of the modules. Another option would be to set the shared variable to the relu()function as an attribute – this would be down on the first call, like this:

```
def relu(X):

with tf.name_scope("relu"):

if not hasattr(relu, "threshold"):

relu.threshold = tf.Variable(0.0, name="threshold")

[...]

return tf.maximum(z, relu.threshold, name="max")
```

There is another option in TensorFlow and this one could provide code that is cleaner and a bit more modular than what we have seen previously. However, this is a little bit trickier to grasp at first but, it is used quite a lot in TensorFlow so it is well worth taking the time to understand it.

The idea is to create a shared variable using the function called get_variable but only if the shared variable is not already in existence. If it is, the same function can be called to reuse that shared variable. Control of the behavior (create or reuse) is done by an attribute in the variable_scope(). For example, the next piece of code creates relu/threshold, which is a variable and it is created as a scale because shape=0 and is set as the initial value:

```
with tf.variable_scope("relu"):
```

```
threshold = tf.get_variable("threshold", shape=(),
initializer=tf.constant_initializer(0.0))
```

If the variable was created when get_variable() was called at an earlier time, an exception will be raised. This stops variables being reused by mistake. You need to explicitly indicate that variable is to be reused and this is done by setting the scope of the reuse attribute in the variable to True – doing this means you do not need to specify the initializer or the shape:

```
with tf.variable_scope("relu", reuse=True):

  threshold = tf.get_variable("threshold")
```

This piece of code fetches the current relu/threshold variable; if it hasn't been created with get_variable() or doesn't exist yet, an exception is raised. An alternative method would be to set reuse to True in the block – simply call the reuse_variables() method from the scope:

```
with tf.variable_scope("relu") as scope:

scope.reuse_variables()

threshold = tf.get_variable("threshold")
```

Warning

Once you have set reuse as True, you cannot set it as False in the block. And, if you were to define the scopes of other variables inside this one, they will inherit reuse=True automatically. Finally, you can only reuse a variable in this way if it has been created by get_variable().

Now we have everything we need; the relu() function now doesn't need to pass the threshold variable as a parameter to have access to it:

```
def relu(X):

with tf.variable_scope("relu", reuse=True):

threshold = tf.get_variable("threshold") # reuse existing variable

[...]

return tf.maximum(z, threshold, name="max")

X = tf.placeholder(tf.float32, shape=(None, n_features), name="X")

with tf.variable_scope("relu"): # create the variable

threshold = tf.get_variable("threshold", shape=(),
initializer=tf.constant_initializer(0.0))
```

```
relus = [relu(X) for relu_index in range(5)]

output = tf.add_n(relus, name="output")
```

Here we have defined the relu() function; we then create the variable called threshold variable – this is built as a scaler that will eventually be initialized to 0.0. Lastly, we call the ReLU function to build five ReLUs. The relu/threshold variable is reused to create the ReLU nodes.

What is a little unfortunate here is that the threshold variable has to be defined external to the relu() function – this is where all the ReLU code is. Fixing this requires that the variable is created in the relu() function with the first call and then reused in other calls. The relu() function doesn't need to take variable sharing or name scopes into consideration; all it does is call get_varaiable(), at which point the threshold variable is created or reused. The remaining code will the relu() function five more times, ensuring that reuse=False is set for the first call and then, for all the other calls, reuse=True.

```
def relu(X):

threshold = tf.get_variable("threshold", shape=(),

initializer=tf.constant_initializer(0.0))

[...]

return tf.maximum(z, threshold, name="max")

X = tf.placeholder(tf.float32, shape=(None, n_features), name="X")

relus = []

for relu_index in range(5):

with tf.variable_scope("relu", reuse=(relu_index >= 1)) as scope:

relus.append(relu(X))

output = tf.add_n(relus, name="output")
```

That's it for TensorFlow for now. You have the basics. We will take it to a more advanced level, specifically in relation to deep neural networks, recurrent neural networks, and convolutional neural networks while also discussing how TensorFlow can be scaled using multiple servers and GPUS, queues and multithreading.

Chapter 9: The Artificial Neural Networks

The next logical step is to start looking at how the human brain was used as the inspiration for intelligent machines. This is the inspiration behind the ANNs – artificial neural networks. Although the airplane had its inspiration from birds, you don't see planes flapping their wings. In the same way, ANNs have evolved to become very different from the biological counterparts. There are researchers who say that we shouldn't even be using this analogy anymore, for example, dropping the word "neurons" in favor of "units".

Deep Learning is based centrally on a core of artificial neural networks. These ANNs are incredibly powerful; they are versatile and they are scalable and this is what makes them perfect for the largest and most complex of the machine learning tasks. For example, you could not use a basic machine learning algorithm for the classification of many billions of images. You couldn't use Siri, Cortana, and other voice recognition systems. A basic algorithm couldn't recommend videos for a specific user from the millions available on services like YouTube. A basic algorithm could not examine vast numbers of previous Go games and then learn how to win over the world champion by playing itself. Artificial neural networks can do all of this and more.

Throughout this chapter, we are going to learn about artificial neural networks, starting from the very first ones ever built, before we look at MLPs or Multi-Layer Perceptions. Then we will learn how to use TensorFlow to implement an MLP to help solve the problems of classifying digit images from the MNIST dataset.

Neurons – From the Biological to the Artificial

It might surprise you to learn that artificial neuron networks are nothing new. In fact, the very first one can be dated back to 1943, a result of work done by Walter Pitts, a mathematician and Warren McCulloch, a neurophysiologist. Together they released a paper called "A Logical Calculus of Ideas Immanent in Nervous Activity". In this paper, they presented a simple model (computational) that showed how neurons potentially work together in the brains of animals using propositional logic to carry out complex computations. That was the very first ANN and has been followed since then by many more, each one different from the last.

These early models were successful and, for many years, there was a strong belief that humans would soon be communing with incredibly intelligent machines. However, during the 1960s, it soon became very clear that this promise was not going to happen as the funding was diverted in other directions, leaving ANNs in the dark for a long time. Interest was revived in the 1980's after new architectures were built and training techniques were improved. But by the start of the following decade, more powerful alternatives were in favor, like the SVM machine leading techniques. This was because these models appeared to offer stronger foundations in theoretical terms and the results they provided seemed to be much better.

Now, more than 30 years later and we are seeing a stronger, more renewed interest in artificial neural networks but how long will it last? There is a lot of evidence to suggest that this time things will be different and ANNs will impact our lives much deeper than before.

These days, we have much more data on hand to train ANNs and the neural networks are almost permanently outperforming any other machine learning techniques on the largest and most complex of tasks. In the last 30 years, computing power has expanded significantly and that gives us what we need to train the larger neural networks in a shorter time. Some of this is because of Moore's Law but we do need to give thanks to gaming – because of that industry, we now have much more powerful GPU cards.

Algorithms for training have also seen improvements and, although they don't look much different to the ones we used 30 years ago, the small changes have effected massive improvements. In terms of theoretical limits, these have shown themselves to be minor. An example is that a lot of people were of the opinion that the training algorithms for ANNs could never survive – all they would do is get jammed in the local optima but, while this does happen in practice, occurrences are very rare. Usually, when it does happen, the algorithms are very near to the global optimum.

Right now, artificial neural networks are in demand and have entered a cycle of funding and good progress. Every day, we see products hit the news with their basis in ANNs and this serves to keep the interest revived which, in turn, leads to more money and more progress, and on it goes.

Biological Neurons

Before we move on to the artificial neurons, we need to understand the biological neuron. This cell is rather odd-looking and is normally located in the cerebral cortex, i.e. the brain. The body of the cell has the nucleus, along with many of the more complex cell components with dendrites, which are extensions that look like branches. There is also one longer extension, the axon. The length of this axon can be anywhere from just a couple of times longer to many thousand times longer than the cell body. The axon splits near its extremity into branches that are known as telodendria; synapses or synaptic terminals are found at the tips of each branch and these connect to the cell body or to the dendrites of the other neurons.

Other neurons send signals, which are electrical impulses, to the biological neurons. When enough signals are received inside of a couple of milliseconds, the biological neuron will send out its own signals. As such, it would seem that the biological neuron's behavior is quite simple, as far as individual neurons go, but they don't work alone. Each biological neuron is part of a network, made up of billions of these neurons; each individual neuron is connected to thousands more. Using a huge network of simple neurons, we can do very complex computations and, while research is still ongoing on the structure of the biological neural networks, some of the brain has already been mapped and this mapping shows that the neurons tend to be formed into successive layers.

Using Neurons for Logical Computations

McCulloch and Pitt came up with a simplified biological neuron model; it was this that later got the name of the artificial neuron. This model had at least one binary input and a single binary output. Artificial neurons will only activate the output when there are more than a specified number of active inputs.

They showed that even using such a simple model, an artificial neuron network could be built to compute just about any logical proposition. For example, let's assume that we have several of these ANNs, each with the ability to perform logical computations on the presumption that, when there are two or more active inputs, the neuron will be activated.

One network is nothing more than an identity function because two input signals are sent from neuron A, neuron C will be activated as well. Should A be switched off, then so will C? Another network will carry out a logical AND – C can only be activated when both A and B are also activated because one input is insufficient for C to be activated. A third network is used to do a logical OR – C will be activated if A or B or both A and B are activated. Lastly, supposing that the activity of a neuron can be inhibited by an input connection, the final network will compute a logical proposition that is somewhat more complex – C will only be activated if A is already active and B has been switched off. If A were permanently active, the output would be a logical NOT – C would be active when B is switched off and B would active when C is switched off.

The Perceptron

One of the most basic ANN structures of all is the Perceptron. It was invented by Frank Rosenblatt in 1957 and is based on an artificial neuron called an LTU, or Linear Threshold Unit. Rather than the binary values of On and Off, this ANN uses numbers for the inputs and outputs and a weight is associated with each of the input connections. LTUs compute weighted sums of all the inputs – z = w 1 x 1 + w 2 x 2 + ... + wn zn = w T . x. A step function is then applied to the resulting sum and the result is output – hw(x) step (z) = step (w T . x).

The Perceptron uses the Heaviside step function the most and this is demonstrated in the next equation. Note that, on occasion, a sign function will be used as an alternative.

$$\text{heaviside}(z) = \begin{cases} 0 & \text{if } z < 0 \\ 1 & \text{if } z \geq 0 \end{cases} \qquad \text{sgn}(z) = \begin{cases} -1 & \text{if } z < 0 \\ 0 & \text{if } z = 0 \\ +1 & \text{if } z > 0 \end{cases}$$

Equation - The Common Perceptron Step Functions

Some linear binary classifications can be done with just one LTU; the inputs are linearly computed and, if the result is higher than a given threshold, the positive class is output; if not, the negative class is output. This is much like the linear SVM or the Logistic Regression classifier.

Let's say that you wanted to use the length and width of the petals as a way of classifying the iris flowers, adding x 0 = 1 as an additional bias feature. To train an LTU means we must find the correct w 0, w 1 and w 2 features – we'll talk about the training algorithm later.

The composition of a Perceptron is one layer of LTUs. Each other LTU neurons are connected to every input. Input neurons, which are passthrough neurons, are used to represent the connections – simply put, whatever input they are given is what they output. Generally, the x 0 = 1 bias feature is added too. Typically, a bias neuron, which is another special neuron, is used to represent the bias feature, and this neuron only outputs 1.

Note

A Perceptron that has a pair of inputs and three outputs has the ability to simultaneously classify instances in no less than three binary classes – this makes it a multi-output classifier.

So, how do we train a Perceptron? Frank Rosenblatt defined a training algorithm that was inspired by Hebb's Rule. Donald Hebb published a book in 1949 called "The Organization of Behavior" and in it, he made the suggestion that the connection between biological neurons is much stronger when one triggers another. Later, Siegrid Löwel coined a phrase that encompasses this – "Cells that fire together, wire together".

Later, this was termed as "Hebb's Rule", otherwise called Hebbian Learning. Basically, when a pair of neurons has the same output, the connection weight in between them is increased. We train a Perceptron on a derivative of this rule; this derivative takes the error network into account and it doesn't build any connections that result in an incorrect output. In more specific terms, a Perceptron is given training instances one at a time providing predictions for each one. Whenever an output neuron produces an incorrect prediction, the Perceptron will strengthen the input connection weights that would have helped in producing the right prediction. You can see the rule demonstrated in the next equation:

$$w_{i,j}^{(\text{next step})} = w_{i,j} + \eta(\hat{y}_j - y_j)x_i$$

Equation - Perceptron Learning Rule With A Weight Update

Let's break the equation down:

- wi j – the connection weight for the ith neuron (input) and the jth neuron (output)
- xi – ith value (input) for the current instance
- j – jth output neuron output for the current instance
- yj – jth output neuron output target for the current instance
- η – learning rate

Each of the output neurons has a linear decision boundary and this means that a Perceptron is not capable of learning any complex patterns, much like the Logistic Regression classifier can't. However, Rosenblatt did demonstrate the Perceptron Convergence Theorem – convergence can happen if the instances are linearly separable.

A single LTU network can be implemented using a Perceptron class in scikit-learn. You would use it as you would expect and the following example shows it in the Iris dataset:

```
import numpy as np

from sklearn.datasets import load_iris

from sklearn.linear_model import Perceptron

iris = load_iris()

X = iris.data[:, (2, 3)] # petal length, petal width

y = (iris.target == 0).astype(np.int) # Iris Setosa?

per_clf = Perceptron(random_state=42)

per_clf.fit(X, y)

y_pred = per_clf.predict([[2, 0.5]])
```

Did you spot that the learning algorithm for a Perceptron is much like that of the Stochastic Gradient Descent? The Perceptron class in scikit-learn is the equivalent of the SGDClassifier but with these parameters:

- loss="perceptron"
- learning_rate="constant"
- eta0=1 (this is the learning rate)
- penalty=None (this signifies that there is no regularization)

Something to be aware of is that, unlike the Logistic Regression Classifiers, a class probability is not an output of a Perceptron. Instead, they use hard thresholds to make predictions and this is a good reason why you should use Logistic Regression rather than a Perceptron.

In 1969, Marvin Minsky and Seymour Papert published a monograph. It was named Perceptrons and it highlighted some of the more serious weaknesses that a Perceptron has. One of the main weaknesses is that a Perceptron is not able to solve some of the more basic problems, such as the Exclusive OR (XOR) problem. The same is true, of course, of most of the linear classification models but more was expected from the Perceptron and this caused a lot of disappointment. A result of this was that connectionism or the study of the neural networks was dropped and many researchers turned to the higher-level problems, like problem solving, logic and search.

However, as it turned out when we stack multiple Perceptrons, some of the limitations are removed. The artificial neural network that results is an MLP – a Multi-layer Perceptron which can be used for solving XOR.

MPL and Backpropagation

MLPs are made up of an input layer, which is a passthrough layer, at least one LTU layer known as hidden layers and an LTU layer called an output layer. There is a bias neuron in each layer except for the output layer and each layer is connected to the next. Where there are at least two hidden layers in an artificial neural network, it is known as a deep neural network or DNN.

Researchers spent many unproductive years attempting to train MLPs but nobody could manage it. However, a revolutionary article was published by D. E. Rumelhart et al in 1986. This article introduced a training algorithm called Backpropagation. Today, it would be a Gradient Descent with a reverse-mode autodiff.

Each training instance is fed to the network by the algorithm; this algorithm will then look at the consecutive layers and compute the output of all the neurons in each layer. This is known as the forward pass. Next, the output error of the network is measured – this is the difference between the output we want and the actual network output. A computation is then done working out the level of contribution that each neuron in the previous hidden layer made to the errors from each output neuron.

Next, the algorithm measures the level of error contributions that came from the neurons in the last hidden layer, and it will continue like this until the input layer is reached. Called the reverse pass, the error gradient is propagated backward within the network, thus allowing an efficient measurement of the gradient across ever connection weight. In short, with backpropagation, both forward and reverse passes will carry out reverse-mode autodiff. To finish, a Gradient Descent step is done on every connection weight across the network and, to do this, the error gradients that were measured earlier are used.

Let me try to make this simple – the backpropagation algorithm will make a forward pass (prediction) on each instance; it will measure the error and then traverse the layers, one at a time, in reverse to measure what contribution to the error came from each of the connections (the reverse pass). Lastly, the connection weights are tweaked a little to bring the error down (the Gradient Descent step).

The authors of this algorithm made one significant change to the structure of the MLP to make the algorithm work as it should – they used a logistic function instead of a step function - $\sigma(z)$ = $1 / (1 + \exp(-z))$. They did this because the step function has only flat segments in it, no gradient. The Gradient Descent will not work when there are only flat surfaces. The logistic function, on the other hand, has a nonzero derivative that is very well defined; this means that Gradient Descent will progress with each step. You can use the backpropagation algorithm in place of logistic functions in some other activation functions, two of the most popular being:

Hyperbolic Tangent Function – tanh (z) = 2σ(2z) – 1

The shape of the hyperbolic tangent function is an S, the same as the logistic function; it is also continuous and it is differentiable. However, rather than 0 to 1, the output values range between -1 and 1. As a result, the output from each layer is pretty much centered on 0 or, in other words, normalized when training begins making convergence much faster.

ReLU Function – ReLU (z) = max (0, z)

The ReLU function is also continuous but, at z = 0, it is not differentiable. This is because there is a sudden change to the slope and this causes bouncing in the Gradient Descent. However, in practical terms, it does work and it is very fast in computation. Perhaps more importantly, because there is no maximum output value, some issues are less likely to happen during Gradient Descent – more about this later in another chapter.

MLPs tend to be used quite a lot for classification. Each of the outputs will correlate to a different binary class. With exclusive classes, like the digit image classification classes 0 to 9, modification of the output layer is done by using a shared SoftMax function in place of the functions for individual activation. Each neuron output is correspondent to the estimated probability of the class that corresponds to it. Note – the signal can only flow from input to output, thus becoming an example of an FNN – a feedforward neural network.

Training an MLP with TensorFlow's High-Level API

Using TensorFlow for training an MLP is a case of using TF.Learn, one of the high-level APIs. This is very similar to the API in scikit-learn. The DNNClassifier is used to train a DNN with one or more hidden layers and the output from the SoftMax output layer will be the estimated class probabilities. Take a look at the next piece of code – a DNN is trained using two hidden layers – one has 100 neurons while the other has 300. The softmax output layer is trained with 10 neurons:

```
import tensorflow as tf

feature_columns =
tf.contrib.learn.infer_real_valued_columns_from_input(X_train)

dnn_clf = tf.contrib.learn.DNNClassifier(hidden_units=[300, 100],
n_classes=10,

feature_columns=feature_columns)

dnn_clf.fit(x=X_train, y=y_train, batch_size=50, steps=40000)
```

Take the MNIST dataset and use StandardScaler in scikit-learn to scale it. Then run the code on the dataset and you might just find that you have a model that can achieve an accuracy of 98% on the test dataset:

```
>>> from sklearn.metrics import accuracy_score

>>> y_pred = list(dnn_clf.predict(X_test))

>>> accuracy_score(y_test, y_pred)

0.98180000000000001
```

You will also find a few convenience functions in the TF.Learn library for model evaluation:

```
>>> dnn_clf.evaluate(X_test, y_test)

{'accuracy': 0.98180002, 'global_step': 40000, 'loss': 0.073678359}
```

Behind the scenes, the neuron layers are created by the DNNClassifier class. The ReLU activation function is used as the basis for this and we can set the hyperparameter activation_fn to change this. The cost function is cross entropy and the softmax function is used for the output layer.

Using Plain TensorFlow to Train a DNN

If you want to have more control of the network structure, you could use the low-level Python API from TensorFlow. In the next part of this chapter, we are going to use that API to build the same model that we built earlier, and then train it on MNIST by implementing Mini-Batch Gradient Descent. Step one is the Construction Phase where the TensorFlow Graph is built. This is followed by the Execution phase where the model is trained by running the graph.

The Construction Phase

It's time to begin. The first job is to import the relevant library, in this case, tensorflow. After that, we will need to provide a number of the inputs and the outputs and then set how many hidden neurons there are in each layer:

```
import tensorflow as tf

n_inputs = 28*28 # MNIST

n_hidden1 = 300

n_hidden2 = 100

n_outputs = 10
```

The next step, as you have done previously, is to have the targets and the training data represented by placeholder nodes. Note that we only have a partly defined shape of X so far. We know that it is going to be a matrix or a 2D tensor and we know that its first dimension will have instances along it; the second dimension will have features and we know there will be 28 x 28 number of features – one feature for one pixel. What we don't know just yet is the number of instances in each training batch. At the moment, the shape of X is (None, n_inputs). We also know that y is going to be a one-dimensional tensor that has a single entry for each instance, but we still don't know what the training batch size is. So for now, the shape will be (None):

```
X = tf.placeholder(tf.float32, shape=(None, n_inputs), name="X")

y = tf.placeholder(tf.int64, shape=(None), name="y")
```

The next job is to create the neural network. X, the placeholder node, is going to represent the input layer. Once we get to the Execution phase, training batches will replace this, one batch at a time. Note that every instance in each training batch will be processed at the same time by the neural network.

The next step is to create the layers – two hidden and one output. The hidden layers are pretty much identical to one another; the only difference is in the inputs that the layers are connected to and how many neurons are in each one. The output layer is also much the same but, rather than the ReLU activation function, this one uses the softmax activation function.

Now we will create the neuron_layer() function; this is what we will use to create the layers, one at a time. We will need to set parameters to specify how many neurons there will be, to specify inputs, the activation function and what we are going to call the layer:

```
def neuron_layer(X, n_neurons, name, activation=None):

with tf.name_scope(name):

n_inputs = int(X.get_shape()[1])

stddev = 2 / np.sqrt(n_inputs)

init = tf.truncated_normal((n_inputs, n_neurons), stddev=stddev)

W = tf.Variable(init, name="weights")

b = tf.Variable(tf.zeros([n_neurons]), name="biases")

z = tf.matmul(X, W) + b

if activation=="relu":

return tf.nn.relu(z)

else:

return z
```

Let's walk through this:

We use the layer name to create the name scope and this has all the computation nodes that the neuron layer requires. This is an optional step really but your TensorBoard graph will look much more attractive if you have properly organized nodes

Second, we look at the shape of the input matrix and we get the second-dimension size so that we can determine how many inputs there are – the first dimension is reserved for instances

The three lines that follow are creating a W variable and this is where the weights matrix will be. This is a two-dimensional tensor that has the connection weights between each individual input and each individual neuron. As such, the shape is (n_inputs, n_neurons). The variable is randomly initialized with a Gaussian, truncated distribution that has a standard deviation of $2/\mathrm{sqrt}(n_{inputs})$.

By using this deviation, convergence is much quicker – we will discuss this tweak later on; for now, just know that tweaks like this can have a significant impact on the efficiency of neural networks. What is important is that the connection weights are initialized randomly for all of the hidden layers. This will eliminate the chances of a symmetry that can't be broken by the Gradient Descent step.

We then create a variable called b for biases. This does not have any symmetry issues because it has been initialized to 0 and there is one bias parameter to every neuron.

The subgraph is then created so that z = X . W + b can be computed. This implementation is vectorized for efficient computation of the inputs' weighted sums and the bias term for each individual neuron that is in the layer. This is done in one go for every instance in the batch.

Lastly, provided 'relu' is set as the activation parameter, this code will return z or it will return relu(z).

That gives us the foundation we need to create the neuron layer so we can now use it to create a deep neural network. The first of the hidden layers will take an input of X; the second will take an input of the output of the previous layer. Lastly, that output layer will take its input as the output of the previous hidden layer.

```
with tf.name_scope("dnn"):

hidden1 = neuron_layer(X, n_hidden1, "hidden1", activation="relu")

hidden2 = neuron_layer(hidden1, n_hidden2, "hidden2",
activation="relu")

logits = neuron_layer(hidden2, n_outputs, "outputs")
```

Note that we have a name scope, just for the purpose of clarity, and before it is put through the softmax activation function, the neural network has an output of logits. We'll talk about the softmax computation later on.

TensorFlow helps with the creation of standard neural network layers by providing a whole heap of useful functions; this means you rarely have to define the neuron_layer() functions like we did in the last code. An example of this is the function called fully_connected – as you would expect, this will create a layer that is fully connected. In this layer, all of the inputs will be connected to all the neurons in the same layer. The function will create all the bias variables and all the weight variables, using the correct strategy for initialization and it also, by default, uses the ReLU activation function – this could be changed with the argument called activation. Later, you will see that the parameters for normalization and regularization are also supported. For now, we are going to make a change to our previous code so that fully_connected() is used instead of neuron_layer(). All you do is import that function and then use the following code to replace the dnn construction part of the code:

```
from tensorflow.contrib.layers import fully_connected

with tf.name_scope("dnn"):

hidden1 = fully_connected(X, n_hidden1, scope="hidden1")

 hidden2 = fully_connected(hidden1, n_hidden2, scope="hidden2")

logits = fully_connected(hidden2, n_outputs, scope="outputs",

activation_fn=None)
```

Our neural network model is now ready; all we need to do now is define the relevant cost function for training it. For this, we are using cross entropy which will, as you know, penalize any model that provides a low probability estimation for the target class.

There are a number of functions in TensorFlow to compute cross entropy and we will be using one called sparse_softmax_cross_entropy_with_logits(). This will base the cross entropy computation on the logits, which are the network outputs before it goes through softmax activation. This function will expect the labels to be formatted as integers from 0 to however many classes there are minus 1 – for us, this will be 0 to 9. The result will be a one-dimensional tensor that contains the cross entropy for each of the instances. After that, the reduce_mean() function from TensorFlow can be used for computing what the mean cross entropy is across all the instances:

```
with tf.name_scope("loss"):

xentropy = tf.nn.sparse_softmax_cross_entropy_with_logits(

labels=y, logits=logits)

loss = tf.reduce_mean(xentropy, name="loss")
```

The neural network model is ready, the cost function is ready, the last thing we need is the definition of a GradientDescentOptimizer. This will minimize the cost function by tweaking the parameters of the model.

```
learning_rate = 0.01

with tf.name_scope("train"):

optimizer = tf.train.GradientDescentOptimizer(learning_rate)

training_op = optimizer.minimize(loss)
```

We have one more very important step to do in this phase; we need to specify how the model is going to be evaluated. All we will do here is use a performance measure of accuracy. For each of the instances, the measure will decide if the prediction from the network is right and it will do this by checking to see if the highest logit and the target class correspond. You can use a function called in_top_k() for this. The return will be a one-dimensional tensor that has many Boolean values – these need to be cast to floats and the average can be computed to provide the overall accuracy of the neural network:

```
with tf.name_scope("eval"):

correct = tf.nn.in_top_k(logits, y, 1)

accuracy = tf.reduce_mean(tf.cast(correct, tf.float32))
```

Then, as you would expect by now, a node must be created for initialization of the variables, and we need a Saver too so that our trained parameters can be saved to disk:

```
init = tf.global_variables_initializer()

saver = tf.train.Saver()
```

And breathe! The construction phase is over. There are less than 40 code lines here but it is an intense piece of code. The input and target placeholders were created; the function was created to build the neuron layer. That layer was used to create the DNN and then we defined a cost function, an optimizer was created and lastly, the performance measure was defined. Now we can head on to the next phase, Execution.

The Execution Phase

Thankfully, this is not so complicated, nor is it quite so long! First, we need to load the MNIST dataset. Previously, we did this using scikit-learn but TensorFlow is a much better way. Not only does it get the dataset, it will scale it between 0 and 1, give it a shuffle, and give us a nice simple function to use that will load the mini-batches one at a time:

```
from tensorflow.examples.tutorials.mnist import input_data

mnist = input_data.read_data_sets("/tmp/data/")
```

Next, we must define how many epochs we are going to run, along with the mini-batch sizes:

```
n_epochs = 400

batch_size = 50
```

Lastly, the model is trained:

```
with tf.Session() as sess:

init.run()

for epoch in range(n_epochs):

for iteration in range(mnist.train.num_examples // batch_size):

X_batch, y_batch = mnist.train.next_batch(batch_size)

sess.run(training_op, feed_dict={X: X_batch, y: y_batch})

acc_train = accuracy.eval(feed_dict={X: X_batch, y: y_batch})

acc_test = accuracy.eval(feed_dict={X: mnist.test.images,

y: mnist.test.labels})

print(epoch, "Train accuracy:", acc_train, "Test accuracy:",
acc_test)

save_path = saver.save(sess, "./my_model_final.ckpt")
```

This piece of code will open a session in TensorFlow and it will run the init node that is used to initialize the variables. After that, the main training loop is run. The code will iterate through the mini-batches that match with the size of the training dataset – this is done at every epoch. We use the next_batch() method to fetch each of the mini-batches; after this, the training operation is run. The code will give the operation the data and the targets for the current mini-batch. When each epoch ends, the model will be evaluated on the last mini-batch as well as on the entire training set and the result is printed out. Lastly, the parameters for the models are saved to disk.

How to Use the Neural Network

Once you have a trained neural network, it can be used for making predictions. That is quite simple to do; we just make use of the construction phase but the Execution phase needs to be changed as such:

```
with tf.Session() as sess:

saver.restore(sess, "./my_model_final.ckpt")

X_new_scaled = [...] # some new images (scaled from 0 to 1)

Z = logits.eval(feed_dict={X: X_new_scaled})

y_pred = np.argmax(Z, axis=1)
```

The code will first load the parameters from the disk. New images that you want to be classified are then loaded — don't forget that the feature scaling you applied to the training data must also be applied here — 0 to 1. The logits node is then evaluated.

To find out what every estimated class probability is, softmax() could be applied to the logits but if all you want to do is predict a class, you just choose the one with the highest logit value — the easiest way to do this is to use the function called argmax().

Fine-Tuning the Hyperparameters

Neural networks are quite flexible and, while this can be a good thing, it is also a huge drawback. Why? Because there are far too many hyperparameters and that makes tweaking difficult. You could use any network topology you could possibly imagine (this means the way the neurons connect with one another); you could use a simple MLP and change how many neurons there are, how many are in each layer, what activation function is used for each layer, the logic for weight initialization and so on. How on earth can you possibly determine what the right combination of hyperparameters is for the task at hand?

One way to find them would be, as we have done previously, to use grid search and cross-validation. However, there are too many hyperparameters and we already know that it can take a lot of time to train neural networks on big datasets. This means that it would only be possible to look through a small piece of the hyperparameter.

Perhaps a better way would be to use a randomized search or you could use a tool that would help you to implement more complex algorithms that will help you search out a decent set of hyperparameters in the shortest possible time. One thing that is very helpful is to have some idea of the values that would be considered reasonable for each individual hyperparameter; that way, the search space can be restricted. The first place to start is the number of hidden layers.

The Number of Hidden Layers

For some problems, the easiest place to start is with one hidden layer and the results will be quite reasonable. We already know that using an MLP that has a single hidden layer, even complex functions can be modeled as long as there are sufficient neurons. For so long, this went a long way toward convincing the researchers that deep neural network investigation was not required but they missed one important fact – there is a higher parameter efficiency with the deep networks than there is with shallow ones. The deep nets use far fewer neurons for modeling than the shallow nets do and this makes them much faster and easier to train.

Why is this? Well, imagine that you are using a piece of drawing software to draw a forest. The instructions say that you cannot use the copy and paste function so each tree has to be drawn individually, one branch and one leaf at a time. If you were able to draw a leaf and then copy and paste it to produce a branch, then copy and paste that to produce a tree, finally copying and pasting that tree to produce an entire forest, it would take you no time at all to draw a forest.

Very often, you find that real-world data is structured in such a way and a DNN will take advantage of this automatically – the hidden layers lower down will model the lower-level structures, the intermediates combine the lower-level structures to produce a model of the intermediate structures while the high layers together with the output layer will take the intermediate structures and put them together in higher-level structures.

This kind of hierarchical structure assists the DNNs to faster convergence for the best solution but it does more than that. It also improves how the DNN generalizes to new sets. For example, let's say that you have a model fully trained to recognize faces in images and now you want a new one trained that will recognize specific hairstyles. To get the training off to a good start, the lower levels of your original network could be used. Rather than having the biases and the weights in the first couple of layers in your new network randomly initialized, each one could be initialized to the corresponding lower-level biases and weights. The network doesn't have to start from the beginning to learn the lower-level structures because it will already recognize them; all it needs to do is learn the high-level structures, in this case, the hairstyles.

To summarize, you can often begin with a couple of hidden layers and attain, for example, 97% or higher accuracy, with one hidden layer containing a couple of hundred neurons, on the MNIST dataset and, using 2 layers and the same amount of neurons, at least 98% accuracy. Both of these would take about the same amount of time. If your problems are more complex, you could increase the number of the hidden layers gradually until such time as overfitting of the training set occurs. For tasks that are incredibly complex, like speech recognition or large classification of images, you would usually need a network that consisted of large numbers of layers, possibly hundreds but these layers would not be fully connected – more about this in a later chapter. You would also need a very large amount of training data. However, it is rare that a network of this size would need to be trained from scratch; more commonly, we would take parts from a network that has already been trained, a state-of-the-art network that already does a similar job, and we would reuse those parts. Training is considerably faster and you won't need so much data.

Number of Neurons per Hidden Layer

The type of the input and the output required by the specific task is what determines the number of neurons in the corresponding layers (input and output). An example of this is the MNIST task. For this, 10 output neurons and 28 x 28 = 784 input neurons are needed. The commonest way to size the hidden layers is to form them into a funnel shape with each layer having fewer neurons than the last. The rationale behind this is that if you have a lot of low-level structures, they can be consolidated into a smaller number of high-level structures. Let's take a typical MNIST neural network; it might have a couple of hidden layers – one containing 300 neurons and the other with 100 neurons. This is not common practice these days – all the hidden layers could be the same size, for example, all of them having 150 neurons. That gives you a single hyperparameter for fine-tuning instead of having one for each layer. As you can with the layers, you can increase the neuron numbers gradually until overfitting begins to happen. Generally, you get better results when the number of layers is increased.

As you have seen, it is not easy to find the optimum number of neurons. Perhaps an easier way would be to choose a model that has more neurons and layers than you need and the implement Early Stopping so it doesn't overfit.

Activation Functions

Most of the time, the ReLU activation function will be used in hidden layers; it computes a little faster than some of the other activation functions and there aren't so many flat surfaces for Gradient Descent to get stuck on. This is down to ReLU not saturating for the bigger input values, whereas the hyperbolic tangent function and the logistic function will both saturate at 1.

As far as the output layer is concerned, the best choice for classification is usually the softmax activation function, so long as you have mutually exclusive classes. If you are doing regression, you don't need an activation function.

You have now been well and truly introduced to the ANN – artificial neural network. In the next few chapters, we will be looking at training deep nets and then we will look at how to distribute the training across several GPUs and servers. To finish the book, we will delve into convolutional networks, autoencoders, and recurrent neural networks, some of the other neural network structures.

Chapter 10: How to Train Deep Neural Nets

In the last chapter, we met the ANNs, the artificial neural networks, and we trained a DNN, a deep neural network. However, it wasn't a very deep DNN, only a shallow one really, with just two hidden layers. So, what would you do if you had a really complex task? Perhaps you need to identify multiple objects from multiple high-res images. In this case, we need a DNN that goes much deeper, maybe one with 10 layers. Each layer would have many hundreds of neurons and each would have thousands of connections. This is not going to be easy.

The first thing you are going to find is the problem of vanishing gradients or you may even face the problem of exploding gradients. Both of these have a profound effect on deep neural networks and they make it very hard to train the lower layers.

Secondly, pretty obvious really, training would be excruciatingly slow on such a large network.

Third, the number of parameters is such a network would reach the millions and we would run a very high risk of overfitting.

How do we get over all of this? Well, that's what we are going to discuss in this chapter; we'll go through each of the problems, one at a time, and look at some techniques that could help solve them.

We'll start by looking at the issue of vanishing gradients and consider some solutions. We'll move on to some of the optimizers that we could use to speed the training up in comparison to the vanilla Gradient Descent. Lastly, we will look at a few of the more commonly used regularization techniques for the larger neural networks. These tools will provide everything you need to start training the very deep nets. Welcome to the world of Deep Learning.

The Problems of Vanishing and Exploding Gradients

In the last chapter, we discussed the backpropagation algorithm and how it works. Basically, the error gradient is propagated by the algorithm as it goes from the output to the input layer. When the cost function gradient has been computed for each of the network parameters, those gradients are used to apply a Gradient Descent step to update the parameters.

The problem we have is that, as the algorithm moves through the layers down to the lower ones, the gradients become smaller and the Gradient Descent update may not change the connection weights on the lower levels. As a result, the training cannot ever converge to a suitable solution. This is the vanishing gradients problem but it can work the other way around – the gradients may grow in size resulting in many of the layers being given considerably large updates to the weight connections, and resulting in the divergence of the algorithm. This is the exploding gradients problem and this tends to be seen more in recurrent neural networks, which is the subject of a later chapter.

More often than not, the DNNs suffer more from instability in the gradients. What this means is that the layers may each learn at completely different speeds. This is one of the reasons why work on DNNs was left untouched for so long, but from about 2010 onwards, progress on understanding it started to move. Xavier Glorot and Yoshua Bengio published a paper called "Understanding the Difficulty of Training Deep Feedforward Neural Networks" and in this paper, they detailed a number of suspects that they had found. One of those suspects was a combination of two popular functions and techniques – the weight initialization technique and the logistic sigmoid activation function – use of normal distribution with a standard deviation of 1 and a mean of 0 to produce random initialization.

What they showed was that by using this combination of initialization and activation there is a greater output variance of each layer than there is input variance. As you move forward through the network, that variance continues to increase, layer by layer, until saturation of the activation function occurs at the top layers. What makes this worse is that the logistic function does NOT have a mean of 0; it is 0.5. The hyperbolic tangent function is the one with a mean of 0 and that behaves in the deep networks just a little better than the logistic function does.

If you look closer at the logistic activation function, you would see that, as the inputs become larger, be they positive or negative, the activation function will saturate at either 1 or 0 and the derivative is very close to 0. As such, when backpropagation starts, it doesn't have much of a gradient to propagate back and what there is of the gradient will continue to dilute as the backpropagation moves down the top layers; when it gets to the bottom layers, there is nothing left.

Xavier and He Initialization

What did Glorot and Bengio propose to solve the problem? What we need is the signal flowing smoothly in both directions – forward, when the predictions are made, and backward for backpropagation. This signal shouldn't vanish, nor should it explode to the point of saturation. For this signal to flow smoothly, Bengio and Glorot argued that the variance of the layer outputs needs to be equal to the variance of the layer inputs. At the same time, there should be equal variance on the gradients before and after it reverses through a layer. For that to be guaranteed, the layer would need to have the same number of both input and output connections. However, a compromise was suggested, one that is proven in practice. We need to randomly initialize the connection weights, as you can see in the following equation – n inputs denotes how many input connections are in the layer where the initialization is happening, and n outputs is the number of output connections for the same layer. This is often called Xavier Initialization or Glorot Initializations, named after the author.

Normal distribution with mean 0 and standard deviation $\sigma = \sqrt{\dfrac{2}{n_{\text{inputs}} + n_{\text{outputs}}}}$

Or a uniform distribution between -r and +r, with $r = \sqrt{\dfrac{6}{n_{\text{inputs}} + n_{\text{outputs}}}}$

Equation - Xavier Initialization – For When The Logistic Activation Function Is Used

This has been shown to speed the training significantly and the success that is seen with Deep Learning today can be, in part, attributed to this. There have been other papers published recently providing strategies that are similar but for other activation functions. For example, the ReLU activation function initialization strategy including the ELU activation and any other variant is often termed the He Initialization, taking the surname of the author.

By default, the Xavier initialization is used by the fully_connected function by default but you use the function called variance_scaling_initializer() to change it to He Intialization, as follows:

```
he_init = tf.contrib.layers.variance_scaling_initializer()

hidden1 = fully_connected(X, n_hidden1, weights_initializer=he_init, scope="h1")
```

> **Note**
>
> Unlike Xavier initialization, He Initialization will only take the fan-in into consideration. Xavier calculates the fan-in to fan-out average. The variance_scaling_initializer() is also set to this as default but you can set argument mode="FAN_AVG" to change this.

Activation Functions That Don't Saturate

Another insight from the Glorot and Bengio paper was that the problems with vanishing and exploding gradients were due partly to choosing the wrong type of activation function. Until then, it had been assumed that if activation functions that were roughly sigmoid were used in biological neurons then these must be the best choice. However, it has since come to light that there are many other activation functions that work in the DNNs a lot better, the ReLU activation function in particular. Much of this is down to the fact that the ReLU function doesn't saturate for the positive values and because it computes much faster.

For one thing, the ReLU activation function isn't perfect. It has its own problems, in particular, the dying ReLUs problem. Some of the neurons die during the training which means they don't output anything but 0. Sometimes as many as 50% of the neurons may die, especially if a large learning rate has been used. If the weights are updated during training in such a way that produces a negative weighted input sum, it will begin to output 0. Once this happens, it is unlikely that the neuron can be revived because when the ReLU function input is negative, the gradient is 0.

Solving this problem could be done by using a ReLU function variant, like the leaky ReLU. The definition of this function is LeakyReLU a(z) = max(az, z). The rate at which the function "leaks" is defined by hyperparameter a – it is the function slope for z < 0 and tends to be set as 0.01. Because the slope is so small, leaky ReLUs can't die; they may go to sleep for a while but they will wake up eventually.

Recently, another paper compared multiple ReLU activation function variants drawing the conclusion that the strict ReLU activation function is always outperformed by the leaky ReLUs. If the setting a = 0.2, which is a massive leak, was used, the result was a much better performance than the smaller a = 0.01 leak. The randomized leaky ReLU (RReLU) was also evaluated; during training, a was randomly chosen from a provided range and fixed for testing purposes to an average value. This also performed well and appeared to reduce the overfitting risk, i.e. like a regularizer does. Lastly, the parametric leaky ReLU (PreLU) was evaluated – in this, rather being a hyperparameter, a is learned in the training – this makes it a parameter that backpropagation can then modify, the same as any other parameter. PreLU was found to outperform ReLU significantly on the larger datasets with images but, with the small datasets, it was more likely to overfit.

Last but by no means least, a paper was published in 2015 by Djork-Arné Clevert et al. In this paper, we were introduced to a new activation function, this one called ELU, or exponential linear unit. The ELU outperformed every ReLU variant in every experiment – training was much faster and neural network produced better test set performance. The definition of ELU can be seen in the following equation:

$$\mathrm{ELU}_\alpha(z) = \begin{cases} \alpha(\exp(z) - 1) & \text{if } z < 0 \\ z & if\ z \geq 0 \end{cases}$$

Equation - ELU Activation Function

Now this might look, at first glance, to be a lot like ReLU but there are some significant differences:

- When $z < 0$, ELU will take negative values. This means the unit can have an output average that is nearer to 0, which mitigates some of the problems with vanishing gradients. When z is a big negative number, the value approached by the ELU function is defined by hyperparameter a. Normally it is set to 1, but like any of the hyperparameters, it can be tweaked.
- The gradient for $z < 0$ is nonzero, thus eliminating the problem of dying units.
- There are no bumps in this function; it runs smoothly all the way and that includes around $z = 0$. This helps Gradient Descent to go much faster because there is less bouncing to the left and the right of $z = 0$.
- The ELU function does have one main drawback; it computes slower than ReLU does and slower than any variant of ReLU and this is because it uses the exponential function. Compensation is provided during training in the form of a much faster rate of convergence. However, when it comes to testing, the ReLU networks are faster than ELU networks.

So, which one do you use on the DNN hidden layers? Generally, you should use them in this order:

- ELU=>Leaky ReLU (and all variants)=>ReLU=>tanh=>logistic. If you want performance at runtime, edge toward the leaky ReLU over ELU.

If you really can't face tweaking more hyperparameters, use the defaults we mentioned earlier – leaky ReLU – 0.01 and ELU – 1. If you have sufficient computing power and some free time, use cross-validation to evaluate some of the activation functions, like ReLU for overfitting and PReLU for large training sets.

You can build a neural network using the elu() function in TensorFlow. All you do, when you call fully_connected, is set the argument activation_fn:

```
hidden1 = fully_connected(X, n_hidden1, activation_fn=tf.nn.elu)
```

There is no predefined leaky ReLU function in TensorFlow but you can easily define your own:

```
def leaky_relu(z, name=None):

return tf.maximum(0.01 * z, z, name=name)

hidden1 = fully_connected(X, n_hidden1, activation_fn=leaky_relu)
```

Batch Normalization

Even if you do use the He Initialization together with ELU or any other ReLU variant, it will cause a significant reduction in vanishing and exploding gradients at the start of training and there is no guarantee that the problems won't reappear while training is ongoing.

In 2015, a paper was published by Sergey Ioffe and Christian Szegedy. In the paper, they proposed Batch Normalization, a technique to address the problems of the vanishing and exploding gradients. At the same time, it addresses the problem of the changing distribution of the inputs in each layer during training – this happens when the parameters change in the layers that come before, known as Internal Covariate Shift.

To do Batch Normalization, we need to do an operation to the model; this goes before each layer's activation function and is used to zero-center and normalize inputs before the result is scaled and shifted with a pair of new parameters on each layer – one parameter for scaling, one for shifting. In simple terms, the model will learn what the mean outputs and the optimal scale are for each layer's inputs.

For the inputs to be zero-centered and normalized, the algorithm must estimate what the standard and mean deviations of the inputs are. To do this, it evaluates those deviations over the mini-batch in use at the time – hence the Batch Normalization. You can see the entire operation in the next equation:

1. $$\mu_B = \frac{1}{m_B} \sum_{i=1}^{m_B} \mathbf{x}^{(i)}$$

2. $$\sigma_B^2 = \frac{1}{m_B} \sum_{i=1}^{m_B} \left(\mathbf{x}^{(i)} - \mu_B\right)^2$$

3. $$\mathbf{\hat{x}}^{(i)} = \frac{\mathbf{x}^{(i)} - \mu_B}{\sqrt{\sigma_B^2 + \epsilon}}$$

4. $$\mathbf{z}^{(i)} = \gamma \mathbf{\hat{x}}^{(i)} + \beta$$

Equation - Batch Normalization Algorithm

Let's break this rather large equation operation down:

- The empirical or observed mean is µB and this will be evaluated over the entire mini-batch called B
- The empirical or observed standard deviation of σB also gets evaluated over the entire mini-batch
- mB represents how many instances the mini-batch contains
- X(i) is the input that has been normalized and zero-centered
- Γ represents the layer's parameter for scaling
- β represents the layer's offset, or the shifting parameter
- ϵ is a tiny number used to eliminate division by zero. The number is generally 10-3 and is known as a smoothing term.
- z (i) represents the Batch Normalization output – the inputs after scaling and shifting

When it comes to testing, the observed deviations cannot be computed by a mini-batch so you would just use the mean and standard deviations for the entire training set. These tend to be computed quite efficiently through the use of a moving average so we have four learned parameters for each of the Batch Normalized layers:

- γ – scale
- β – offset
- μ = mean
- σ – standard deviation

It was demonstrated by Ioffe and Szegedy that use of this technique brought about a huge improvement in every deep neural net on which they tried it. The problem of the vanishing gradients was reduced to the point that use of activation functions that saturate, like tanh and the logistic activation function, was possible. It was also found that the DNNs were significantly less sensitive to initialization of the weights. Larger learning rates could be used which served to make the training process faster.

Perhaps more specifically, they found that when Batch Normalization was applied to a "state-of-the-art" model for image classification, the same accuracy was produced as the original model but with 14 times fewer steps. Batch Normalization also acts as a regularizer so there is a much lower requirement for other techniques, like dropout, which we talk about later in this chapter.

However, when you use Batch Normalization, the model becomes a bit more complex, even though the first hidden layer will normalize the input data for us, so long as it has been batch normalized. There is also a runtime penalty – slower predictions are made by the neural network because each layer requires more computations. If you want lightning-fast predictions, you may want to try ELU with He Initialization first.

Using TensorFlow to Implement Batch Normalization

In TensorFlow, we find a function called batch_normalization(). This will center the inputs and normalize them, but you will need to compute the mean and the standard deviations. This can be done, as discussed earlier, either on the mini-batch data while training or the full dataset while testing. The deviations then need to be passed to the function as parameters and you will also need to take care to create the parameters for scaling and offset (not forgetting the need to be passed to the function). It can be done but it isn't the best way. Instead, use a function called batch_normal() which will do it all automatically. You have a choice – directly call it or tell fully_connected() that you want it used, like this:

```
import tensorflow as tf

from tensorflow.contrib.layers import batch_norm

n_inputs = 28 * 28

n_hidden1 = 300

n_hidden2 = 100

n_outputs = 10
```

```
X = tf.placeholder(tf.float32, shape=(None, n_inputs), name="X")

is_training = tf.placeholder(tf.bool, shape=(), name='is_training')

bn_params = {

'is_training': is_training,

'decay': 0.99,

'updates_collections': None

}

hidden1 = fully_connected(X, n_hidden1, scope="hidden1",

normalizer_fn=batch_norm, normalizer_params=bn_params)

hidden2 = fully_connected(hidden1, n_hidden2, scope="hidden2",

normalizer_fn=batch_norm, normalizer_params=bn_params)

logits = fully_connected(hidden2, n_outputs,
activation_fn=None,scope="outputs",

normalizer_fn=batch_norm, normalizer_params=bn_params)
```

Let's break this down.

The first few lines need no explanation; then we have the placeholder, is_training and this will evaluate True or False. We use this to let batch_norm() know whether the mean and standard deviations in training should be used or whether it should use the running averages that it tracks during testing.

The next thing to do is define a dictionary that is used to define the parameters that are passed

$$\hat{v} \leftarrow \hat{v} \times \text{decay} + v \times (1 - \text{decay})$$

to batch_norm() including the is_training parameter. That dictionary is called bn_params. The algorithm makes use of exponential decay when the running averages are computed and this is why we need to provide the decay parameters. If the running average $\hat{v}$ is given a new value of v, it is updated through this equation:

Good values for decay tend to be near to 1, like 0.9, 0.999, etc. – the larger the dataset, the more 9's you want; the same applies to small mini-batches. Then, we set updates_collections to None so that the running averages are updated by batch_norm() before Batch Normalization is done during the training. If you omit this parameter, TensorFlow will add the operation to update running averages to an operation set that you need to run manually.

Finally, we call fully_connected() so the layers can be created using batch_norm(). This function will have the nb_params parameters to normalize the inputs before the activation function is called.

By default, batch_norm() will center the inputs, normalize them and shift them; it will not scale them. This is fine for the layers that either doesn't have any activation function or has the ReLU activation function because the weights on the next layer will do the scaling. If you use any of the other activation functions, bn_params needs to be given "scale": True.

It shouldn't have escaped your notice that the definition of the three preceding layers was nothing short of repetitive and this was down to there being a number of identical parameters. We can avoid this repetition with parameters by creating an argument scope. To do this, we use arg_scope(); parameter one is a list of the functions while the other parameters are automatically passed to those functions. We can change the last three lines of our code like this:

```
[...]

with tf.contrib.framework.arg_scope(

[fully_connected],

normalizer_fn=batch_norm,

normalizer_params=bn_params):

hidden1 = fully_connected(X, n_hidden1, scope="hidden1")

hidden2 = fully_connected(hidden1, n_hidden2, scope="hidden2")

logits = fully_connected(hidden2, n_outputs, scope="outputs",

activation_fn=None)
```

It doesn't really look any better than it did before in this example, but if you had more layers, for example, 10, and each needs an activation function, a normalizer, an initializer, a regularizer and more, this makes it much easier to read your code.

The remainder of this construction phase will flow the same guidelines as in the last chapter – the cost function is defined, an optimizer is created, the code is told to minimize the cost function, the evaluation operations are defined, a Saver is created, and on it goes.

The Execution phase is much the same as before with a single exception. When you have an operation you need to run that is dependent on the batch_norm layer, the placeholder, is_training, must be set as True or False:

```
with tf.Session() as sess:

sess.run(init)
```

```
for epoch in range(n_epochs):

[...]

for X_batch, y_batch in zip(X_batches, y_batches):

sess.run(training_op,

feed_dict={is_training: True, X: X_batch, y: y_batch})

accuracy_score = accuracy.eval(

feed_dict={is_training: False, X: X_test_scaled, y: y_test}))

print(accuracy_score)
```

That is all there is to it. This is only a small example and with just two layers Batch Normalization is likely to have too much of a positive effect but when it comes to the much deeper neural networks, it can make a stupendous difference.

Gradient Clipping

Gradient clipping is one of the more popular ways to reduce the problem of exploding gradients. Quite simply, during backpropagation, the gradients are clipped so that they cannot go over a specified threshold – this does tend to be very useful in the recurrent neural networks which we will explain later in this book. Generally, Batch Normalization is used the most but it is still good to have some idea of Gradient Clipping and how it is implemented.

TensorFlow has a function called minimize() for optimizers. This function will compute the gradients and it will apply them, leaving you to call compute_gradients() first, followed by the creation of an operation that will use a function called clip_by_function to clip the gradients. Lastly you use the optimizer's method of apply_gradients() to create the operation that applies to those clipped gradients:

```
threshold = 1.0

optimizer = tf.train.GradientDescentOptimizer(learning_rate)

grads_and_vars = optimizer.compute_gradients(loss)

capped_gvs = [(tf.clip_by_value(grad, -threshold, threshold), var)

for grad, var in grads_and_vars]

training_op = optimizer.apply_gradients(capped_gvs)
```

The training_op will then be run at each of the training steps. The gradients are computed, they are clipped between -0.1 and 1.0 and then applied. You can fine-tune the threshold hyperparameter.

Reusing Layers and Models

In general, you should not train a massive DNN from the start. Instead, always look for a neural network that does something similar to your task and then you can take the lower layers from the network and reuse them. We call this Transfer Learning. Training is much faster and you don't need anywhere near as much training data. Let's say that you can get into a neural network that was trained in classifying images into categories. There were 100 categories including vehicles, plants, animals and so on. Now you want another DNN trained in classifying specific vehicle types. Both these tasks are very alike so you should try to use some of the layers in the first neural network.

In the same way, you can reuse parts of a TensorFlow model. All you do is restore the original model and then train it to do a new task:

```
[...] # construct original model

with tf.Session() as sess:

saver.restore(sess, "./my_original_model.ckpt")

[...] # Train it on a new task
```

However, you won't need, nor will you want to reuse the entire model, only a part of it. The easiest solution is to change the configuration of the Saver so that it will restore just a small subset of the original model's variables. The next code shows how we restore the first three hidden layers:

```
[...] # build a new model with the same definition as before for
hidden layers 1-3

init = tf.global_variables_initializer()

reuse_vars = tf.get_collection(tf.GraphKeys.TRAINABLE_VARIABLES,

scope="hidden[123]")

reuse_vars_dict = dict([(var.name, var.name) for var in reuse_vars])

original_saver = tf.Saver(reuse_vars_dict) # saver to restore the
original model

new_saver = tf.Saver() # saver to save the new model

with tf.Session() as sess:

sess.run(init)

original_saver.restore("./my_original_model.ckpt") # restore layers 1
to 3
```

```
[...] # train the new model

new_saver.save("./my_new_model.ckpt") # save the whole model
```

So, what have we done here? Well, we construct a new model ensuring that the hidden layers from one to three in the original model are copied. Next, we retrieve all of the variables that the default trainable=True had just created and retain those that have a scope that matches "hidden[123]", the regular expression. In short, we are going to get any trainable variable that is in hidden layer one, two, and three.

The next step is to create the dictionary that will map each variable's name from the original model to the new model – you should try to keep the names exactly the same. A Saver is then created to restore just those specific variables, followed by another Saver that will save the new model in its entirety, not just the first three layers.

A session is started and all the model variables are initialized; the variables from the first three layers of the original model are restored and, lastly, the model is trained and saved.

Models from Other Frameworks

If another model was used to train the framework, in order to reuse it the weights need to be manually loaded. For example, if the models were trained using Theano then you need to use the Theano code. Then you would manually assign the weights to the right variables. This can be time-consuming and just a little on the boring side. For example, look at the following piece of code, showing you how to copy the biases and the weight from hidden layer one in a model trained with another framework:

```
original_w = [...] # Load the weights from the other framework

original_b = [...] # Load the biases from the other framework

X = tf.placeholder(tf.float32, shape=(None, n_inputs), name="X")

hidden1 = fully_connected(X, n_hidden1, scope="hidden1")

[...] # # Build the rest of the model

# Get a handle on the variables created by fully_connected()

with tf.variable_scope("", default_name="", reuse=True): # root scope

hidden1_weights = tf.get_variable("hidden1/weights")

hidden1_biases = tf.get_variable("hidden1/biases")

# Create nodes to assign arbitrary values to the weights and biases

original_weights = tf.placeholder(tf.float32, shape=(n_inputs,
n_hidden1))
```

```
original_biases = tf.placeholder(tf.float32, shape=(n_hidden1))

assign_hidden1_weights = tf.assign(hidden1_weights, original_weights)

assign_hidden1_biases = tf.assign(hidden1_biases, original_biases)

init = tf.global_variables_initializer()

with tf.Session() as sess:

sess.run(init)

sess.run(assign_hidden1_weights, feed_dict={original_weights:
original_w})

sess.run(assign_hidden1_biases, feed_dict={original_biases:
original_b})

[...] # Train the model on your new task
```

Freeze Lower Layers

It is absolutely possible that the lower layers from the original deep neural network have already learned how to look at images and detect any low-level features that will prove useful in both of the classification tasks described above. So you would be able to use these layers in another model exactly as they are. When you train a new deep neural network, it is best to freeze the weights on these layers. If you do this, the weights on the higher levels will train much easier – they don't need to learn a target that moves. Freezing the lower layers in training is quite easy; just provide the optimizer with a list of the variables that are going to be trained – make sure that you do not include the lower-level variables:

```
train_vars = tf.get_collection(tf.GraphKeys.TRAINABLE_VARIABLES,

scope="hidden[34]|outputs")

training_op = optimizer.minimize(loss, var_list=train_vars)
```

At the start, we get the variables for training from the output layer and from hidden layers three and four. This omits any of the variables from layers one and two. Next, this restricted list is given to the optimizer function called minimize(). Layers one and two have now been frozen and they will not move while the training happens. These are referred to as frozen layers.

Caching the Layers

Because these layers are not going to change, the output from the top frozen layer for each instance can be cached. Because the training will iterate over the entire dataset multiple times, you realize a massive boost in speed as the frozen layers only need to be gone through once per instance and not once per epoch. For example, the entire training set could first be run through the low layers (providing you have sufficient RAM):

```
hidden2_outputs = sess.run(hidden2, feed_dict={X: X_train})
```

Then, instead of training instance batches, when the training is happening you build batches of the layer two outputs and pass them to the training operation:

```
import numpy as np

n_epochs = 100

n_batches = 500

for epoch in range(n_epochs):

shuffled_idx = rnd.permutation(len(hidden2_outputs))

hidden2_batches = np.array_split(hidden2_outputs[shuffled_idx],
n_batches)

y_batches = np.array_split(y_train[shuffled_idx], n_batches)

for hidden2_batch, y_batch in zip(hidden2_batches, y_batches):

sess.run(training_op, feed_dict={hidden2: hidden2_batch, y: y_batch})
```

The training operation that we defined to freeze the first two layers is run on the last line. It is given a batch of the second layer outputs and the batch targets. Because we have already told TensorFlow what the output of layer two was, it won't attempt an evaluation of it nor will it evaluate any of the nodes on which hidden layer two depends.

The Upper Layers – Tweak, Drop, or Replace

You should, normally, replace the original model's output layer because it probably won't be that useful for your new task. It might not even possess the correct number of outputs that the new task requires.

In the same way, the hidden layers at the top of the original model are not going to be anywhere near as useful as the hidden lower layers – the most useful higher-level features for your new model will likely be quite different from those that the original model found useful. You need to find the correct number of reusable layers.

The first thing you can do is freeze the copied layers. Then you can train the model and check its performance. Next, unfreeze a couple of the higher hidden levels and tweak them using backpropagation – check to see if there is any improvement in performance. If you have plenty of training data, you can unfreeze more layers. Conversely, if you only have a small amount of training data, you unfreeze fewer levels.

If good performance is still proving elusive and you don't have much training data, drop the hidden layers from the top and freeze all the rest. Continue iterating until you have the correct number of reusable layers. If you have more data, rather than dropping the uppermost hidden layers, try replacing them and add a few more hidden layers.

Unsupervised Pre-training

Let's assume that you have a very complex task to do but little in the way of labeled data on which to train it. Not only that, you are struggling to find another model that has been trained on something similar. What do you do? Have you got to train this complex model from scratch? Not necessarily. The first thing you should do is attempt to find and gather some more labeled data but, if this proves to be an expensive option or is too hard to achieve, you can do something called unsupervised pre-training. What this means is, provided you have enough unlabeled data, you can try training each layer individually, one at a time. You start at the bottom and work your way up and, on each layer, you use an algorithm designed to detect unsupervised features, like an RBM – Restricted Boltzmann Machine.

Each of the layers is trained on the output from the previous layers that have been trained – every layer is frozen except for the one that is being trained. When every layer has been trained like this, you can then use supervised learning to tune the network, for example using backpropagation.

This is a very long and time-consuming method but it does work on most occasions. This technique is responsible for interest in neural networks being revived and has also played a large part in the growing success of Deep Learning. Up until 2010, it was common for this kind of pre-training to be done on deep nets. It took solving the problems of the vanishing gradient to make backpropagation the go-to for training the deep neural nets. However, these days, it still tends to be a preferred option to use unsupervised pre-training, but with autoencoders instead of RBMs. When complex tasks need to be solved, there is no similar trained model that you can use and you have loads of unlabeled but not much in the way of labeled training data.

Pre-training on Auxiliary Tasks

Another option you could use to get or generate some labeled training data is to first use an auxiliary task to train a network and then you can reuse the bottom layers for your task. The layers in the first network will learn the feature detectors that are likely to be reused by the next neural network.

Let's say that you want a system that will recognize certain faces but you don't have many pictures of those faces. This is not enough to train a good classifier. It isn't practical to gather in hundreds of images of each face, but what you could do is gather many images of random faces and then train your first network to detect whether two pictures that are different contain the same face. A network like this would be able to learn a decent facial detector. If you then reused the lower layers in your new network, you could train a classifier to recognize faces with very little training data.

It isn't always expensive to gather unlabeled data but it can be expensive to label that data. There is one technique that you could use – label every example as "good" and then you can corrupt those good examples to generate multiple new instances – those corrupted examples would be labeled as "bad". For example, let's say that you download many millions of sentences; you label all of them 'good' and then, in each sentence randomly change one word. The new sentences are then given the "bad" label. Provided your neural network can detect that "The cat scratched" is good but "The cat be" is a bad one, then that network probably already knows a fair bit about language; that means you can reuse the lower layers for other tasks centered around language processing.

Another way is to train a network so each training instance has a score as an output and then check that the score for a good instance is higher than the score for a bad instance by at least a certain margin. This is known as max margin learning and we use a cost function to check it.

Fast Optimizers

It isn't a five-minute job to train a large DNN; in fact, it can be excruciatingly slow. We have already looked at four techniques you can use to speed things up so you get a good solution:

- Using the right initialization for the connection weights
- Using the right activation function
- Batch Normalization
- Reusing lower layers of a network already trained up

Another way to boost your training speed is by using a fast optimizer. You want one that is faster than the normal optimizer for Gradient Descent. We will look at some of those in this section, the more popular ones are:

- Momentum
- Nesterov Accelerated
- AdaGrad
- RMSProp
- Adam

I'm going to tell you now; Adam is the one you should use most of the time. If you are not bothered about learning the way it works, all you need to do is put AdamOptimizer in place of GradientDescentOptimizer. That one small change can provide a significant boost to speed. There are three hyperparameters attached to Adam that can be tuned as well as the learning rate. While the default values are normally okay, it would be helpful to know what they do in case you need to do any tweaking. Adam is a combination of several optimizers so we'll start by looking at those.

Momentum Optimization

We all know what momentum is but let's start by imagining a smooth gentle slope. If you roll a ball from the top, it will start quite slowly. As it descends, it picks up speed, or momentum, until, provided there is air resistance or friction, it will reach terminal velocity. That is Momentum Optimization and it was first mooted in 964 by Boris Polyak. In complete contrast, the normal Gradient Descent descends the slope in small steps so it takes longer to get to the bottom.

With Gradient Descent, remember that to update the weights (θ), it subtracts the cost function gradient J(θ) regarding the weights ($\nabla_\theta J(\theta)$) multiplied by η (learning rate). The full equation would be $\theta \leftarrow \theta - \eta \nabla_\theta J(\theta)$. Gradient Descent isn't bothered what the gradients from earlier are; it simply doesn't care. If there is a tiny local gradient, then Gradient Descent takes it very slowly.

By contrast, Momentum Optimization does care what the earlier gradients were and, for every iteration it will take the local gradient and add it to m (the momentum vector) which is multiplied by η, the learning rate, and to update the weights, it will subtract the momentum vector. In simpler terms, the gradient isn't for speed, it is for acceleration. The algorithm has a way of simulating a friction mechanism so the momentum cannot grow too large – β, which is a new hyperparameter with a very simple name – Momentum. This needs to be set between 0, which is high friction, and 1, which is no friction. Typically, a momentum value would be 0.9.

$$1. \qquad m \leftarrow \beta m + \eta \nabla_\theta J(\theta)$$

$$2. \qquad \theta \leftarrow \theta - m$$

Equation - Momentum Algorithm

It is easy enough to verify that, provided the gradient stays constant, the maximum weight update size (i.e. terminal velocity), is equal to the gradient multiplied by η (learning rate) multiplied by $1/(1-\beta)$.

Let's say that $\beta = 0.9$; the terminal velocity would be the same as 10 x the gradient x learning rate. So if you used Momentum Optimization goes 10 times the speed of Gradient Descent.

This means that Momentum can get out of plateaus a great deal faster than Gradient Descent, which tends to get stuck. More specifically, earlier we learned that the cost function looks much like an elongated bowl when the inputs have differing scales. While Gradient Descent shoots down the steeper slope at a fair rate, it takes much, much longer to traverse the valley. By contrast, Momentum rolls down the valley picking up speed until it gets to the optimum, which is the bottom.

If you have a DNN that does not use Batch Normalization, the top layers usually end up with different scales in the inputs and Momentum Optimization can help out quite a bit here. Momentum can also help to get you past local optima.

You can implement Momentum in TensorFlow very easily; take GradientDescentOptimizer out and input MomentumOptimizer; sit back and real in the profits.

```
optimizer = tf.train.MomentumOptimizer(learning_rate=learning_rate,
momentum=0.9)
```

Momentum does have one drawback; you have an additional hyperparameter to tune up. However, the value of 0.9 for Momentum seems to work in practice and will be faster than Gradient Descent for almost all occasions.

Nesterov Accelerated Gradient

In 1983, Yurii Nesterov proposed a variant that is faster than standard Momentum on almost every occasion. That variant is called NAG, or Nesterov Accelerated Gradient (sometimes called Nesterov Momentum Optimization). The idea behind NAG is that the cost function should be measured slightly ahead of the local position, toward the momentum. You can see this algorithm in the equation below. The only real difference between NAG and Momentum is that instead of just θ, $\theta + \beta m$ is used to measure the gradient:

$$1. \quad m \leftarrow \beta m + \eta \nabla_\theta J(\theta + \beta m)$$

$$2. \quad \theta \leftarrow \theta - m$$

Equation - Nesterov Accelerated Gradient Algorithm

So why does this work? It works because, generally, the direction the Momentum optimizer points in is the right one – it points to the optimum – so, by using a gradient that is further in that direction than the original position, you get a result that is a bit more accurate.

Let's say that $\nabla 1$ is the cost function gradient that has been measured at the starting point of θ and $\nabla 2$ is the gradient at $\theta + \beta m$. The Nesterov update will be a little nearer to the optimum. Small improvements like this add up over time with the result being that NAG is faster than standard Momentum. Not only that, when the weights are pushed across the valley by the momentum, $\nabla 1$ carries on pushing across while $\nabla 2$ pushes back to the bottom resulting in fewer oscillations and faster convergence. NAG is almost always faster than Momentum and using it is very easy – when you create your MomentumOptimizer, set use_nesterov=True:

```
optimizer = tf.train.MomentumOptimizer(learning_rate=learning_rate,

momentum=0.9, use_nesterov=True)
```

AdaGrad

Let's go back to the elongated bowl. Gradient Descent begins by speeding down the steep slope and then slows down as it goes to the valley's bottom. What would be very nice and very useful would be the algorithm detecting this early enough that the direction could be corrected to point more toward the global optimum.

AdaGrad can do this; it simply scales the gradient vector down on the steeper dimensions:

$$1. \quad s \leftarrow s + \nabla_\theta J(\theta) \otimes \nabla_\theta J(\theta)$$

$$2. \quad \theta \leftarrow \theta - \eta \, \nabla_\theta J(\theta) \oslash \sqrt{s + \epsilon}$$

Equation - AdaGrad Algorithm

Step 1 squares the gradients and puts them into the vector called s. $\otimes$ is representing the multiplication element by element. The vectorized form is the same as the computation si ← si + (∂ / ∂ θi J(θ))2 for each si element of the s vector. Basically, each si will accumulate the partial derivative squares of the cost function regarding the θi parameter. If the ith dimension cost function is steeper, then si will get larger with every iteration.

Step 2 is much the same as Gradient Descent but there is a difference – a factor of sqrt(s+ϵ) is

$$\theta_i \leftarrow \theta_i - \eta \, \partial / \partial \theta_i \, J(\theta) / \sqrt{s_i + \epsilon}$$

used to scale the gradient vector down. This time, $\otimes$ represents the division element by element and to eliminate the risk of division by zero, a smoothing term of ϵ is used and this is normally set 10-10.

This algorithm is decaying the learning rate. This is done much quicker for the steeper dimensions than those that have gentle slopes and this is known as an adaptive learning rate. This will help the updates to be pointed more directly at the global optimum and one of the biggest benefits is that the η learning rate hyperparameter does not need as much tuning.

AdaGrad is a good choice for quadratic problems that aren't too difficult but, when used on neural networks, it tends to stop early. This is because the learning rate has been scaled down so much that it stops completely before it gets to the global optimum.

RMSProp

While AdaGrad is a bit too quick to slow and global optimum convergence never happens, and this can be fixed with RMSProp. What this does is only accumulates the gradients that result from the recent iterations rather than accumulating them from the start of the training. The following equation shows you how this works – it uses exponential decay in step 1:

$$1. \quad s \leftarrow \beta s + (1 - \beta) \nabla_\theta J(\theta) \otimes \nabla_\theta J(\theta)$$

$$2. \quad \theta \leftarrow \theta - \eta \, \nabla_\theta J(\theta) \oslash \sqrt{s + \epsilon}$$

Equation - RMSProp Algorithm

B is the decay rate and it is normally set as 0.9. And yes, we have yet another new hyperparameter but it is unlikely to need much, if any tuning because the default value tends to do just fine.

There is, as you probably guessed, an RMSPropOptimizer class in TensorFlow and implementing it is quite simple:

```
optimizer = tf.train.RMSPropOptimizer(learning_rate=learning_rate,

momentum=0.9, decay=0.9, epsilon=1e-10)
```

With the exception of the simplest of problems, the RMSProp optimizer tends to produce higher performance than AdaGrad and it performs somewhat better than both Nesterov and Momentum. Until Adam Optimization came out, this was the preferred algorithm for many of the top researchers.

Adam Optimization

Adam is the short version of Adaptive Moment Estimation and this takes RMSProp and Momentum and combines the ideas. Like Momentum, Adam tracks the average of the exponential decay of the previous gradients and, like RMSProp, it tracks the average of the exponential decay of the previously squared gradients, as you can see in the following equation:

1. $$m \leftarrow \beta_1 m + (1 - \beta_1) \nabla_\theta J(\theta)$$

2. $$s \leftarrow \beta_2 s + (1 - \beta_2) \nabla_\theta J(\theta) \otimes \nabla_\theta J(\theta)$$

3. $$m \leftarrow \frac{m}{1 - \beta_1^{\,T}}$$

4. $$s \leftarrow \frac{s}{1 - \beta_2^{\,T}}$$

5. $$\theta \leftarrow \theta - \eta m \oslash \sqrt{s + \epsilon}$$

Equation - Adam Algorithm

- T is representing the iteration number which begins at 1.

Start by looking at the first, second and fifth steps; you can see just how similar Adam is to RMSProp and Momentum. There is one difference – in step 1, the exponential decay average is computed and not the exponential decay sum. These are actually the same with the exception of a constant factor – the decay average is $1 - \beta_1$ multiplied by the decay sum.

The third and fourth steps are more a technicality – because initialization of m and s was at 0, both have a bias to 0 when training starts so these steps are used for boosting m and s at the start.

β_1 is the decay hyperparameter for Momentum and this tends to be, as you now know, initialized to 0.9 and β_2, which is the decay hyperparameter, tends to be initialized at 0.999. As we saw earlier, the ϵ smoothing term initialization is normally a tiny number, like 10-8 and, as these are the defaults for the AdamOptimizer class in TensorFlow, you would just use the following:

```
optimizer = tf.train.AdamOptimizer(learning_rate=learning_rate)
```

Because Adam is classed as an algorithm for adaptive learning alongside AdaGrad and RMSProp, it doesn't need anywhere near as much learning hyperparameter tuning and the default value, which is $\eta = 0.00$, is often used, making Adam one of the easiest to use, even better than Gradient Descent.

How to Train Sparse Models

All the previous algorithms provide us with dense models; almost every parameter will be a nonzero parameter. But what if you wanted a model that was lightning fast at runtime? What if you needed a model that took up less memory? In that case, you would probably prefer a sparse model over a dense one.

One way that this could be achieved is to train the model as normal and then remove the tiny weights by setting them to 0. Or you could apply ℓ_1 regularization, ensuring it is strong during the training – this will make the optimizer set as many weights to 0 as it can, as we saw in Lasso Regression earlier in the guide.

However, there will be times when techniques such as these are simply not enough. However, there is another option – Dual Averaging. You will sometimes see this called FTRL – Follow The Regularized Leader and, when you use this with ℓ_1 regularization, it very often results in sparse models. There is a variant of this in TensorFlow called FTRL-Proximal which is in the class called FTRLOptimizer.

Learning Rate Schedules

It isn't always easy to find the best learning rate – set too high and training may diverge; too low and it will converge eventually but not for an inordinately long time. You could set it a little high and it will move fast to start with but will wind up skipping around the optimum; it won't settle unless one of the adaptive learning rates we talked about (AdaGrad, Adam or RMSProp) is used, but even then it can take time. If your computing budget is limited, training may need to be interrupted before convergence and the result will be a suboptimal solution.

You could train your network repeatedly over a small number of epochs making use of a number of different learning rates and then compare the learning curves. A good learning rate will be quick to learn and you get convergence fairly quickly. You can do much better than having a constant learning rate. Provided you begin with a high rate and then when progress slows down you reduce that rate, a good solution can be found quicker than with the optimal constant rate. How do we reduce the learning rate? Well, there are a few ways to do this and all come under the umbrella of learning schedules. The most commonly used of these are:

Predetermined Piecewise Constant

An example of this would be to start by setting your learning rate as $\eta_0 = 0.1$; once 50 epochs have been done, you would then set it to $\eta_0 = 0.001$. This can work reasonably well but you do need to do some tinkering to get the learning rates right and to work out when they should be used.

Performance Scheduling

To use this, the validation error needs to be measured every N steps, much the same as you do with Early Stopping, and when the error ceases to drop, the learning rate is reduced by a factor of λ.

Exponential Scheduling

The learning rate is set to t: $\eta(t) = \eta_0 \cdot 10^{-t/r}$, which is the function of the iteration number. This does work very well but 0 and r do need to be tuned. After every r steps, the learning rate drops by a factor of 10.

Power Scheduling

The learning rate is set to $\eta(t) = \eta_0 (1 + t/r)^{-c}$, where c is the hyperparameter, usually set to 1. This is much like exponential scheduling but with a slower dropping learning rate.

Using TensorFlow to implement a learning schedule is very easy:

Once the hyperparameter values have been set, a non-trainable variable called global_step is created and initialized to 0. This is to monitor the iteration number in the training. Next, an exponentially decaying learning rate is defined, using $\eta_0 = 0.1$ and r = 10,000 and the exponential_decay() function in TensorFlow. Then we use that decaying learning rater to create the optimizer – we are using the Momentum optimizer. Lastly, we call the minimize method() for the purpose of creating a training operation. Because we pass this to the variable called global_step and incrementation is all taken care of for us.

<u>Using Regularization to Avoid Overfitting</u>

Typically, a deep neural network will have parameters numbering in the thousands, sometimes millions. Because there are so many parameters, the DNN has a great deal of freedom and that means it is able to fit a wide range of complex datasets. But this is its downside – it makes the network prone to overfitting.

When you have millions of parameters there isn't much you can't fit and we're now going to look at some of the regularization techniques that have proven popular for the neural networks along with using TensorFlow to implement them including:

- Early Stopping
- $\ell1/\ell2$
- Dropout
- Max-norm
- Data augmentation

Early Stopping

To eliminate the chance of overfitting, one of best solutions is Early Stopping. Simply stop the training when performance begins to drop on the validation set. You can use TensorFlow to implement this and you do this by evaluating your model at regular intervals on a validation set – it could be every 50 steps. A 'winner' snapshot should be saved provided it is better than the 'winner' snapshots before it. Count how many steps are between that 'winner' and the last one and stop the training when this number reaches a given limit, for example, 1500 steps. Then the last 'winner' snapshot can be restored.

Early stopping is good in practice but better performance can usually be achieved if you combine with one or more other techniques for regularization.

$\ell1$ and $\ell2$ Regularization

Just as we did for the linear models, $\ell1$ and $\ell2$ regularization can be used to constrain the connection weights of a neural network but you can't usually constrain the biases. Using TensorFlow, you can do this by adding the right regularization terms to the cost function. For example, let's say that you have a single hidden layer and it has weights (weights1) and a single output that has weights (weights2); $\ell1$ regularization can be applied like this:

```
[...] # construct the neural network

base_loss = tf.reduce_mean(xentropy, name="avg_xentropy")

reg_losses = tf.reduce_sum(tf.abs(weights1)) +
tf.reduce_sum(tf.abs(weights2))

loss = tf.add(base_loss, scale * reg_losses, name="loss")
```

However, if your network has multiple layers, this isn't the most convenient approach. TensorFlow does provide another way, a much better way. There are functions, like fully_connected() and get_variable(), that create variables and that will also accept *_regularizers for each of the variables, for example, weights_regularizer. If a function takes arguments in the form of weights and then returns a corresponding regularization loss, that function can be passed. There are three functions that return functions like this:

- $\ell1$_regularizer()
- $\ell2$_regularizer()
- $\ell3$_regularizer()

The next piece of code makes things clearer:

```
with arg_scope(

[fully_connected],
```

```
weights_regularizer=tf.contrib.layers.l1_regularizer(scale=0.01)):

hidden1 = fully_connected(X, n_hidden1, scope="hidden1")

hidden2 = fully_connected(hidden1, n_hidden2, scope="hidden2")

logits = fully_connected(hidden2, n_outputs,
activation_fn=None,scope="out")
```

What we have done is created a neural network that has two hidden layers and an output layer. The network will also create nodes to compute the $l1$ regularization loss that corresponds to each of the layers' weights. These nodes are automatically added by TensorFlow to a collection that has all of the regularization losses; you just need to do the following to add them to the overall loss:

```
reg_losses = tf.get_collection(tf.GraphKeys.REGULARIZATION_LOSSES)

loss = tf.add_n([base_loss] + reg_losses, name="loss")
```

Dropout

Dropout is one of the most commonly used of all the regularization techniques or DNNs. It was first proposed in 2010 by G E Hinton and more detail was provided by Nitish Srivastava et al in a published paper. Since then, it has gone on to be one of the most successful. By adding dropout, even some of the state-of-the-art networks experienced a boost in accuracy by about 1 to 2%. This doesn't sound like much but when that network model is already showing an accuracy of about 95%, an extra percent or two in accuracy means the error rate drops from about 5% to about 3%, or by about 40%.

It isn't a difficult algorithm. At each of the training steps, each neuron, and that includes input but no output neurons will have a probability (p) of being 'dropped out' temporarily – for the duration of the training step it will be effectively ignored but will become active in the next one. p is the hyperparameter for the dropout rate and it is usually set at 50%. Once the training is done, the neurons are no longer dropped and that is pretty much it for dropout - except for one tiny little technical detail.

This detail is quite important, too. Let's assume that p = 50. During the testing phase, a neuron is connected to about two times more input neurons than it was during training. This needs to be compensated for and to do that, the input weights for each neuron need to be multiplied by 0.5 once training has finished. If we don't do this, the neurons will each get an input signal that is about twice the size the network trained and that will not result in very good performance. Perhaps in more general terms, the input connection weights should be multiplied individually by 1 – p, which is the keep probability. Alternatively, the outputs from each neuron could be divided by the keep probability during the training phase. While not perfectly equivalent, these alternatives do work quite well.

To use TensorFlow to implement dropout, the dropout() function can simply be applied to the input layer and then to the output of each hidden layer. When training is taking place, the dropout() function will drop some items randomly, i.e. by setting 0 and then divides the items that are left by the keep probability. Once training is finished, the dropout() function doesn't do anything.

The next code will apply the dropout regularization to our neural network with three layers:

```
from tensorflow.contrib.layers import dropout

[...]

is_training = tf.placeholder(tf.bool, shape=(), name='is_training')

keep_prob = 0.5

X_drop = dropout(X, keep_prob, is_training=is_training)

hidden1 = fully_connected(X_drop, n_hidden1, scope="hidden1")

hidden1_drop = dropout(hidden1, keep_prob, is_training=is_training)

hidden2 = fully_connected(hidden1_drop, n_hidden2, scope="hidden2")

hidden2_drop = dropout(hidden2, keep_prob, is_training=is_training)

logits = fully_connected(hidden2_drop, n_outputs, activation_fn=None,

scope="outputs")
```

Warning

The dropout() function should be used in the tensorflow.contrib.layers and not in tensorflow.nn. The first will turn off when it isn't in training (no-op) which is exactly what you need; the second one does not.

As you did for Batch Normalization, is_training must be set to True when in training and to False when in testing.

If you see that your model is overfitting, raise the dropout rate by reducing the hyperparameter called keep_prob. If the model is underfitting, then increase keep_prob to decrease the dropout rate. If you have large layers, increase the dropout while decreasing the rate for small layers.

Convergence tends to be quite a bit slower with dropout but you do get a much better model provided you tune it properly.

Max-Norm Regularization

There is another technique that works quite well for the neural networks; it's called max-norm regularization and it works like this. For each individual neuron, it will take the incoming connections, like $\| w \|_2 \leq r$ (hyperparameter r is for max-norm and $\| . \|_2$ is the norm for ℓ2) and it constrains the weights w for each one.

This constraint tends to be implemented through the computation of $\|w\|_2$ following each of the training steps and, if required clipping w ($w \leftarrow w \frac{r}{\|w\|_2}$).

When we reduce r, we increase how much regularization is done and we reduce the risk of overfitting. Max-norm regularization can help eliminate or at least reduce the problems of vanishing and exploding gradients but only if Batch Normalization hasn't been used.

There is no max-norm regularizer built into TensorFlow but it isn't difficult to implement. The next piece of code will create a node called clip_weights – this clips the weights variable on the second axis so that a maximum norm of 1.0 is set for each row vector:

```
threshold = 1.0

clipped_weights = tf.clip_by_norm(weights, clip_norm=threshold,
axes=1)

clip_weights = tf.assign(weights, clipped_weights)
```

This operation would then be applied after every training step, like this:

```
with tf.Session() as sess:

[...]

for epoch in range(n_epochs):

[...]

for X_batch, y_batch in zip(X_batches, y_batches):

sess.run(training_op, feed_dict={X: X_batch, y: y_batch})

clip_weights.eval()
```

Hold on, how do we get to the weights variable for all the layers? That's easy; just use a variable scope, as you can see below:

```
hidden1 = fully_connected(X, n_hidden1, scope="hidden1")

with tf.variable_scope("hidden1", reuse=True):
```

```
weights1 = tf.get_variable("weights")
```

Or, the root variable scope could be used

```
hidden1 = fully_connected(X, n_hidden1, scope="hidden1")

hidden2 = fully_connected(hidden1, n_hidden2, scope="hidden2")

[...]

with tf.variable_scope("", default_name="", reuse=True): # root scope

weights1 = tf.get_variable("hidden1/weights")

weights2 = tf.get_variable("hidden2/weights")
```

If you don't know the name of a variable, you have two options – find out through TensorBoard or use the function called global_variables() and print the names of all the variables:

```
for variable in tf.global_variables():

print(variable.name)
```

This solution should do just fine but it isn't the neatest. A better way would be to find a max_norm_regularizer() function and then use it in the same way as with the ℓ2_regularizer() function, like this:

```
def max_norm_regularizer(threshold, axes=1, name="max_norm",

collection="max_norm"):

def max_norm(weights):

clipped = tf.clip_by_norm(weights, clip_norm=threshold, axes=axes)

clip_weights = tf.assign(weights, clipped, name=name)

tf.add_to_collection(collection, clip_weights)

return None # there is no regularization loss term

return max_norm
```

A parameterized function, max_norm(), is returned and this can be used as you use any other regularizer:

```
max_norm_reg = max_norm_regularizer(threshold=1.0)

hidden1 = fully_connected(X, n_hidden1, scope="hidden1",

weights_regularizer=max_norm_reg)
```

Be aware that you do not need to add a regularization loss term to the overall loss function when you use max_norm regularization so the function will return None. However, the clip_weights operation has still got to be run after every training step so the clips_node weight is added, by max_norm(), to a collection of special clipping operations, all max_norm. You must fetch the operations and run them after every training step, like this:

```
clip_all_weights = tf.get_collection("max_norm")

with tf.Session() as sess:

[...]

for epoch in range(n_epochs):

[...]

for X_batch, y_batch in zip(X_batches, y_batches):

sess.run(training_op, feed_dict={X: X_batch, y: y_batch})

sess.run(clip_all_weights)
```

Now that is a lot neater and cleaner.

Data Augmentation

There is one last technique to talk about – data augmentation. This regularization technique involves the use of existing training instances to generate new ones and this gives the training set an artificial boost. This helps to cut the risk of overfitting, which is why it is classed as a regularization technique. The trick is in generating training instances that are realistic. In idealistic terms, the human eye should not be able to determine the training instances that were generated from those that weren't. Just adding a lot of white noise will not provide any help here either; the applied modifications have got to be learnable, something that white noise isn't.

For example, let's say you have a model designed to classify mushrooms. The images in the training dataset can be rotated, shifted, and resized slightly by different amounts and the resulting images added to the set. This will force the model to have more tolerance to orientation, size, and position of the mushrooms in each image. If you wanted it to have more tolerance to lighting conditions, you would generate multiple images with differing contrasts. Assuming that each mushroom in each image is symmetrical, the images can also be horizontally flipped, and if you combine the two transformations, your training set can be vastly increased in size.

Often the preferred method is to have the training instances generated as you go instead of taking up valuable storage space and bandwidth by doing it beforehand. In TensorFlow, you will find a number of operations to manipulate images including:

- Shifting (transposing)
- Rotating
- Resizing
- Cropping
- Flipping

You can also adjust the hue, brightness, saturation, and contrast of the images in addition to the above operations. This makes data augmentation dead easy to implement for the image datasets.

Next, we look at how to use TensorFlow across multiple devices and networks.

Chapter 11: Using TensorFlow Across Servers and Devices

In the previous chapter, we looked at a few of the techniques used to speed training considerably – Batch Normalization, initializing weights better, faster, better optimizers and more. However, even with all these faster techniques, it can still take days, sometimes weeks, to train a very large network on one machine that has one CPU.

We are now going to look at how TensorFlow can help to distribute the work across several GPUs and CPUs, running them parallel. The first thing to do is distribute the work across several devices on one machine and then move on to multiple machines.

Compared to many of the other frameworks for neural network testing, TensorFlow has one of the best systems of support for distributed computing. With TensorFlow, you have total control over the way in which your graph is replicated across servers and devices. You also get a lot of flexibility in the ways that you can synchronize and parallelize the operations, with a good choice of parallelization approaches to use.

Throughout this chapter, we will discuss some of the common ways to parallelize neural network execution and training. Rather than having to wait for weeks for an algorithm to finish, we could bring that time down to just hours saving a considerable amount of time and giving you the flexibility to experiment far easier with different models, as well as give your existing models new data and re-training them.

Some other useful ways for parallelization include using it to explore huge hyperparameter spaces when you tune your model or the efficient running of large network ensembles. Before we get to that stage, we need to learn how it all works and the best place to start is to take several graphs and parallelize them over multiple GPUs on one machine.

Multiple Devices, One Machine

One of the easiest ways to realize a performance boost is to add more GPU cards to one machine. Much of the time this will be more than sufficient and you won't require any more than one machine. An example of this is training a neural network on one machine with eight GPU cards, which is just as fast as using multiple machines with 16 GPU cards. How could this be? Because when you have several machines, there is a delay in network communications.

To begin with, we will look at setting up your environment to allow TensorFlow to use several cards on a single machine. Then we will move on to distribution of operations across all available devices and parallel execution.

Installation

Running TensorFlow on multiple cards first requires determining whether your GPU cards have got a Nvidia Compute Capability equal to or greater than 3.0. This includes the Titan and K range of cards but you can check compatibility of any card at https://developer.nvidia.com/cuda-gpus.

The next step is to download the right versions of the CUDA library and the cuDNN library and install them. We also need to set some environment variables so that TensorFlow can find these installations. The best option is to go directly to the TensorFlow website as installation instructions tend to go out of date very quickly and they will be the most up-to-date at any given time.

CUDA or Compute Unified Device Architecture is a Nvidia library that gives developers the ability to use GPUs that are CUDA-enabled for many different computations, not just for accelerating graphics. cuDNN or CUDA Deep Neural Network is another Nvidia library, this one is GPU-accelerated and provides primitives for use by DNNs. These include some of the more common computations, like normalization, activation layers, convolutions (backward and forward), as well as pooling, which we'll be discussing in the next chapter. You will need a Nvidia developer account because cuDNN is part of the Deep Learning SDK. Both CUDA and cuDNN are used by TensorFlow to control GPUs and accelerate the computations.

Lastly, install TensorFlow with GPU support and then open a Python shell. You need to make sure that TensorFlow is able to detect CUDA and cuDNN and use them properly. To do this, we import TensorFlow and create a session:

```
>>> import tensorflow as tf

I [...]/dso_loader.cc:108] successfully opened CUDA library
libcublas.so locally

I [...]/dso_loader.cc:108] successfully opened CUDA library
libcudnn.so locally

I [...]/dso_loader.cc:108] successfully opened CUDA library
libcufft.so locally

I [...]/dso_loader.cc:108] successfully opened CUDA library
libcuda.so.1 locally

I [...]/dso_loader.cc:108] successfully opened CUDA library
libcurand.so locally

>>> sess = tf.Session()

[...]

I [...]/gpu_init.cc:102] Found device 0 with properties:

name: GRID K520

major: 3 minor: 0 memoryClockRate (GHz) 0.797

pciBusID 0000:00:03.0
```

```
Total memory: 4.00GiB

Free memory: 3.95GiB

I [...]/gpu_init.cc:126] DMA: 0

I [...]/gpu_init.cc:136] 0: Y

I [...]/gpu_device.cc:839] Creating TensorFlow device

(/gpu:0) -> (device: 0, name: GRID K520, pci bus id: 0000:00:03.0)
```

That looks ok. TensorFlow has detected both libraries and detected the GPU card by using CUDA.

Management of GPU RAM

TensorFlow will, by default, use all the RAM from all the GPUs when you run the graph for the first time so you can't start another program running while the first one is working. Try to, and you will get an error like the following:

```
E [...]/cuda_driver.cc:965] failed to allocate 3.66G (3928915968
bytes) from

device: CUDA_ERROR_OUT_OF_MEMORY
```

One way around this to run each individual process on separate GPU cards and the easiest way to do this is to set the environment variable called CUDA_VISIBLE_DEVICES so that each process see only the GPU card appropriate to it. For example, two programs could be run like this:

```
$ CUDA_VISIBLE_DEVICES=0,1 python3 program_1.py

# and in another terminal:

$ CUDA_VISIBLE_DEVICES=3,2 python3 program_2.py
```

The first program sees only the GPU cards with the numbers 0 and 1 and the second program will see only those numbered 2 and 3 and everything will work just as it should.

Another way would be to tell TensorFlow that you want just a fraction of the memory grabbed. For example, for TensorFlow to get 40% of the memory from each GPU, a ConfigProto object needs to be created, the gpu_options.per_process_gpu_memory_fraction of the object set to 0.4 and a session created with this configuration:

```
config = tf.ConfigProto()

config.gpu_options.per_process_gpu_memory_fraction = 0.4

session = tf.Session(config=config)
```

Now you can use the same GPU cards to run two programs in parallel.

While both of the programs are running, run the command nvidia-smi and it should show you that each of the processes makes use of approximately 40% of each card's RAM.

One more way would be to tell TensorFlow to get the memory only when it is required. This means setting config_gpu_options.allow_growth as True. Keep in mind that, once TensorFlow has grabbed the memory, it will not release it, and the reason for this is to eliminate the risk of memory fragmentation. Because of this, there is the chance that you could run out of memory at some point. This option is not the easiest method to guarantee deterministic behaviors so you probably want to avoid using it and rely on the first two options.

Okay, we have our GPU-enabled installation in TensorFlow. It works. Now we just need to learn how to use it.

Placing The Operations on The Devices

In 2015, a preliminary TensorFlow white paper was released and in it, a dynamic placer algorithm was introduced. This algorithm automatically and somewhat magically distributes the operations across the available devices. At the same time, it will take other things into consideration, such as:

- Measured computation times from when the graph was previously run;
- Estimations of the input and output tensor size to each of the operations;
- How much RAM each device has available;
- Delay in communication while data is transferred in and out of the devices;
- User constraints and hints;
- Much more.

However, this algorithm, sophisticated as it is, has never been released as part of the open-source TensorFlow because it is internal to Google. It was left out of this TensorFlow version as it appears to be that in practical terms, it is less capable in performing efficient placement than a set of user-specified placement rules. However, the dynamic placer is being worked on by TensorFlow and may, in time, be sufficient to be released. Until then, we use the simple placer, a very basic placer that does the job.

Simple Placement

When a graph is run and a node that hasn't been placed onto a device requires evaluation by TensorFlow, the simple place is used to put the node on the device, along with any other node that hasn't yet been placed. These are the rules that the simple placer respects:

- If a node was placed on a device when the graph was previously run, it will be left on the device, or
- If the node was pinned to a device by the user, it will be put onto that specific device, or

- It will default to GPU number 0 or, if no GPU is available, to the CPU.

What it boils down to is that it is really up to you to place the operations on the correct device. If you do nothing, the entire graph gets placed on whichever device is the default one. Pinning nodes requires a device block to be created and that requires the device() function. For example, the next piece of code will on the variable called a and the constant called b onto the CPU; however, the multiplication node called c has not been pinned on any device so it will go to the default on2:

```
with tf.device("/cpu:0"):

a = tf.Variable(3.0)

b = tf.constant(4.0)

c = a * b
```

Note

There isn't a way of pinning nodes to a specific CPU nor is there any way to use a subset of all the CPUs; instead, "/cpu:0" aggregates all the CPUs on multiple CPUs on one system.

Logging Placements

The next thing to do is check that the constraints we defined have been respected by the simple placer. To do this, log_device_placement is set to True so that, whenever the placer places a node, it will log a message. For example:

```
>>> config = tf.ConfigProto()

>>> config.log_device_placement = True

>>> sess = tf.Session(config=config)

I [...] Creating TensorFlow device (/gpu:0) -> (device: 0, name: GRID K520,

pci bus id: 0000:00:03.0)

[...]

>>> x.initializer.run(session=sess)

I [...] a: /job:localhost/replica:0/task:0/cpu:0
```

```
I [...] a/read: /job:localhost/replica:0/task:0/cpu:0

I [...] mul: /job:localhost/replica:0/task:0/gpu:0

I [...] a/Assign: /job:localhost/replica:0/task:0/cpu:0

I [...] b: /job:localhost/replica:0/task:0/cpu:0

I [...] a/initial_value: /job:localhost/replica:0/task:0/cpu:0

>>> sess.run(c)

12
```

The log messages are the lines starting with "I" (information). When a session is created, a message is logged by TensorFlow, telling us that a GPU card has been found. Then when the graph is run for the first time, when variable a is initialized in this case, the simple placer is also run and this will put each of the nodes onto the device to which it has been assigned. As you can see from the log messages, each node has been placed onto "/cpu:0" with the exception of one – the multiplication node. This is placed onto "/gpu:0", which is the default device. For now, disregard the /job:localhost/replica"0/task:0 prefix – we will discuss it shortly.

Note that the placer is not used when the graph is run a second time for c to be computed; this is because every node that is needed for TensorFlow to compute c have been placed already.

Dynamic Placement

When a device block is created, rather than using a device name, a function can be specified instead. This function then gets called by TensorFlow for each of the operations that are to be placed in the device block and the device name that the operation is being pinned n must be returned by the function. For example, in the next code, all the variable nodes are pinned to "/cpu:0" and the other nodes are pinned to "/gpu:0":

```
def variables_on_cpu(op):

if op.type == "Variable":

return "/cpu:0"

else:

return "/gpu:0"

with tf.device(variables_on_cpu):

a = tf.Variable(3.0)

b = tf.constant(4.0)

c = a * b
```

Kernels and Operations

For any TensorFlow operation to run on any device that device must have an implementation called a kernel. Some operations will have both CPU and GPU kernels. For example, where integer variables are concerned, there is no GPU kernel in TensorFlow so, when TensorFlow attempts to place the variable called i on GPU 0 the following code would fail:

```
>>> with tf.device("/gpu:0"):

...  i = tf.Variable(3)

[...]

>>> sess.run(i.initializer)

Traceback (most recent call last):

[...]

tensorflow.python.framework.errors.InvalidArgumentError: Cannot
assign a device

to node 'Variable': Could not satisfy explicit device specification
```

Here, TensorFlow is making the inference that the variable has to be of type int32; as you can see, an integer has been used for the initialization value. Let's say that, instead of 3, the initialization value was changed to 3.0 or if dtype=tf.float32 were explicitly set at the time the variable was created, everything would work well.

Soft Placement

If you were to attempt to pin an operation to a device where there is no kernel for the operation, by default you would get an exception, the one you saw earlier when TensorFlow tried to direct the operation to a device. If you wanted TensorFlow to go back on the CPU, the allow_soft_placement option would need to be set to True:

```
with tf.device("/gpu:0"):

i = tf.Variable(3)

config = tf.ConfigProto()

config.allow_soft_placement = True

sess = tf.Session(config=config)

sess.run(i.initializer) # the placer runs and falls back to /cpu:0
```

Up to now, we have talked about placing nodes on devices. Now it's time to see how they are going to be run in parallel by TensorFlow:

Parallel Execution

When a graph is run on TensorFlow, it will begin by locating a list of all the nodes that must be evaluated and then it will count the number of dependencies each node has. Tensorflow will them evaluate those nodes with zero tendencies, which are the source nodes. If these are put on separate devices then the parallel evaluation will take place. Put them on the same device and evaluation happens in different threads so they too can run in parallel, either in separate CPU cores or GPU threads.

On each of the devices, TensorFlow will manage a thread pool for the parallelization of operations. These pools are known as inter-op thread pools. Some of the operations have kernels that are multi-threaded, i.e. they can make use of other pools that are known as intra-op thread pools.

Let's say that you have three operations, A, B, and C. All of them are source ops so they can all be evaluated immediately. A and B are placed on GPU 0, being sent to the inter-op thread pool of that device; parallel evaluation can then happen. Operation A contains a multi-threaded kernel; the computations are divided into three and the intra-op thread pool will execute all three in parallel. Operation C is placed on the inter-op thread pool for GPU 1.

Once operation C has finished, D and E's dependency counters are decremented to 0, meaning both are sent for execution by the inter-op thread pool.

Tip

It is possible to control how many threads are in each inter-op pool and you do this by setting the option for inter_op_parallelism_threads. Note that the initial session will create those inter-op thread pools and, unless you set use_per_session_threads to True, the pools will be reused by subsequent sessions. To control how many threads are in each intra-op pool, you need to set the option for intra_op_parallelism_threads.

Control Dependencies

Sometimes it is better to wait to evaluate an operation even when all the operations that it is dependent on have already been executed. For example, if an operation requires a large amount of memory but the value of that operation isn't needed until much later, it's best to postpone evaluation until the last minute so that RAM required for other operations isn't taken up needlessly.

Another example would be a set of operations that are dependent on data that is external to the device. If all the operations were run simultaneously, the communication bandwidth of the device would be saturated and all of the operations would be waiting on I/O, also blocking any other operation that has data it needs to communicate. It would be much better to execute operations like this in sequence, thus allowing other operations to be performed in parallel.

Postponing evaluation of some of the nodes is quite simple; all you do is add control dependencies. The next code is telling TensorFlow that x and y are to be evaluated once a and b have been evaluated, not before:

```
a = tf.constant(1.0)

b = a + 2.0

with tf.control_dependencies([a, b]):

x = tf.constant(3.0)

y = tf.constant(4.0)

z = x + y
```

As z is dependent on x and y, there is the implication that z also cannot be evaluated until after a and b, even though it hasn't been explicitly set out in the control_dependencies() block. Also, because b is also dependent on a, the previous code could be simplified – instead of [a, b], a control dependency could be created on [b] but, sometimes, explicit is much better.

So, you now know:

- How operations are placed on multiple devices
- How parallelism can be used to execute the operations
- How control dependencies are created for optimizing that parallel execution

Now it's time to distribute those computations over multiple servers.

Multiple Devices, Multiple Servers

For a graph to be run on multiple servers, a cluster must first be defined. Clusters are made up of at least one TensorFlow server – these are known as tasks and are spread over multiple machines. Each of the tasks belongs to a specific job, which is nothing more than a group of tasks with a name. The tasks are grouped by common roles, like "worker" jobs which are used for computations, or 'ps' jobs, which stands for parameter server and are used for tracking the parameters of the model.

Next, you will see the specification of a cluster that defines those two jobs – "worker" and "ps". "ps" has one job and "worker" has two. In the example, two Tensorflow servers or tasks are hosted on Machine A, each server listening on a different port. One is a part of the "ps" job, and one is a part of the "worker" job. Machine b hosts a single server which is part of "worker":

```
cluster_spec = tf.train.ClusterSpec({
```

```
"ps": [

"machine-a.example.com:2221", # /job:ps/task:0

],

"worker": [

"machine-a.example.com:2222", # /job:worker/task:0

"machine-b.example.com:2222", # /job:worker/task:1

]})
```

For a TensorFlow server to be started, a Server object needs to be created and then passed to the cluster specification, so that server communication can happen, and to its task number and job name. For example, if you wanted the first worker task to be started, the following code would be run on Machine A:

```
server = tf.train.Server(cluster_spec, job_name="worker",
task_index=0)
```

Normally, it would be easier to run one task on one machine but, as you can see from the last example, TensorFlow will easily let you run multiple tasks on one machine. If the machine has multiple servers, it is important to make sure that all the servers don't attempt to use the RAM from every GPU.

If you only want the process to run that TensorFlow server, the main thread can be blocked and this is done by telling the thread it must wait until the server has finished – you do this by using a method called join(). If you don't do this, as soon as the main thread has exited, the server is killed. Because the server cannot be stopped at the moment, this will block forever:

```
server.join() # blocks until the server stops (i.e., never)
```

Open a Session

When you have all your tasks running, although they aren't doing anything at the moment, a session can be opened. You can do this from one of the clients in one of the processes on one of the machines on any server – you can even use a process that is running a task – and then that session can be used the way you would any local session. Look at this example:

```
a = tf.constant(1.0)

b = a + 2

c = a * 3

with tf.Session("grpc://machine-b.example.com:2222") as sess:
```

```
print(c.eval()) # 9.0
```

What we have here is a client code that is creating a graph, opening a TensorFlow server session on Machine B - this will be the Master – and then tells it that c needs to be evaluated. The Master begins by putting the operations into the right devices. In our code, because no operation had been pinned to any device, they were all put on their defaults – for this example, the GPU device for machine B. Then it continues to evaluate c as it has been told to do and the result is returned.

Services – Master and Worker

The client is using the Google Remote Procedure Call protocol, otherwise known as gRPC, for communication with the server. This is one of the most efficient of the frameworks to call remote functions and to gather their outputs, and it can do it across a wide range of languages and platforms. gRPC is based on HTTP2 – this opens the connection and will keep it open throughout the session so that bidirectional communication is enabled when the connection has been enabled. The data is transmitted as protocol buffers via this communication pathway – protocol buffers are another piece of open-source technology from Google and are a particularly lightweight format for the interchange of data.

Please keep in mind that the TensorFlow cluster servers may communicate with one another so you must ensure that the right firewall ports are open.

Each of the servers in the TensorFlow cluster will provide two services – the Master and the Worker service. The Master will allow sessions to be opened by the clients and used to run graphs. It will take responsibility for coordinating the computations across the tasks with a reliance on the Worker to take care of executing the computations and gathering in results from other tasks.

This is a very flexible architecture because one client is able to open several sessions in a single thread and connect to several servers. One server is able to handle several sessions from one or more clients simultaneously. You can choose between running a single client for each task, usually inside the same process, or you can have one client that controls all the tasks.

Pinning Operations

Device blocks can be used to pin operations to any device, regardless of which task manages it. To do this you simply specify the name of the job, the task index, the type of device, and the device index. An example is shown in the code below, where we are pinning a to the CPU belonging to the first task listed in the job called "ps" – the CPU for Machine A, in other words. Next, b is pinned to the second GPU that the first task listed in "worker" manages – GPU 1 on Machine A. Lastly, we don't pin c to any device so it is placed on its default by the Master – GPU 0 for machine B.

```
with tf.device("/job:ps/task:0/cpu:0")
```

```
a = tf.constant(1.0)

with tf.device("/job:worker/task:0/gpu:1")

b = a + 2

c = a + b
```

If you don't specify the type and index of the device, TensorFlow defaults to the default device of the task. If you were, for example, to pin an operation to "/job:ps/task:0", it would be placed on the CPU for Machine A – the device that the first task in the "ps" job defaults to. If you were to leave the task index out as well, for example, "/job:ps", TensorFlow will go to :/task:0" by default. And if the job name were left out along with the task index, it would default to the Master task of the session.

Sharding Variables

You will soon see, when a neural network is trained on a distributed setup, one of the most common patterns is using a set of parameter servers to store the model parameters, for example, the "ps" job tasks, leaving the remaining tasks to concentrate on computations, for example, the "worker" job tasks.

When you have huge models that have millions of parameters, sharding is a very useful technique. The parameters can be sharded over many parameter servers and this will help keep the risk of saturation down on the network card of any parameter server. It would be very time-consuming to pin each variable to a parameter server manually. But once again, TensorFlow comes to the rescue with a function called replica_device_setter(). This function takes care of distributing the variables using a Round-Robin method over all of the "ps" tasks. Let's look at an example; this code is pinning five variables across two servers:

```
with tf.device(tf.train.replica_device_setter(ps_tasks=2):

v1 = tf.Variable(1.0) # pinned to /job:ps/task:0

v2 = tf.Variable(2.0) # pinned to /job:ps/task:1

v3 = tf.Variable(3.0) # pinned to /job:ps/task:0

v4 = tf.Variable(4.0) # pinned to /job:ps/task:1

v5 = tf.Variable(5.0) # pinned to /job:ps/task:0
```

Rather than the number of ps_tasks being passed, cluster=cluster_spec can be passed instead, resulting in TensorFlow counting how many tasks are in the "ps" job.

If you were to create different operations, aside from variables, in the block, they will automatically be pinned to "/job:worker" by TensorFlow, and this defaults to the first device that is the first task in the "worker" managed. You could set the worker_device parameter to pin them to any other device but embedded device blocks are a better way. If you define a job, a device, or a task in an outer block, an inner block can override it, like this:

```
with tf.device(tf.train.replica_device_setter(ps_tasks=2)):

v1 = tf.Variable(1.0)  # pinned to /job:ps/task:0 (+ defaults to /cpu:0)

v2 = tf.Variable(2.0)  # pinned to /job:ps/task:1 (+ defaults to /cpu:0)

v3 = tf.Variable(3.0)  # pinned to /job:ps/task:0 (+ defaults to /cpu:0)

[...]

s = v1 + v2 # pinned to /job:worker (+ defaults to task:0/gpu:0)

with tf.device("/gpu:1"):

p1 = 2 * s # pinned to /job:worker/gpu:1 (+ defaults to /task:0)

with tf.device("/task:1"):

p2 = 3 * s # pinned to /job:worker/task:1/gpu:1
```

This code example makes the assumption that we only have CPU parameter servers. This is typical because the parameters only need to be stored and communicated; there are no intense computations to be done.

Using Resource Containers to Share State Across Sessions

If you use a local session and not a distributed session, the session will manage the state of each variable. When the session ends, the values of every variable are then lost. If you have several local sessions, they cannot share states, even if they are both on the same graph; each session will retain a copy of each variable. Conversely, if you were using a distributed session, resource containers are used to manage the variable state on the cluster; the session takes no part in management. So, let's say that you have a variable called x; it's been created using a specific client session and it will be available to all other sessions that share the cluster, regardless of which server the session is connected to (they can be on different servers and they could still share). Look at this piece of client code:

```
# simple_client.py

import tensorflow as tf

import sys

x = tf.Variable(0.0, name="x")
```

```
increment_x = tf.assign(x, x + 1)

with tf.Session(sys.argv[1]) as sess:

if sys.argv[2:]==["init"]:

sess.run(x.initializer)

sess.run(increment_x)

print(x.eval())
```

Let's say that you have a TensorFlow cluster; it runs on port 2222 on A and B machines. The following command will launch the client, telling it a session needs to be opened on A and the variable needs to be initialized, incremented, and its value printed:

```
$ python3 simple_client.py grpc://machine-a.example.com:2222 init

1.0
```

If you then use the net command to launch it, the client connects to the machine B server and reuses that variable called x without a request being made for variable initialization:

```
$ python3 simple_client.py grpc://machine-b.example.com:2222

2.0
```

This works both ways. If you want a variable shared over multiple sessions, it's an easy way to do it. However, if you want independent computations run on one cluster, you need to take care that you don't accidentally use the same variable names. There is a way to make sure none of your names clash, and that is to use a wrapper – the construction phase can be wrapped up inside one variable scope with unique names for each individual computation, like this:

```
with tf.variable_scope("my_problem_1"):

[...] # Construction phase of problem 1
```

A better option is to use a container block:

```
with tf.container("my_problem_1"):

[...] # Construction phase of problem 1
```

Rather than using the default container, with a name of "" (an empty string), a container that is dedicated to problem 1 is used. An advantage to this is that we can keep the names of the variables short; it is also easy to reset a container that has been named. The following command connects to the server that is on A and requests it resets the container with the name of "my_problem_1"; this frees up the resources that the container used and closes any open sessions on the server. If you want to reuse any variable that this container managed, the variable needs to be initialized:

```
tf.Session. Reset("grpc://machine-a.example.com:2222",
["my_problem_1"])
```

Variable sharing across sessions is much easier with a resource container and more flexible too. Let's say that you have four clients – A, B, C, and D. Each runs a different graph in the same cluster but they do share variables. A and B share one variable called x – the default container manages this variable. C and D share another x variable, this time managed by "my_problem_1" container. Client C is able to share variables that are managed by both containers.

Resource containers can as be used to help preserve the state of readers and queues – both stateful operations – so we'll start by looking at queues.

TensorFlow Queues and Asynchronous Communication

Queues are a really good method of exchanging data between several sessions. For example, one of the more popular uses for it is a client-created graph that will load the data for training and then put it into a queue while, at the same time, another client-created graph will pull that data from the graph and use it for training a model. This can provide a considerable speed boost to training because there is no need to wait for the mini-batches at each step.

There are a few different queues in TensorFlow and the easiest is called a FIFO queue – First-In-First-Out. The following example shows you a FIFO queue being created for the storage of up to 10 tensors, each tensor having a pair of float values:

```
q = tf.FIFOQueue(capacity=10, dtypes=[tf.float32], shapes=[[2]],

name="q", shared_name="shared_q")
```

Warning

Sharing variables across multiple sessions requires the specification of the same name and the same container at both ends. TensorFlow queues use shared_name rather than a name attribute so specifying it is very important, regardless of whether the name is the same you must also use the same container.

Enqueuing Data

An enqueue operation needs to be created if you want data pushed into a queue. This code is pushing three instances into the queue:

```
# training_data_loader.py

import tensorflow as tf
```

```
q = [...]

training_instance = tf.placeholder(tf.float32, shape=(2))

enqueue = q.enqueue([training_instance])

with tf.Session("grpc://machine-a.example.com:2222") as sess:

sess.run(enqueue, feed_dict={training_instance: [1., 2.]})

sess.run(enqueue, feed_dict={training_instance: [3., 4.]})

sess.run(enqueue, feed_dict={training_instance: [5., 6.]})
```

Rather than queuing each instance individually, several can be enqueued simultaneously with the operation called enqueue_many:

```
[...]

training_instances = tf.placeholder(tf.float32, shape=(None, 2))

enqueue_many = q.enqueue([training_instances])

with tf.Session("grpc://machine-a.example.com:2222") as sess:

sess.run(enqueue_many,

feed_dict={training_instances: [[1., 2.], [3., 4.], [5., 6.]]})
```

Both of the above examples are doing the same thing – enqueuing the same tensors into the queue.

Dequeuing Data

If you want the training instances pulled out of the queue at the other end, a dequeue operation must be used:

```
# trainer.py

import tensorflow as tf

q = [...]

dequeue = q.dequeue()

with tf.Session("grpc://machine-a.example.com:2222") as sess:

print(sess.run(dequeue)) # [1., 2.]

print(sess.run(dequeue)) # [3., 4.]
```

```
print(sess.run(dequeue)) # [5., 6.]
```

Generally, it will be preferable to pull an entire mini-batch at the same time, and not just one instance after another. To do this, a dequeue_many operation must be used and you must specify the size of the mini-batch:

```
[...]

batch_size = 2

dequeue_mini_batch= q.dequeue_many(batch_size)

with tf.Session("grpc://machine-a.example.com:2222") as sess:

print(sess.run(dequeue_mini_batch)) # [[1., 2.], [4., 5.]]

print(sess.run(dequeue_mini_batch)) # blocked waiting for another
instance
```

When there is no more room in the queue, the enqueue operation blocks until a dequeue operation is used to pull some items out. Conversely, when you have an empty queue or you have used dequeue_many() and you have fewer items than the specified mini-batch size, the dequeue operation blocks until an enqueue operation has been used to push enough items into the queue.

Tuple Queues

The items in a queue do not have to be single tensors; they can be tuples of tensors, of varying shapes and types. The following queue has tensor pairs stored – each pair consists of a type int32 and shape () and a type float32 and shape [3,2]:

```
q = tf.FIFOQueue(capacity=10, dtypes=[tf.int32, tf.float32],
shapes=[[],[3,2]],

name="q", shared_name="shared_q")
```

Tensor pairs must be supplied to the enqueue operation, with each pair representative of one item:

```
a = tf.placeholder(tf.int32, shape=())

b = tf.placeholder(tf.float32, shape=(3, 2))

enqueue = q.enqueue((a, b))

with tf.Session([...]) as sess:

sess.run(enqueue, feed_dict={a: 10, b:[[1., 2.], [3., 4.], [5.,
6.]]})
```

```
sess.run(enqueue, feed_dict={a: 11, b:[[2., 4.], [6., 8.], [0.,
2.]]})

sess.run(enqueue, feed_dict={a: 12, b:[[3., 6.], [9., 2.], [5.,
8.]]})
```

At the other end, a pair of dequeue operations are created by dequeue():

```
dequeue_a, dequeue_b = q.dequeue()
```

These operations should be run together:

```
with tf.Session([...]) as sess:

a_val, b_val = sess.run([dequeue_a, dequeue_b])

print(a_val) # 10

print(b_val) # [[1., 2.], [3., 4.], [5., 6.]]
```

Warning

Running dequeue_a alone will result in a pair being dequeued and the first element only being returned with element two being lost. In the same way, if dequeue_b is run alone, you will lose the first element.

If you use dequeue_many, a pair of operations is returned:

```
batch_size = 2

dequeue_as, dequeue_bs = q.dequeue_many(batch_size)

You can use it like this:

with tf.Session([...]) as sess:

a, b = sess.run([dequeue_a, dequeue_b])

print(a) # [10, 11]

print(b) # [[[1., 2.], [3., 4.], [5., 6.]], [[2., 4.], [6., 8.], [0.,
2.]]]

a, b = sess.run([dequeue_a, dequeue_b]) # blocked waiting for another
pair
```

Closing Queues

Queues can be closed to send a signal to other sessions indicating that there will be no more enqueued data:

```
close_q = q.close()

with tf.Session([...]) as sess:

[...]

sess.run(close_q)
```

Any new enqueue or enqueue_many operations that come after this will result in an exception being raised when you try to execute them. If there are any pending requests, these are honored unless q.close(cancel_pending_enqueues=True) is called. Any new dequeue or dequeue_many operation executions will continue to be successful so long as the queue contains sufficient items; if there are insufficient queued items, these operations will fail.

If a dequeue_many operation is in use and you have some instances in the queue but not as many as the specified mini-batch size, the items will all be lost. Instead, it might be better to use an operation called dequeue_up_to, which works in much the same way as dequeue_many until you close a queue or there are fewer instances than batch_size specifies; in these cases, the items will just be returned.

RandomShuffleQueue

TensorFlow also has support for other queues one of which is called RandomShuffleQueue. This can be used in the same way as the FIFOQueue but the items are dequeued randomly. This is very useful during training when you want the instances shuffled at each epoch.

First, we create a queue:

```
q = tf.RandomShuffleQueue(capacity=50, min_after_dequeue=10,

dtypes=[tf.float32], shapes=[()],

name="q", shared_name="shared_q")
```

We specify a minimum for the number of items that have to stay in the queue following a dequeue operation by using min_after_dequeue. This will make sure that there are sufficient instances left for there to be enough randomness – once the queue has been closed, that limit will be ignored.

Now, let's assume that you have a queue of 22 floats – 1. to 22. You could dequeue them in this way:

```
dequeue = q.dequeue_many(5)

with tf.Session([...]) as sess:

print(sess.run(dequeue)) # [ 20. 15. 11. 12. 4.] (17 items left)

print(sess.run(dequeue)) # [ 5. 13. 6. 0. 17.] (12 items left)
```

```
print(sess.run(dequeue)) # 12 - 5 < 10: blocked waiting for 3 more
instances
```

PaddingFIFOQueue

Another queue supported by TensorFlow is the PaddingFIFOQueue. You can use this the same as you do a FIFOQueue and it will accept tensors that have a fixed rank along any dimension and are of variable sizes. When you use dequeue_many or dequeue_up_to with PaddingFIFOQueue, each of the tensors will be padded on each variable dimension with zeros so that it is an equal size to the largest tensor the mini-batch contains.

For example, let's enqueue some 2D tensors or matrices which are of arbitrary sizes:

```
q = tf.PaddingFIFOQueue(capacity=50, dtypes=[tf.float32],
shapes=[(None, None)]

name="q", shared_name="shared_q")

v = tf.placeholder(tf.float32, shape=(None, None))

enqueue = q.enqueue([v])

with tf.Session([...]) as sess:

sess.run(enqueue, feed_dict={v: [[1., 2.], [3., 4.], [5., 6.]]}) #
3x2

sess.run(enqueue, feed_dict={v: [[1.]]}) # 1x1

sess.run(enqueue, feed_dict={v: [[7., 8., 9., 5.], [6., 7., 8.,
9.]]}) # 2x4
```

If you were to dequeue the items one at a time you would get the tensors back that you enqueued. However, if you dequeue multiple items at once, the tensors will be padded automatically by the queue. For example, if all three items were dequeued at once, all of the tensors would be zero padded to provide 3 x 4 tensors – this means the first dimension has a maximum size of 3 (the first item) and the second dimension has a maximum size of 4 (the third item):

```
>>> q = [...]

>>> dequeue = q.dequeue_many(3)

>>> with tf.Session([...]) as sess:

...    print(sess.run(dequeue))

[[[ 1. 2. 0. 0.]
```

```
 [ 3.  4.  0.  0.]

 [ 5.  6.  0.  0.]]

[[ 1.  0.  0.  0.]

 [ 0.  0.  0.  0.]

 [ 0.  0.  0.  0.]]

[[ 7.  8.  9.  5.]

 [ 6.  7.  8.  9.]

 [ 0.  0.  0.  0.]]]
```

Queues of this type are very useful when you have inputs of variable length, for example, a sequence of words.

Ok, we've covered how to distribute computations over several servers and devices, how to share the variables across multiple sessions, and how to use queues with asynchronous communication. Before you can even think about using all this to start training your neural networks, there is one more subject we need to talk about – the efficient loading of training data.

Load the Data from the Graph

Up until now, it has been assumed that the training data would be loaded by the clients and fed to the cluster using placeholders. This works very well for the simple setups but it really isn't that efficient because the training data is transferred multiple times:

- First, it is taken from the filesystem and given to the client;
- Second, it is taken from the client and given to the Master task;
- Third, when required, it may be taken from the Master task and given to other tasks.

If you have multiple clients training different networks with the same data, such as you would have with hyperparameter tuning, it gets even worse. If each of the clients were to load the data at the same time, you could end up with the network bandwidth or the file server becoming saturated.

Preloading into Variables

If you are working with datasets that fit into memory, a better way would be to load the data just once, assign it to a variable which can then be used in the graph. We call this preloading and, in this way, the data is transferred just once – it is taken from the client and given to the cluster. However, depending on whether it is needed by other operations and by which ones, the data might still need to be moved from one task to another.

This piece of code loads the entire dataset into one variable:

```
training_set_init = tf.placeholder(tf.float32, shape=(None,
n_features))

training_set = tf.Variable(training_set_init, trainable=False,
collections=[],

name="training_set")

with tf.Session([...]) as sess:

data = [...] # load the training data from the datastore

sess.run(training_set.initializer, feed_dict={training_set_init:
data})
```

To stop the optimizers attempting to tweak the variable, trainable=False must be set. You should also ensure that collections=[] is set so that the variable cannot be added the collection called GraphKeys.GLOBAL_VARIABLES. This collection is used to save checkpoints and restore them. Also, with this example, it is assumed that your training set consists of type float32 values only and that includes the labels. If you have any other data type, you require one variable for each type.

Reading the Data From the Graph

Reader Operations are a good choice if your training set won't fit into memory. These can read the data straight from the filesystem, meaning that the data doesn't have to go through the clients. There are several readers in TensorFlow for different file formats including:

- CSV
- Binary records – fixed length
- TFRecords – TensorFlow format, based on the protocol buffers

We'll concentrate on CSV. Let's assume that we have a file called my_test.csv. It has training instances in it and to read it, you create some operations. Let's also assume that the file has the content you see below in it – x1 and x2 are float features and a binary class is represented by an integer target:

```
x1, x2, target

1. , 2. , 0

4. , 5 , 1

7. , , 0
```

First, to read the file, a TextLineReader needs to be created. This will open a file that we specify and will read the lines one at a time. This operation is stateful in the same way as queues and variables are, which means its state is preserved across several graph runs, tracking the file that is being read and where it is in the file:

```
reader = tf.TextLineReader(skip_header_lines=1)
```

Next, a queue is created so that the reader will know which file is next to be read. An enqueue operation is also created along with a placeholder; these push specified file names to the queue and we finish with an operation that will close the queue when all the files are read:

```
filename_queue = tf.FIFOQueue(capacity=10, dtypes=[tf.string],
shapes=[()])

filename = tf.placeholder(tf.string)

enqueue_filename = filename_queue.enqueue([filename])

close_filename_queue = filename_queue.close()
```

Now we can create a read operation – this reads the records or lines one at a time and, for each one, we get a key-value pair returned. The key is the unique identifier for the record and is a string made up of the file name followed by a colon and then a line number, while the value is a string that has the line content:

```
key, value = reader.read(filename_queue)
```

Now the file can be read one line at a time. But we're not quite ready yet. First, we need the features and the target and, to get these, the string needs to be parsed:

```
x1, x2, target = tf.decode_csv(value, record_defaults=[[-1.], [-1.],
[-1]])

features = tf.stack([x1, x2])
```

Line one gets the values from the current line by using the CSV passer from TensorFlow. When one of the fields is missing, the default values are used. In our example, the x2 feature is missing its third training instance. The defaults are also used to work out what type each field is – we have an integer and two floats.

Lastly, the training instance together with its target is pushed to a RandomShuffleQueue – this will be shared with the training graph so that mini-batches can be pulled, and an operation is created to close out the queue when we have no more instances to push to it:

```
instance_queue = tf.RandomShuffleQueue(

capacity=10, min_after_dequeue=2,

dtypes=[tf.float32, tf.int32], shapes=[[2],[]],
```

```
name="instance_q", shared_name="shared_instance_q")

enqueue_instance = instance_queue.enqueue([features, target])

close_instance_queue = instance_queue.close()
```

That seems like a lot of work – all we want to do is read the file! Not only that, the graph has only been created and not run yet. To do that:

```
with tf.Session([...]) as sess:

sess.run(enqueue_filename, feed_dict={filename: "my_test.csv"})

sess.run(close_filename_queue)

try:

while True:

sess.run(enqueue_instance)

except tf.errors.OutOfRangeError as ex:

pass # no more records in the current file and no more files to read

sess.run(close_instance_queue)
```

First, the session is opened; the filename "my_test.csv" is enqueued and the queue is then closed because there are no more filenames to be enqueued. Next, an infinite loop is run so the instances are enqueued one at a time. The operation, enqueue_instance, is dependent on the next line being read by the reader, so with each iteration, a new record or line is read until the end of the file. Then, the reader will try to read the queue of filenames so it knows what file is to be read next; because you have closed the queue, an OutOfRange exception is thrown. If you had left the queue open, it would stay blocked until we either closed it or added another filename.

Last, the instance queue is closed – this stops the training operations that pull from the queue getting blocked forever. For the training graph, the shared instance queue must be created and the mini-batches dequeued:

```
instance_queue = tf.RandomShuffleQueue([...],
shared_name="shared_instance_q")

mini_batch_instances, mini_batch_targets =
instance_queue.dequeue_up_to(2)

[...] # use the mini_batch instances and targets to build the
training graph
```

```
training_op = [...]

with tf.Session([...]) as sess:

 try:

for step in range(max_steps):

sess.run(training_op)

except tf.errors.OutOfRangeError as ex:

pass # no more training instances
```

The first mini-batch has the first pair of CSV file instances and the second will have the last CSV instance.

Be aware that sparse tensors are not handled very well by TensorFlow queues so if you are using sparse training instances, after the instance queue the records need to be parsed.

This only uses a single thread to read and push records to the queue. If you had multiple threads reading from multiple files with multiple readers at the same time, you would get a better throughput and we'll look at this now.

Multi-threaded Readers

If you want multiple threads to read instances at the same time, you could use the threading module to create and manage Python threads. However, there are two tools in TensorFlow that can help make this much easier – both are classes and are called Coordinator and QueueRunner.

Coordinators are simple objects with one purpose – to coordinate the stopping of multiple threads. First, a coordinator needs to be created:

```
coord = tf.train.Coordinator()
```

Next, the threads that need to stop at the same time are given to the coordinator – the main loop will look like this:

```
while not coord.should_stop():

[...] # do something
```

A request can be made for all threads to stop by any of the threads. To do this, we call a coordinator method called request_stop():

```
coord.request_stop()
```

Once called, all threads will complete their current iteration and then stop. If you call another coordinator method called join() and pass it to the thread list, you will be able to wait for the threads to finish:

```
coord.join(list_of_threads)
```

To run multiple threads, each of which repeatedly runs an enqueue operation, you would use a QueueRunner. This will fill the queue up very fast and, when the queue is closed, an OutOfRangeError is thrown for the next thread that attempts to push an item onto the queue. The thread catches this error and will then pass a message to all the other threads, indicating to stop using the coordinator.

The next code example demonstrates the use of a QueueRunner for five separate threads, each reading instances at the same time and pushing those instance to the instance queue:

```
[...] # same construction phase as earlier

queue_runner = tf.train.QueueRunner(instance_queue,
[enqueue_instance] * 5)

with tf.Session() as sess:

sess.run(enqueue_filename, feed_dict={filename: "my_test.csv"})

sess.run(close_filename_queue)

coord = tf.train.Coordinator()

enqueue_threads = queue_runner.create_threads(sess, coord=coord,
start=True)
```

Line one is creating the QueueRunner and telling it that it needs to run five threads, all repeating the same operation, enqueue_instance, over and over again. Next a session is started and the file names are enqueued to read – in our case, this is "my_test.csv".

Then a coordinator is created and the QueueRunner will use this to stop, as we discussed. Lastly, the QueueRunner creates the threads and starts them. All the training instances are read by the threads and then pushed to the instance queue, after which, they will all stop.

This is somewhat more efficient than the method we saw earlier but there is still more we can do to make it even better. At this point, the same file is being read by all the threads but we can make them read from different files simultaneously as long as we sharded the data across several CSV files. We make the threads do this through the creation of multiple readers. To do this, a small function needs to be written so the reader can be created along with the nodes responsible for reading and pushing each instance to the queue:

```
def read_and_push_instance(filename_queue, instance_queue):
```

```
reader = tf.TextLineReader(skip_header_lines=1)

key, value = reader.read(filename_queue)

x1, x2, target = tf.decode_csv(value, record_defaults=[[-1.], [-1.],
[-1]])

features = tf.stack([x1, x2])

enqueue_instance = instance_queue.enqueue([features, target])

return enqueue_instance
```

Next, the queues are defined:

```
filename_queue = tf.FIFOQueue(capacity=10, dtypes=[tf.string],
shapes=[()])

filename = tf.placeholder(tf.string)

enqueue_filename = filename_queue.enqueue([filename])

close_filename_queue = filename_queue.close()

instance_queue = tf.RandomShuffleQueue([...])
```

Lastly, the QueueRunner is created but with a list containing the enqueue operations. Each operation makes use of a different reader so all the threads are reading from different files at the same time:

```
read_and_enqueue_ops = [

read_and_push_instance(filename_queue, instance_queue)

for i in range(5)]

queue_runner = tf.train.QueueRunner(instance_queue,
read_and_enqueue_ops)
```

The Execution phase remains as it was before – the file names are pushed, a coordinator is created, and the QueueRunner threads are created and started. The difference this time is that different files are read by the threads simultaneously until there are none left to read; at this point, the QueueRunner closes the queues, stopping other operations that pull from it from being blocked.

More TensorFlow Convenience Functions

There are a few more convenience functions in TensorFlow that help read the training instances by simplifying some of the more common tasks. We'll talk here about a couple of the more popular options, starting with the string_input_producer(). This will take a one-dimensional tensor that has a filename list; it will create a thread to push the filenames one at a time to a filename queue and will close the queue once the last name has been pushed. If you provide a specific number of epochs, string_input_producer() will go through each filename once per epoch; a QueueRunner is created for thread management and is then added to the collection called GraphKeys.QUEUE_RUNNERS.

You will need to call tf.train.start_queue_runners() if you want all the QueueRunners in the collection to start. Forgetting to start QueueRunner means the filename is open and has nothing in it; the result is your readers are blocked forever.

Other producer functions can be used to create queues and a QueueRunner for the enqueue operation and they are:

- input_producer()
- range_input_producer()
- slice_input_producer()

A list of tensors is provided to the function called shuffle_batch(), which will then create the following:

- A RandomShuffleQueue
- A QueueRunner – the tensors are enqueued to GraphKeys.QUEUE_RUNNER
- A dequeue_many – for mini-batch extraction from the queue

This makes life so much easier. One single process can manage a multi-threaded pipeline of inputs that feed the queue together with a training pipeline that extracts the mini-batches from the queue and reads them. You should also take some time to examine other functions that do something similar, such as:

- batch()
- batch_join()
- shuffle_batch_join()

You now have all the tools you need to begin training your neural networks and running them efficiently across a TensorFlow cluster containing several servers and devices. Before we continue, let's do a quick recap.

You learned how to:

- Work with multiple GPUs
- Set up a TensorFlow cluster and start it
- Distribute the computations over the devices and servers on the cluster

- Use containers to share stateful ops, like variable, readers and queues across sessions
- Coordinate several graphs using queues to work asynchronously
- Efficiently read the inputs by using readers, coordinators and queue runners

Now we can parallelize some neural networks

How to Parallelize Networks on a Cluster

For the remainder of this chapter, we will look at some of the ways to parallelize multiple neural networks. First, we look at putting one network on one device and then move on to training one network over several devices and servers.

One Network, One Device

The easiest way to train a neural network and run it on a cluster is to use the code you use for one device on one machine and then modify it slightly so that, when the session is created, the Master server address is specified. That is pretty much it. Your code runs on the default device for the server but, if you wanted to change the device that runs the graph, all you do is place the construction phase of your code into a device block.

It becomes easy to train your neural networks and run multiple ones in parallel when you run multiple client sessions in parallel. By that, each session would be run in a different thread or within a different process and then connected to different servers. These sessions would then require a certain amount of configuration so they can use different devices. Running your networks across all available devices and all available machines in the TensorFlow cluster will result in an almost linear speed boost. For example, you could train 100 networks on 50 servers, each one with two GPUs, and it would take just a fraction longer than training one network on one GPU.

This is one of the best solutions to tune hyperparameters; each of the cluster devices trains a model with its own hyperparameters. The more computing power at your disposal, the more hyperparameter space is open to you.

This solution is also ideal to host web services that take huge numbers of QPS (queries per second) and your neural network needs to make a prediction on each of those queries. All you need to do is replicate the network over all the cluster devices and then send the queries over all the devices too. The more servers you have, the more QPS you can handle, but you will not experience any reduction in the time it takes to process one request because the network still needs to make a prediction and you still have to wait for it.

Note

There is one more option and that is to use TensorFlow Serving to serve the networks. TensorFlow Serving is open-source, released in 2016 by Google and it was designed as a way to serve machine learning models with vast numbers of queries, especially those built using TensorFlow. TensorFlow Serving can handle versioning too so if you have a newer version of your model it can be deployed and TensorFlow Serving will manage it. You can also play with different algorithms without any interruption to the service and finally, more servers can easily be added because it can take a heavier load.

Replication – In-Graph vs. Between-Graph

There is also a way of parallelizing the training of a network ensemble – each neural network needs to be put on a different device. But, when you want the ensemble to run, the predictions that each network makes need to be aggregated to produce the overall prediction from the ensemble and doing this takes a little coordinating.

There are two main ways to handle these ensembles or another type of graph that has large numbers of computations.

You could create a large graph that has every one of the neural networks in it. Each network would be pinned to its own device and you would have all the computations you needed for the individual network predictions to be aggregated. All you would do then is create a single session to a specified server on the cluster and leave it to do everything. It will even wait until all the predictions have been made before it aggregates them. This type of replication is called in-graph.

The other way is to create a graph for each network and then manually handle the synchronization between them. This is between-graph replication, a little more complex to implement. One of the more popular implementations of between-graph replication is to use queues to coordinate the graphs' executions. You would have a set of clients, each handling one network. These clients read from the input queue and write to the prediction queues dedicated to each network while a separate client will read all the inputs, pushing them to the input queues while copying each input to each queue. Lastly, there is one more client that reads a prediction from each of the prediction queues and aggregates them so you get the prediction for the network ensemble.

Each solution has its own pros and cons. The first solution, in-graph replication, is much easier to implement because you don't need to handle multiple clients and queues. However, it is much easier to organize between-graph replication into modules that are bounded and are easy to test, not to mention the flexibility this solution provides. For example, to stop the ensemble failing should a network client crash or a network take too long to make a prediction, you could place a dequeue timeout into the client that aggregates the predictions. With TensorFlow, when you call run(), you can pass RunOptions with timeout_in_ms to set a specific timeout:

```
with tf.Session([...]) as sess:

[...]

run_options = tf.RunOptions()

run_options.timeout_in_ms = 1000 # 1s timeout

try:

pred = sess.run(dequeue_prediction, options=run_options)

except tf.errors.DeadlineExceededError as ex:

 [...] # the dequeue operation timed out after 1s
```

You can also set a session configuration option of operation_timeout_in_ms but, this time, should any of the operations continue for longer than the given delay, the run() function will time out:

```
config = tf.ConfigProto()

config.operation_timeout_in_ms = 1000 # 1s timeout for every
operation

with tf.Session([...], config=config) as sess:

[...]

try:

pred = sess.run(dequeue_prediction)

except tf.errors.DeadlineExceededError as ex:

[...] # the dequeue operation timed out after 1s
```

Parallelizing Your Model

Until now, each network has been run on a single device but what if we wanted a single network to run across multiple devices? To do this, you would need to break your model down into several pieces and each piece would be run on a different device. This is how to parallelize a model, in machine learning terms it is usually known as model parallelism. If you are working with fully connected networks, it is best to avoid this method as you won't get a great deal out of it.

At first glance, it might seem that the easiest way to break your model down is to split by layers, placing each one on a different device but this doesn't actually work. The reason why is every layer must wait for the output of the last layer before it can act. Another way, perhaps, would be a vertical slice, placing the left side of each layer onto one device and the right side onto another. This would be a little better because it would be possible for each half to work parallel to one another. However, there is still a problem – each half needs the output from both halves so there is quite a lot of communication across devices – you would see this on the graph as a series of dashed arrows. This would more than likely mitigate any of the benefits you might have received from the parallel computation – cross-device communication is notoriously slow, particularly when separate machines are involved.

You will see in the next chapter that there are some network architectures, like the convolutional networks, whose layers are connected to the lower layers only partially. That means the efficient distribution of pieces across multiple devices is much easier. And, in a future chapter, we also discuss the recurrent neural networks – these have multiple layers consisting of memory cells. If you were to do a horizontal split on a network like that, putting each of the layers onto a separate device, only one of those devices is active at the first step; on step two, two will be active, and so on. By the time the signal has been propagated to the output layer, all of the devices are active at the same time. There is still much cross-device communication but, because the cells are complex, this cross-device communication penalty is often wiped out or reduced by the benefits of running multiple complex cells in parallel.

Simply put, parallelizing your model can significantly speed up the running and/or training of some network types but not all of them. You need to pay special attention and make sure your tuning is correct, such as ensuring that the devices that communicate the most with one another are all run on one machine.

Parallelizing Your Data

Otherwise known as data parallelism, this is another way of training your neural network. All you do is replicate the neural network onto each device; a training step is then run on all of the replicas at the same time. A different mini-batch is used for each replica and the gradients from each one are aggregated and the model parameters are updated. There are two ways that this can be done – through synchronous or asynchronous updates.

Synchronous Updates

When you use synchronous updates, the aggregator will not do a computation of the average until all the gradients have been made available. Then it aggregates the gradients and updates the parameters of the model, thus applying the computation result.

When the replica has completed the gradient computation, it cannot move on until the parameters have all been updated. When they have, it can go to the next mini-batch. The problem with using this method is that not all devices are the same speed. That means the faster devices have to wait for the slower ones at each of the training steps. Not only that, the parameters are copied to each device almost simultaneously, as soon as the gradients have been applied and this could result in saturation of the server bandwidth.

You can reduce the waiting time by ignoring those gradients that come from the bottom end group of replicas (the slowest few), usually around 10%. Let's say that you run 20 replicas but opt to aggregate only the gradients that are in the top 18 (the fastest), ignoring the slowest two. Once the parameters have been updated, those 18 can begin work on the next mini-batch immediately; they will not need to wait for the last two. You will often see this described as a setup with 18 replicas and two spares.

Asynchronous Updates

When you use asynchronous updates when a replica completes computation of the gradients, the model parameters can immediately be updated. There is no need for aggregation of all the gradients and there is no need for synchronization. The replicas will work independently of one another and, because there is no waiting for all replicas to finish each step, more steps can be run every minute. Not only that, even though there is still a need to copy the parameters at each step to every device, this doesn't need to happen at the same time; each replica can do this at different times and that means we reduce the risk of saturation.

Using asynchronous updates with data parallelism is one of the better choices – it is simple, there are no delays while we wait for synchronization and the bandwidth is used far more efficiently. However, even though it has been shown to work in practice, it is somewhat surprising that it actually does work. Why?

Because, by the time a replica has finished the gradient computation based on the parameter values there at the time, those parameters will have undergone several more updates from some of the other replicas and we have absolutely no guarantee that the gradients computed by the first replica will still be pointing the right way. Gradients that are out of date are called stale gradients and they have several downsides – convergence is much slower, noise can be introduced, along with wobble effects, and the training algorithm may even diverge.

We can reduce these effects a little by:

- lowering the learning rate
- dropping the stale gradients or scaling them down
- changing the size of the mini-batch

Using a single replica, get the first few epochs off and running – this is the warm-up phase. Stale gradients cause more damage at the beginning of the training when the gradients are much larger. At this point, the parameters haven't yet settled into the cost function valley (remember the elongated bowl) so different replicas could push those parameters in different directions.

The Google Brain Team published a paper in 2016 in which several approaches were benchmarked. The data parallelism using synchronous updates with spare replicas was deemed the most efficient of the approaches, as well as the fastest to converge and results in a much better model. However, research is still ongoing in this area so hold fire and don't discard asynchronous updates out of hand just yet.

Bandwidth Saturation

It matters not whether you choose synchronous updates or asynchronous updates with data parallelism. The model parameters still need to be communicated from the servers to each replica when each training step begins and the gradients in the opposite direction when each step ends. What this means is, somewhere along the line there will be no performance gains to be had by adding another GPU because of the time it takes to move the data to and from the RAM of the new GPU and maybe across the network too will more than take care of any speed boost you may have gained by breaking the load down. All you achieve by adding more GPUs is slowing the training and increasing the saturation.

Tip

If you have quite small models that have trained using a large training set, it is usually better to train those models using one machine and one GPU. Denser models or the larger ones tend to increase the risk of saturation quite severely because they have many more gradients and parameters that need transferring. Saturation isn't so severe for the smaller models but you also don't gain much in terms of parallelization either. Saturation is not so severe for the larger sparse models because the gradients are usually zero, thus communication is more efficient.

If you go beyond a couple of dozen GPUs on denser models or a couple of hundred for sparse models then saturation will kick in and you will notice a degradation in performance. There is plenty of active research on this right now to try to find a way around this problem so there is likely to be some progress down the line. For now, the teams are studying several areas including:

- Lossy model compression
- P2P architecture instead of centralized parameter servers
- Better optimization of what the replicas require to communicate and when
- Plus more areas

While we wait, there are some steps you can take to lessen the saturation issues:

- Use fewer servers to group the GPUs on rather than spreading them too thin; this stops network hopping about when it doesn't really need to.
- Shard your parameters so they go over several parameter servers.
- Drop the float precision for the model parameter to 16 bits (tf.float16) for 32 bits (tf.float32). This will halve how much data needs transferring without having a negative effect on performance or convergence rate.

While 16-bit precision is the preferred minimum as far as 8-bit once training is complete so that the model size is reduced and the computations are faster. We call this quantizing and it is very useful when you need to deploy a pre-trained model and run it on a mobile device.

Implementing Data Parallelization with TensorFlow

Using TensorFlow to implement data parallelism requires that you first decide whether you are using in-graph or between-graph replication. Then you need to decide between synchronous or asynchronous updates. Without using any code, I'll explain how each combination would be implemented:

In-graph Replication and Synchronous Updates

One large graph is built with every model replica, each on a different device, along with some nodes for aggregating the gradients and then feed them to an optimizer. The code will open the session to the cluster and repeatedly run the operation.

In-graph Replication and Asynchronous Updates

One large graph is created with one optimizer for each replica and one thread for each replica is run; the optimizer for the replica is run repeatedly.

Between-graph Replication and Asynchronous Updates

Several independent clients are run usually with a separate process for each. Each client will train the model replica as if it were the only one but the parameters are shared with all the other replicas through a resource container.

Between-graph Replication and Synchronous Updates

Again, you have several clients and each one will train a replica using shared parameters. This time though, the optimizer is wrapped inside a SyncReplicasOptimizer. All replicas will use this in the same way they would use any optimizer but this one is sending the gradients to queues, one for each variable. This is read by the optimizer of one replica, known as the chief; this then aggregates the individual gradients, applies them, and then writes a token, which goes to each replica's token queue. This is to tell the replica that it can continue on to the next gradients. With this approach, you can have spare replicas.

Once you are familiar with the contents of this chapter and have practiced, you will be able to use it to train deep neural networks across multiple GPUs and servers. To aid you, in the next couple of chapters we are going to be looking at a couple of the most important architectures before we look at Reinforcement Learning.

Chapter 12: Working with Convolutional Neural Networks

In 1996, world Chess champion Gary Kasparov was beaten by Deep Blue, a supercomputer designed and built by IBM. However, quite apart from that, until now computers have not been able to perform seemingly simple tasks reliably. So what makes tasks like recognizing spoken words or picking out kittens in pictures seem so easy to humans and not to computers? It comes down to perception and consciousness. Perception is mostly outside the realms of human consciousness but within specialized sensory modules in our brains. By the time information reaches human consciousness, it already has a number of high-level features attached to it.

For example, if you were to look at an image of fluffy kittens, there is no way that you can't NOT see those kittens – you don't have that choice. You can't NOT notice that the kittens are fluffy and cute and you do not know how you recognize cute kittens; you just do. Because of this, we cannot place trust in subjective experiences; perception is quite complex and to understand it we need to understand how the sensory modules in the brain work.

Since the 1980's, CNNs (Convolutional Neural Networks) have used image recognition after emerging from in-depth studies on the visual cortex of the human brain. In the last decade CNNs have achieved performance on some visual tasks, very complex ones that can only be described as superhuman. This was thanks mainly to a significant jump in computational power, and partly to how much training data is available and the tricks we discussed earlier to train the deep neural nets.

CNNs are used to power self-driving cars, services for image searches, video classification systems, and a whole lot more. Not only that, CNNs are not only used for visual tasks; they can do many other things including NLP (natural language processing) and voice recognition. However, for now, we will concentrate our efforts on the visual applications. Throughout this chapter, we will look at the CNNs, where they came from, their building blocks, and how to use TensorFlow to implement them. Lastly, we will take a quick look at some of the best CNNs.

The Visual Cortex Architecture

Between 1958 and 1959, Torsten Wiesel and David Hubel conducted several experiments using cats staring at screens with black dots, repeating them a few years later on monkeys. These experiments provided critical insights into how the visual cortex was constructed, leading to both being awarded the Nobel Prize for Physiology or Medicine in 1981. One of the things their experiments showed was that the local receptive field in many visual cortex neurons is quite small; this means that reactions to visual stimuli only occur in a small part of the visual field.

It is possible to overlap the receptive fields of each neuron and this results in the entire visual field being tiled with these fields. The authors also demonstrated that some of the neurons will only react to images that show horizontal lines, while others will react only to images of differently orientated lines. It is possible for a pair of neurons to have the exact same receptive field but to react to different orientations. It was also noted that some of the neurons have quite large receptive fields and that they were more reactive to complex patterns that were made up of several of the smaller patterns. This led Wiesel and Hubel to deduce that the high-level large neurons rely on the outputs from their smaller neighbors. This is a pretty powerful architecture that allows all kinds of patterns, complex or otherwise to be detected across the entire visual field.

These studies were the inspiration behind the neocognitron, first introduced in 1980 and it was this that evolved, over the years, into what is now called the convolutional neural network. In 1998 a paper was published by Patrick Haffner, Yann LeCun, Yoshua Bengio and Leon Bottu introducing the LeNet-5 architecture, famous for being used to recognize check numbers in handwriting. There are a few building blocks in this architecture that we are already familiar with – sigmoid activation functions and fully connected layers, for starters. It also gives us two more blocks – the convolutional layers and the pooling layers, which we will look at next.

Note

Before we go any further, why could we not use a normal deep neural network containing fully connected layers for any tasks involving image recognition? DNNs only works well on small images, like those in the MNIST dataset. If you feed it larger images, the DNN will break down because there are too many parameters required. An example would be an image of 100 x 100 made up of 10,000 pixels; if the initial layer has 1000 neurons, this would result in 10 million connections being needed – and 1000 neurons are very restrictive in what information gets transmitted to the next layer. Instead, the CNN corrects this problem with partially connected layers.

Convolutional Layers

The convolutional layer is the single most important layer in any convolutional neural network. The first convolutional layer contains neurons that are only connected to the image pixels that are in their own receptive field. Remember, in previous chapters the neurons were connected to every pixel in the input images.

In the second convolutional layer, each of the neurons is connected to the neurons that are inside a small rectangle of the first layer. This kind of architecture leaves the network to focus on the low-level features in hidden layer one, add them to the high-level features on hidden layer two, and so on through the layers. This structure is hierarchical and is very common in real-world images which is why CNNs work for image recognition tasks.

Note

Up to this point, we only looked at multi-layer neural networks with layers made up of lengthy neuron lines; each input image had to be flattened to 1D before it was given to the network. Now, each of the layers is 2D and this makes it so much easier to match the neurons and their inputs.

Let's say we have a layer and a neuron at the location row i, column j connects to the neuron outputs from the layer before, in rows i to i + fh and columns j to j + fw. fh is the height of the receptive field while fw is the width. For a layer to have identical height and width to that of the previous layer, the inputs can be zero padded.

We can also connect large input layers to small layers and this is done by spreading the receptive fields out. The space between each consecutive field is known as the stride. If you wanted to connect an input layer of 5 x 7 with zero padding to a layer of 3 x 4, you could use 3 x 3 receptive fields and add a stride of 2. The stride can be the same in both directions or it can be different. So a neuron in the upper layer at row i and column j, connects to the neuron outputs at rows i x sh to i x sh + fh and columns j x sw x fw. sh is the vertical stride and sw is the horizontal stride, fh and fw remain as the height and width of the receptive fields.

Filters

We can use small images to represent the weights of the neuron, the image no bigger than the neuron's receptive field. Let's say that we have two weights – these are called filters or convolution kernels. The first weight is a matrix of 7 x 7 padded with zeros and a central column of 1's. A neuron using this weight would only take note of the central column, ignoring everything else in their receptive field. This is because all the inputs are multiplied by zero except for the central column inputs. The second weight, or filter, is the same but it has a central row of 1's; again the neuron will ignore all but that central row.

Now, let's assume that all the neurons in one layer make use of the same bias term and the same vertical row filter. As you feed the input to the network, the output will show the vertical line more enhanced while the rest is blurred. If the neurons used the horizontal column filter and the same bias terms, the horizontal line is enhanced and the rest gets blurred. So, if you had a neuron layer with each neuron using the same filter, you get a feature map and this will show you all the parts of the image that are the nearest to the filter. When you train a CNN, the network will find the filter that is the most useful for the task it is performing and it will then learn to combine those filters into patterns that are computationally more complex.

Stacking Several Feature Maps

Up to this point, each convolutional layer has been shown as a thin, two-dimensional layer – we have done this for the sake of simplicity. However, the reality is that each layer is actually made up of multiple feature maps each of equal size, so a more accurate representation would be 3D. In one map, all the neurons have the same parameters, both bias term and weights, but when you have several maps each may have different parameters. The receptive field of the neuron remains as it was earlier but it is extended over the feature maps of all previous layers. Put simply, a convolutional layer will give its inputs several filters at the same time and this makes the layer fully able to detect several features anywhere within the inputs.

Note

Because all of the neurons in one feature map make use of all the same parameters, there are significantly fewer parameters in the model. What it also means, more importantly, is that when the CNN learns a pattern in one area, it will recognize it anywhere else. By contrast, the DNN will only recognize a pattern in the location it learned it, and nowhere else. Not only that, the input images are made up of several sublayers, one for each color channel. Typically, these are red, green and blue – RGB. Conversely, a grayscale image has a single channel but other images may have many more channels, such as satellite images that can capture additional light frequencies, like infrared.

A neuron in feature map k, in row i column j, in a specified convolutional layer called l, will connect to the neuron outputs of the last layer, l – 1, in rows i x sw to i x sw + fw, columns j x sh to j x sh + fh across every feature map in that layer. All of the neurons in row i, column j in all the different feature maps will connect to the outputs from the same neurons from the last layer.

The equation below summarizes these explanations, showing how the output of a specified neuron in one convolutional layer is computed. It isn't a very pretty equation because there are a lot of indices but all it is doing is calculating the weighted sum from all the inputs and the bias term:

$$z_{i,j,k} = b_k + \sum_{u=1}^{f_h} \sum_{v=1}^{f_w} \sum_{k'=1}^{f_{n'}} x_{i',j',k'} \cdot w_{u,v,k',k} \quad \text{with} \begin{cases} i' = u.s_h + f_h - 1 \\ j' = v.s_w + f_w - 1 \end{cases}$$

Equation – Computation of the Neuron Output in a Convolutional Layer

To break this down:

- $z_{i,j,k}$ – the output of a neuron in row i, column j, in the layer l convolutional layer of feature map k
- sh and sw are the strides (horizontally and vertically), while fh and fw are the receptive field's height and width. $f_{n'}$ represents how many feature maps are in layer l – 1, which is the layer that came before
- $x_{i',j',k'}$ represents the output of a neuron in layer l – 1, in row i, column j of a feature map called k – note, if the last layer was an input layer, this will be channel k
- b_k represents the bias term for the feature map called k, in layer l. Think of this as a dial, used to change the brightness level of the feature map
- $w_{u,v,k',k}$ represents the connection weight between any of the neurons in the feature map in layer l; the input is in row u, column v, feature map k.

TensorFlow Implementation

Each input image is represented in TensorFlow by a 3D shape tensor, consisting of height, width and channels. Mini-batches are a 4D tensor shape of size, height, width and channels. On a convolutional layer, the weights are represented as 4D tensor shapes, of fh, fw, fn and fn'. The convolutional layer bias terms are represented quite simply as a 1D tensor shape, f.

Here's an example. The next code snippet will load two images using load_sample_image() from scikit-learn. This will load a pair of color images, one is a flower and the other is a Chinese temple. Next, two filters are created, both 7 x 7 – one has a central vertical line while the other has a central horizontal line. These filters are then applied to both of the images. To do this, the conv2d() function from TensorFlow is used to build a convolutional layer – a stride of 2 and zero padding are used. Lastly, a feature map is plotted as a result:

```
import numpy as np

from sklearn.datasets import load_sample_images

# Load sample images

dataset = np.array(load_sample_images().images, dtype=np.float32)

batch_size, height, width, channels = dataset.shape

# Create 2 filters

filters_test = np.zeros(shape=(7, 7, channels, 2), dtype=np.float32)

filters_test[:, 3, :, 0] = 1 # vertical line

filters_test[3, :, :, 1] = 1 # horizontal line

# Create a graph with input X plus a convolutional layer applying the
2 filters

X = tf.placeholder(tf.float32, shape=(None, height, width, channels))

convolution = tf.nn.conv2d(X, filters, strides=[1,2,2,1],
padding="SAME")

with tf.Session() as sess:

output = sess.run(convolution, feed_dict={X: dataset})

plt.imshow(output[0, :, :, 1]) # plot 1st image's 2nd feature map

plt.show()
```

Most of this should be self-explanatory by now but there is one line that needs further explanation – the conv2d() line:

- X represents the input mini-batch and, as demonstrated earlier, it is a 4D tensor
- filters represent the filter set being applied, also a 4D tensor
- strides is a 1D array with four elements. The vertical stride (sh) and the horizontal stride (sw) are the central elements and elements one and four must be currently equal to 1. At some point they may be used to specify a batch stride, enabling some instances to be skipped over, and a channel stride, to skip some channels or maps from the feature maps on the previous layer.
- padding must be set to VALID or to SAME.

If padding is set to VALID, no zero padding is used by the convolutional layer and some of the rows and columns to the right and the bottom of the input image may be ignored. This will depend on what the stride is.

If padding is set to SAME, zero padding is used where needed. If this is the case, the number of output neurons will equal the input neurons divided by stride and rounded up, i.e. ceil (13/5) = 3. The zeros are then placed around the inputs relatively evenly.

The downside to convolutional layers is that they have many hyperparameters; it is down to you to decide how many filters you need, what their width and height are, what strides to use, and the type of padding. You could find the right hyperparameters using cross-validation but this takes a lot of time. Later, we'll see some of the best hyperparameter values that are in practice when we look at CNN architectures.

Memory Requirements

Convolutional neural networks have another downside to them – the vast amount of RAM needed by the convolutional layers. This is more so during the training phase and the reason for this is that all the intermediate values have to be computed in the forward pass of backpropagation; reverse pass won't work otherwise.

Let's look at an example. You have a convolutional layer; the filters are 5 x 5 and the output is 200 feature maps, each 150 x 100 in size, with a stride of 1 and padding set to SAME. If the input is an RG image of 150 x 100 RGB = three channels), then we have a parameter number of (5 x 5 x 3 + 1) x 200 = 15,200 - +1 is for the bias terms. This number, 15,200 is actually quite a small one if you compare it to a layer that is fully connected. However, each one of the feature maps, 200 in total, has 150 x 100 neurons; each of those neurons must take the 5 x 5 x 3 = 75 inputs and compute the weighted sum; this equals 225 million float multiplications. Again, not so much as the fully connected layer but, in terms of computations, it is still intensive. And, if 32-bits are used to represent each feature map, the output from the convolutional layer will take up 200 x 150 x 100 x 32 = 96 million bits of RAM (around 11.4 MB). That doesn't sound vast but that is just for a single instance. If you had a training batch of 100 instances then this layer alone will account for more than 1 GB of RAM.

When a prediction is being made for a new instance, known as inference, the RAM that one layer takes up may be released on the computation of the next layer. In real terms, you need only as much RAM as two consecutive layers require. However, for training, everything that is computed in the forward pass has got to be kept for the reverse pass so you would need an absolute minimum of the total RAM needed by all of the layers; i.e. if you have 10 layers, each using 1 GB RAM, you would need a minimum of 10 GB RAM.

Tip

If an out-of-memory error crashes the training, reduce the size of the mini-batch. You can also use a stride to reduce the dimensionality or you could take a layer or two out. Alternatively, use 16-bit floats and not 32-bit floats. You could even try to distribute the CNN over several devices.

Now we'll move on to the pooling layer, the second of the CNN building blocks.

The Pooling Layer

When you have grasped the way that convolutional layers work, pooling layers are really quite simple. The goal of a pooling layer is to shrink or subsample the input image so that the computational load is reduced, along with the memory usage and how many parameters there are. Together these cut the risks of the model overfitting the data. By making the image size smaller, the neural network has a little more tolerance for location invariance or image shifting.

As we found with the convolutional layers, every neuron in a pooling layer connects to the outputs of some of the neurons from the previous layer and, again, these neurons are in a small receptive field, rectangular in shape. You are responsible to define the size, the type of padding, and the stride, just as before, but the pooling layer does not have any weights. All this layer does is use an aggregate function, such as mean or max to aggregate all the inputs.

The most common pooling layer is the max pooling layer. Let's assume that we have a pooling kernel of 2 x 2, a stride of 2 and we have no padding. The only value to go to the next layer is the max input; everything else is dropped. This kind of pooling layer is incredibly destructive; even though it is very small and has a small stride, the output is twice as small in both directions and that means it has an area that is four times smaller and 75% of the input values are dropped.

Pooling layers tend to work independently on each input channel so the input and output depths will be the same. Alternatively, you can pool over the dimension of the depth which results in the height and width (spatial) dimensions of the image remain as they are but there will be fewer channels.

It is quite a simple matter to use TensorFlow to implement a max pooling layer. This code snippet will use a 2 x 2 kernel to create a max pooling layer, with a stride of 2, and with no padding. The kernel is then applied to every image in the dataset:

```
[...] # load the image dataset, just like above

# Create a graph with input X plus a max pooling layer

X = tf.placeholder(tf.float32, shape=(None, height, width, channels))

max_pool = tf.nn.max_pool(X, ksize=[1,2,2,1],
strides=[1,2,2,1],padding="VALID")

with tf.Session() as sess:

output = sess.run(max_pool, feed_dict={X: dataset})

plt.imshow(output[0].astype(np.uint8)) # plot the output for the 1st
image

plt.show()
```

In the ksize argument, we find the kernel shape on all four of the input tensor's dimension – the size of the batch, the height, the width, and the channels. Right now, there is no support in TensorFlow to pool over several instances so element one of ksize has got to be equal to 1. On top of that, there is no support for pooling over the spatial and the depth dimensions so ksize[1] and ksize[2] must be equal to 1 OR ksize[3] must be equal to 1.

If you wanted an average pooling layer instead, you would replace max_pool() with avg_pool().

There you have it, everything needed for a convolutional neural work to be created. Now we look at some of the different CNN architectures to see how they work.

Common CNN Architectures

A typical architecture for a convolutional neural network will stack some convolutional layers, each having a ReLU layer after it, followed by a pooling layer. This is then repeated through the model and, as it moves through the network, the image will shrink in size but it will also get deeper, which means it will have more feature maps. This is down to the convolutional layers. At the top we add a regular neural network of feedforward type made up of several fully connected layers interspersed with the ReLUs; the prediction is output by the last layer, for example, a softmax layer from which the output is estimated class probabilities.

Tip

One of the most common mistakes made is to use over-sized output kernels. For a less computationally heavy load, you could stack kernels, each 3 x 3, on top of one another rather than one single 9 x 9 kernel.

Some significant advances have been made in this field over the years as different variations of the basic architecture have been developed. One of the best progress measures is the error rate shown in competitions, such as the ILSVRC ImageNet challenge, where the top-5 image classification error rate fell in five years, from 26% to 3%. This error rate is the number of the test images where the correct number was not included in the top 5 predictions of the system. The images are 256 pixels, which are large and there are 1,000 classes, some subtle.

One of the best ways to understand how a convolutional neural network works is to look at how the winning entries have evolved so we'll start with the LeNet-5 architecture from 1998 and then look at three of the ILSVRC challenge winners – AlexNet in 2012, GoogLeNet in 2014 and ResNet in 2015.

LeNet-5

This is one of the more common CNN architectures, created in 1998 by Yann LeCun. It is mostly used to recognize handwritten digits and is composed of fully connected, convolution, avg pooling, and an input layer. The output layer has an RBF activation function and all the others, with the exception of the output layer, have tanh activation functions – the output layer has none. There are a few other things to note as well:

The images in the MNIST dataset are 28 x 28 but zero padding takes them to 32 x 32 pixels. They are normalized before they are given to the network. No padding is used for the rest of the network and this is why the size keeps reducing as the image moves through the network.

The avg pooling layers are a bit more complex than they usually are – each of the neurons will compute the mean of its own outputs; this is then multiplied by a learnable coefficient, of which there is one for each map. A learnable bias term is added, again, there is one for each map. Lastly, the activation function is applied.

Most of the neurons in a C3 map connect to the neurons in just three or four of the S2 maps, rather than all six of them.

The output layer is somewhat special. Rather than computing the input and weight vector dot product, each of the neurons will compute the Euclidean distance between its own input and weight vectors and output the square. The amount of the image that belongs to a specific digit class is measured by each output. The cross entropy function is the preferred function because it will penalize the bad predictions, produce gradients that are larger and converge much faster.

AlexNet

The winner of the ImageNet ILSVRC Challenge in 2012 was AlexNet and it won by a very large margin. It's top -5 error rate was 17% - its nearest competitor achieved only 26%. AlexNet CNN architecture was developed by Alex Krizhevsky, Geoffrey Hinton, and Ilya Sutskever. It is a lot like LeNet-5 but significantly bigger and deeper; it was also the first CNN architecture to stack the convolutional layers on top of one another rather than having a pooling layer atop each convolutional layer.

To cut the risk of overfitting, two regularization techniques were used; dropout was the first to be applied, with a dropout rate of 50%. This was applied to the outputs of the F8 and F9 layers during training. Second, data augmentation was performed by shifting the images randomly by different offsets, horizontally flipping them and tweaking the lighting conditions.

AlexNet also makes use of a normalization step immediately following the ReLU step in layers C1 and C3. This is called Local Response Normalization (seen in the equation below) and it makes the neurons that have the strongest activation on the inhibit neurons that are located in the same place but on different feature maps. This is done to encourage specialization of the different feature maps; they are pushed apart and forced to explore more feature ranges, with an ultimate improvement in generalization.

$$b_i = a_i \left(k + \alpha \sum_{j=j_{low}}^{j_{high}} a_j^2 \right)^{-\beta} \quad \text{with} \quad \begin{cases} j_{high} = \min \left(i + \frac{r}{2}, f_n - 1 \right) \\ j_{low} = \max \left(0, i - \frac{r}{2} \right) \end{cases}$$

Equation - Local Response Normalization

Breaking this equation down:

- b_i – the normalized output from the neuron in i (feature map) as row u, column v. Do note – only the neurons at this row and column are considered in the equation so u and v do not get shown
- a_i – activation of the neuron following ReLU, before normalization
- k, α, β, and r – hyperparameters – k_i is bias, r is depth radius
- f_n – indicates how many feature maps there are

Let's say that r = 2; if a neuron has got a strong activation, the activation of those neurons on the feature maps immediately below and above the neuron's feature map will be inhibited.

The hyperparameters are set in AlexNet as:

```
r = 2, α = 0.00002
```

```
β = 0.75, and k = 1
```

The TensorFlow operation, local_response_normalization() may be used to implement this step.

ZF Net is a variation of AlexNet that won the ILSVRC challenge in 2013. Developed by Rob Fergus and Matthew Zeiler, it is very like AlexNet but some of the parameters have been tweaked.

GoogLeNet

Christian Szegedy et al are responsible for GoogLeNet. They work for Google Research and their CNN architecture won the ILSVRC in 2014 with a top-5 error rate under 7%. Much of this fantastic performance came from the neural network being significantly deeper than its predecessors and this could happen because GoogLeNet uses inception modules. These give GoogLeNet the ability to make more efficient use of the parameters than many of the previous CNNs. It has about 6 million parameters, around ten times fewer than AlexNet's 60 million.

Let's look at how an inception module might be built. We could have a 3 x 3 kernel with a stride of 2 and padding set to SAME. The notation for this would be 3 x 3 + 2(S). The input signal is copied first and then given to four separate layers. The activation function for each convolutional layer is ReLU.

The second lot of convolutional layers have a kernel size of 1 x 1, 3 x 3, and 5 x 5. These different sizes allow for the capture of patterns that are at different scales. Each layer has a stride of 1 and padding set to SAME, and that includes the layer for max pooling. This means that all the outputs have identical widths and heights to their inputs which, in turn, makes it possible for the outputs to be concatenated in the last depth concat layer along the depth dimension. What that means is the feature maps are stacked from all of the top layers. Implementation of the concatenation layer is possible through TensorFlow with the concat() operation with a depth of axis = 3.

Now, why would an inception module have 1 x 1 kernel convolutional layers? Surely they can't capture features – they look at the pixels individually, not as a whole. Well, these layers do more than one thing.

First and foremost, the configuration of these layers is designed to output considerably fewer feature maps than their inputs. This means they are bottleneck layers and help reduce dimensionality. This comes in hand before the 3 x 3 convolution and the 5 x 5 convolutions because these two layers are very expensive in computation terms.

Secondly, each of the convolutional layer pairs – 1 x 3, 3 x 3 and 1 x 5, 5 x 5 – act as one very powerful layer that can capture patterns that are so much more complex. Rather than one linear classification being swept across the image, in the way a single layer does, this combination of two layers will sweep a dual-layer neural network instead.

Put simply, the inception module is a hyped-up convolutional layer that can output feature maps with the capability to capture far more complex patterns that are at different scales.

> **Warning**
>
> For each inception layer that gets added, you are adding six more hyperparameters because the number of the kernels for each layer is classed as a hyperparameter.

Now we'll look at an example of the GoogLeNet architecture. It is incredibly deep, a very tall stack that has nine inception modules, each one containing three layers. Before the kernel size, you will see the number of feature maps that each convolutional layer and each pooling layer outputs. The six numbers for the inception modules is representative of how many feature maps are output by each of the convolutional layers, all of which use the ReLU activation function.

Let's break the network down:

Layers one and two are used to divide the height and width of the image by 4, meaning the area is divided by 16. This cuts down on computational load.

Next, the Local Response Normalization layer makes sure that a variety of features are learned by the previous layers.

This is followed by two more convolutional layers – the first is the bottleneck layer. As we said earlier, this pair could be thought of as one powerful layer.

Another Local Response Normalization layer does the same -makes sure the features variety is learned by the last layers.

Now we have a max pooling layer that will reduce the weight and the height of the image by 2, again making computation faster.

Next, that tall stack of inception modules, nine in total, with a couple of max pooling layers weaved in to speed the net up and reduce the dimensionality.

Next, we have an average pooling layer with a kernel that is the same size as the feature maps with a padding of VALID. This will output feature maps of 1 x 1. This is known as global average pooling and, in effect, it forces feature maps out of the previous layers. These maps are confidence maps for each of the target classes – if an averaging step were used, other feature types would be destroyed. Using this means it isn't necessary to have multiple fully connected layers at the top of the convolutional neural network like there is in AlexNet. This cuts down the number of network parameters and keeps overfitting risks to a minimum.

The final layers are a dropout layer for regularizations followed by a fully connected layer that has an activation function that outputs class probability estimations.

This is a simplified version; a full GoogLeNet architecture would have a pair of auxiliary classifiers connected to the top of the third inception module and the sixth one. Each would have one avg pooling layer, one convolutional, two fully connected and one softmax activation layer.

In training, their loss was aggregated with the overall loss with the goal of attempting to reduce the problem of vanishing gradients and of regularizing the network. However, their effect was too minor to be of any real importance.

ResNet

Finally, we have the 2015 winner of the ILSVRC challenge, ResNet, or Residual Network, developed by Kaiming He et al. ResNet showed a top-5 error rate of lower than 3.6% and this was done with a very deep CNN of 152 layers. The key to training networks of this depth is in the use of skip connections, sometimes known as shortcut connections. The signal that is fed into a layer also gets added to the output from a layer somewhere up the stack. Let's look into why this could be considered useful.

The goal when you train a neural network is to make that network model a function h(x). If input x was added to the network output, i.e. a skip connection is added, the network is then forced into modeling f(x) – h(x) and not just h(x). this is known as residual learning.

When a regular neural network is initialized, its weights are very near zero. As a result, the network output values will also be near zero. Add a skip connection into the mix and the output from the resulting network will be a copy of that networks inputs. In short, it will start by modeling the identity function. If the target function is near to this which is usually the case, training is considerably faster.

If you were to add multiple skip connections, the network would be able to move forward even if some of the layers hadn't begun to learn. With skip connections, the signal can work its way across the entire network very easily. You can think of the deep residual network as being a stack of residual units; each unit is an individual small network with its own skip connection.

Here's an example of the ResNet architecture. It is actually quite a simple one, beginning like GoogLeNet and ending like it too. What it doesn't have is the dropout layer. In between, it is a stack of residual units that go to a great depth, each unit made up of two convolutional layers with BN (Batch Normalization) and the ReLU activation. It uses 3 x 3 kernels and spatial dimensions are preserved at a stride of 1 and padding set to SAME.

With a ResNet architecture, every few residual units the feature map numbers are doubled while their width and height are cut in half – this is done with a convolutional layer that has a stride of 2. When this happens, the residual unit inputs can't be directly added to the outputs because their shapes are different. To solve this, the inputs get put through a convolutional layer of 1 x 1, with a stride of 2 and the correct amount of feature maps.

ResNet-34 is a variant of ResNet with just 34 layers – the only layers counted are the convolutional and the fully connected layers. Each layer has three residual units with an output of 64 feature maps, four residual units with an output of 128 maps, six residual units with an output of 256 maps and three residual units with an output of 512 maps.

Any ResNet that goes deeper than that, like the ResNet – 152, will have residual units that are a little different. Rather than a pair of 3 x 3 convolutional layers with, let's say, 256 feature maps, there are three layers – the first is a convolutional layer of 1 x 1 and 64 feature maps; this will be the bottleneck layer. Second is a 3 x 3 layer that has 64 feature maps and third, a 1 x 1 convolutional layer with 256 feature maps restoring the depth to its original. In ResNet-152, there are three residual units that have an output of 256 maps, eight residual units with 512 maps, 36 residual units with 1,025 maps and three residual units with 2,048 maps.

It should be clear to you now that the field of CNNs is a fast moving one. New architectures are being developed every year, each trying to improve on its predecessor. A trend is becoming clear – CNNs continue to get deeper and deeper, as well as getting considerably lighter, and there are fewer parameters required. Right now, ResNet is the simplest and the most powerful. While it is the one to use at the moment, there may be better ones coming in the future. In 2016, the ILSVRC winners, the Chinese Trimps-Soushen team achieved a top-5 error rate of less than 3%, achieved by training a combination of the earlier models and bringing them together into an ensemble. However, depending on what the task is, the reduction in error rate may be worth the additional complexity, or it may not.

Other architectures that you may want to look at when you get time are the VGGNet13, 2014 ILSVRC runner-up and Inception-v414, a merger of the ResNet and GoogLeNet ideas that achieve a top-5 error rate of near to 3%.

TensorFlow Convolution Operations

To finish this chapter, we'll look briefly at some of the other convolutional layers offered by TensorFlow:

- **Conv1d()** – to create convolutional layers for one-dimensional inputs. This can be useful when natural language processing tasks are being done because a 1D array of words can be used to represent a sentence, with some of the nearby words covered by the receptive field.
- **Conv3d()** – to create convolution layers for three-dimensional inputs, like a 3D PET scan, for example.
- **Atrous_conv2d()** – to create an atrous convolutional layer. In French, à trous means "with holes". This is the same as using normal convolutional layers with filters dilated through the insertion of holes – columns and rows of zeros. An example would be a 1 x 3 filter that is equal to [[1, 2, 3]] with a dilation rate of 4 – the result would be a dilated filter [[1, 0, 0, 0, 2, 0, 0, 0 3]]. What this does is it provides a larger receptive field to the convolutional layer at no extra cost in terms of computation and with no need for more parameters.
- **Conv2d_transpose()** – to create a transpose convolutional layer, alternatively known as a deconvolutional layer, used for upsampling images. To do this, it will put zeros in between the inputs, much like a normal convolutional layer with a fractional stride. Upsampling can be very useful for segmentation of images. The feature maps in a typical CNN will reduce in size as you go through the network so if you needed an image output that was of equal size to the input you would need to add an upsampling layer.
- **Depthwise_conv2d()** – used to creating depth wise convolutional layers. These apply all the available filters to all of the individual input channels independently. As such, if you have fn' input channels and fn filters, the output would be fn x fn' feature maps.

- **Separable_conv2d()** – to create a separable convolutional layer; this will act in the first instance as a depthwise layer. Then it will apply a convolutional area of 1 x 1 to the feature maps that result. This means that filters can be applied to arbitrary input channel sets.

That completes our look at convolutional neural networks; time to move onto recurrent neural networks.

Chapter 13: Using Recurrent Neural Networks

Imagine that you are playing a ball game; the batter smacks the ball hard. You begin to run trying to guess which way the ball will go. You watch it and change your direction to match it and then you catch it. We predict the future all the time. You might automatically finish your partner's sentence, or you anticipate that coffee will be on the table at breakfast. If you think about everything you do in the course of one day, you might find that you predict the future more often than you realize.

In this chapter, we look at recurrent neural networks otherwise called RNNs. These are a class of neural nets that have the ability to predict the future up to a certain point. They can take time series data, such as stock prices, and analyze it, indicate when it is the best time to buy and to sell. Self-drive cars, or autonomous systems, are able to anticipate the trajectory of the vehicle and avoid collisions.

In more general terms, they work on sequences that are of arbitrary lengths and not on inputs of fixed size like the neural nets we have seen so far do. For example, as an input they can take documents, sentences, and samples of audio and turn them into something useful for NLP systems (natural language processing), like speech-to-text systems, automatic translation, or sentiment analysis, i.e. reading a movie or a book review and determining how the rater felt about the book or movie.

Because the RNNs have such an ability to anticipate a situation, they are highly capable of being incredibly creative. You could ask an RNN to predict the most likely note to come next in a tune and then pick a note at random and play it. Then you would ask the RNN what the next likely note is, play it and then repeat, over and over again. In a very short time, your RNN will have composed a melody. In a similar way, they can generate captions for images, complete sentences, and much, much more. While the results are still quite basic, in years to come there is no way of knowing what they could be capable of doing.

We are going to be looking at the basic concepts that underlie the recurrent neural networks, the biggest problem faced by them – the vanishing and exploding gradients – and two of the most common solutions to fight those problems – LSTM and GRU cells. We will also look at using TensorFlow to implement an RNN and how a machine translation system is composed.

Recurrent Neurons

Until now, most of what we have learned has been feedforward types of neural network. In these, the activations only go from the input to the output layers. Recurrent neural networks tend to look very much the same but they also have connections that point in the other direction.

We're going to start by looking at one of the simplest RNNs, made up of a single neuron that receives inputs, which produces an output and then sends it straight back to itself. At each frame or time step t, the recurrent neuron will get the inputs x(t) in addition to the output that comes from itself from the previous frame, y(t-1). This miniature network can be represented against the time axis and is known as Unrolling the Network Through Time.

A recurrent neural layer is quite easy to create. At each of the time steps t, each neuron will get the input vector x(t) and the output vector that both come from the last time step y(t-1). Both inputs and outputs are now vectors – when there is only one neuron, the output will be a scalar.

Each of the recurrent neurons has got two lots of weights – one set for the inputs x(t) and one set for the outputs that came from the last step y(t-1). For the sake of simplicity, we will call these vectors w x and w y. the next equation shows you how the output is computed for one recurrent neuron. Note the b is for the bias term and φ (.) represents the activation function:

$$y_{(t)} = \phi\left(x_{(t)}^T \cdot w_x + y_{(t-1)}^T \cdot w_y + b\right)$$

Equation – Output of One Recurrent Neuron for One Instance

As it is for the feedforward networks, the output for an entire layer can be computed in one hit for a mini-batch. The next equation shows you how we do this taking the previous equation and vectorizing it:

$$Y_{(t)} = \phi\left(X_{(t)} \cdot W_x + Y_{(t-1)} \cdot W_y + b\right)$$

$$= \phi\left(\left[X_{(t)} \quad Y_{(t-1)}\right] \cdot W + b\right) \quad \text{with} \quad W = \begin{bmatrix} W_x \\ W_y \end{bmatrix}$$

Equation – Output of an Entire Layer of Recurrent Neurons for an Entire Mini-batch (All Instances)

Breaking this equation down:

- Y(t) – a matrix of m x n neurons; in this are the outputs for the layer at the time step t for each mini-batch instance – m represents how many instances there are and n neurons represent how many neurons there are.
- X(t) – a matrix of m x n inputs; in this are the inputs for all of the instances – n inputs represents how many input features there are.
- W x – a matrix of n inputs x n neurons; in this are all the connection weights for all the inputs at the current time step.
- W y – a matrix of n neurons x n neurons; in this are the connection weights for all outputs from the last time step.

- W x and W y – weight matrices; these often get concatenated into one weight matrix, W of shape – n inputs + n neurons.
- b – vector of the size n neurons; in this are the bias terms for each neuron.
- Take note that Y(t) is a function of (t) while Y(t-1) is a function of X(t-1) and so on. This results in Y(t) being a function of every input because time t = 0 (that is to say that X(0), X(1), ..., X(t)). t = 0 is the first time step and that means there aren't any inputs from before so it is assumed that they are all zeros.

Memory Cells

We now know that, at time step t, the recurrent neural output is a function of every output from the previous time steps. In theory, it could be seen as having some type of memory. Any part of the neural network that preserves any kind of state across the time steps is known as a memory cell or just a cell. One recurrent neuron is a basic cell, as is one layer of recurrent neurons. Later we will be looking at some of the more powerful, complex cell types.

Generally, the state of a cell at time step t, which you will see noted as h(t) – h for hidden – is a function of some of the inputs from that time step plus the cell state at the last time step – h(t) = f(h(t-1). The output from time step t, which is noted as y(t), is a function of the last cell state plus the current inputs. With the basic cells we've talked about up to now, the output will be equal to the cell state, but with the more complex cells, this will not always happen.

Input and Output Sequences

A recurrent neural network is able to take an input sequence and produce an output sequence at the same time. For example, RNNs are very useful when you want to predict stock prices and other time series; you give it the prices from the last N number of days and the output must be the prices moved by a day into the future, i.e. from N – 1 day before to one day ahead.

You could provide a sequence of inputs to the network and ignore every output except for the final one. Put simply, this kind of network is called a sequence-to-vector network. Let's say that you provide a sequence of words to your network; this sequence relates to a review on a recent book. The output would be a sentiment score, based on the words, for example from -1[didn't like] to +1 [loved].

Conversely, you could give your network one input at the first time step providing zeros for all subsequent time steps and leave it to output a sequence; this is called a vector-to-sequence network. An example would be an image as the input and an image caption as the output.

Finally, you could have an encode, which is a type of sequence-to-vector output and follow this with a decoder, which is a type of vector-to-sequence output. This is very useful when you want to do translations, say from French to English or vice versa. You give the network a sentence in the first language; the encoder converts into a single vector and the decoder takes the vector, decodes it back to a sentence in the second language. This is a two-step model known as an Encoder-Decoder and it is a much better way of translating that trying to do it as you go using a sequence-to-sequence RNN. Why? Because the final words in that sentence will affect the first words of the new translation so it's best to wait until the entire sentence is there before making the translation.

All this sounds very promising so it's time to get busy with TensorFlow again and do some coding.

Using TensorFlow to Implement Basic RNNs

First, we are going to use TensorFlow to implement a basic RNN model but we are not going to use any of the built-in RNN operations. This will enable you to see what goes on behind the scenes. We are creating a recurrent neural network that has five recurrent neurons on one single layer and we will use the tanh activation function. We are going to take it as read that the RNN will run over just two time steps and at each one, it will take size 3 input vectors. This code will build this and unroll it through two time steps:

```
n_inputs = 3

n_neurons = 5

X0 = tf.placeholder(tf.float32, [None, n_inputs])

X1 = tf.placeholder(tf.float32, [None, n_inputs])

Wx = tf.Variable(tf.random_normal(shape=[n_inputs,
n_neurons],dtype=tf.float32))

Wy =
tf.Variable(tf.random_normal(shape=[n_neurons,n_neurons],dtype=tf.flo
at32))

b = tf.Variable(tf.zeros([1, n_neurons], dtype=tf.float32))

Y0 = tf.tanh(tf.matmul(X0, Wx) + b)

Y1 = tf.tanh(tf.matmul(Y0, Wy) + tf.matmul(X1, Wx) + b)

init = tf.global_variables_initializer()
```

This looks very much like a feedforward neural network with two layers but there are a couple of twists to it:

- First, both layers share bias terms and weights;
- Second, the inputs are fed in at each layer and result in outputs at each layer.

Running this model requires us to feed the inputs in at both of the time steps:

```
import numpy as np

# Mini-batch: instance 0,instance 1,instance 2,instance 3
```

```
X0_batch = np.array([[0, 1, 2], [3, 4, 5], [6, 7, 8], [9, 0, 1]]) # t
= 0

X1_batch = np.array([[9, 8, 7], [0, 0, 0], [6, 5, 4], [3, 2, 1]]) # t
= 1

with tf.Session() as sess:

init.run()

Y0_val, Y1_val = sess.run([Y0, Y1], feed_dict={X0: X0_batch, X1:
X1_batch})
```

In this mini-batch, we have four instances and each one has an input sequence with two inputs exactly. On the last line, Y0_val and Y1_val have the network inputs from both of the time steps for all the instances and neurons in the mini-batch:

```
>>> print(Y0_val) # output at t = 0

[[-0.2964572 0.82874775 -0.34216955 -0.75720584 0.19011548] #
instance 0

[-0.12842922 0.99981797 0.84704727 -0.99570125 0.38665548] # instance
1

[ 0.04731077 0.99999976 0.99330056 -0.999933 0.55339795] # instance 2

[ 0.70323634 0.99309105 0.99909431 -0.85363263 0.7472108 ]] #
instance 3

>>> print(Y1_val) # output at t = 1

[[ 0.51955646 1. 0.99999022 -0.99984968 -0.24616946] # instance 0

[-0.70553327 -0.11918639 0.48885304 0.08917919 -0.26579669] #
instance 1

[-0.32477224 0.99996376 0.99933046 -0.99711186 0.10981458] # instance
2

[-0.43738723 0.91517633 0.97817528 -0.91763324 0.11047263]] #
instance 3
```

That was quite easy but bear in mind we only had two time steps; if you want your RNN to run over 100 steps then you are going to have a pretty large graph.

Next, we'll create this model again but this time, we will use the RNN operations in TensorFlow.

Unrolling Through Time - Static

The function called static_rnn() is used to chain cells so that we have an unrolled RNN network. This next code will create an identical model to the last one:

```
X0 = tf.placeholder(tf.float32, [None, n_inputs])

X1 = tf.placeholder(tf.float32, [None, n_inputs])

basic_cell = tf.contrib.rnn.BasicRNNCell(num_units=n_neurons)

output_seqs, states = tf.contrib.rnn.static_rnn(

basic_cell, [X0, X1], dtype=tf.float32)

Y0, Y1 = output_seqs
```

The first thing we did was create some input placeholders, just like last time. Next, a BasicRNNCell was created – you could think of this as being a kind of factory, one that churns out copies of the cell to build the unrolled RNN – we get a cell copy for each of the time steps.

Next, the static_rnn() function is called, passed to the cell factory and to the input tensors; we tell the function what the data type of the inputs is so that the state matrix can be created – by default, this will be full of zeros. Static_rnn() will then call the _call_function() of the factory once for every input, creating a copy of the cell each time (twice, in this case). Each copy will have 5 recurrent neurons on one layer and both copies will share the weights and the bias terms. These cells are then chained together. Two objects are returned by static_rnn(); first, a Python list that has the output tensors for both time steps, second, a tensor that has the final network states in it. With basic cells like this one, the final state is equal to the last output we got.

If we were using, say, 50 time steps, it would be somewhat unwieldy to define that many placeholders and that many output tensors. Plus, when it came to executing the code, you would need to give the network each of those placeholders and you would need to manipulate each of the outputs. Time-consuming or what! We can make this easier.

With the next code we are building this same RNN model but this time, we are doing it so it will take a single placeholder of shape – [None, n_steps, n_inputs] – the first dimension is the mini-batch size.

The list of input sequences is extracted for each of the time steps. X_seqs is a Python list that contains the n_steps tensors of shape – [None, n_inputs]; again, the first dimension is the size of the mini-batch. To do this, we need to use the transpose() function to change dimensions one and two around so that we now have our time steps in the first one. Next, a Python list is extracted, containing the tensors on the first dimension, which will be one tensor for each times step – this is done with the unstack() function – and the next two code lines remain as they were before.

Lastly, all the output tensors are merged into one tensor with the stack() function and the first two dimensions are swapped so we get our final tensor of shape – [None, n_steps, n_neurons], with None being the size of the mini-batch.

```
X = tf.placeholder(tf.float32, [None, n_steps, n_inputs])

X_seqs = tf.unstack(tf.transpose(X, perm=[1, 0, 2]))

basic_cell = tf.contrib.rnn.BasicRNNCell(num_units=n_neurons)

output_seqs, states = tf.contrib.rnn.static_rnn(

basic_cell, X_seqs, dtype=tf.float32)

outputs = tf.transpose(tf.stack(output_seqs), perm=[1, 0, 2])
```

Now we can give the network one tensor with all the sequences from the mini-batch:

```
X_batch = np.array([

# t = 0 t = 1

[[0, 1, 2], [9, 8, 7]], # instance 0

[[3, 4, 5], [0, 0, 0]], # instance 1

 [[6, 7, 8], [6, 5, 4]], # instance 2

[[9, 0, 1], [3, 2, 1]], # instance 3

])

with tf.Session() as sess:

init.run()

outputs_val = outputs.eval(feed_dict={X: X_batch})
```

And the output will be one outputs_val tensor for all the instances, all the neurons and all the time steps:

```
>>> print(outputs_val)

[[[-0.2964572 0.82874775 -0.34216955 -0.75720584 0.19011548]

[ 0.51955646 1. 0.99999022 -0.99984968 -0.24616946]]

[[-0.12842922 0.99981797 0.84704727 -0.99570125 0.38665548]

[-0.70553327 -0.11918639 0.48885304 0.08917919 -0.26579669]]

[[ 0.04731077 0.99999976 0.99330056 -0.999933 0.55339795]
```

```
[-0.32477224 0.99996376 0.99933046 -0.99711186 0.10981458]]

[[ 0.70323634 0.99309105 0.99909431 -0.85363263 0.7472108 ]

[-0.43738723 0.91517633 0.97817528 -0.91763324 0.11047263]]]
```

However, we are still building a graph that has one cell for every time step and, with 50 time steps we would have an ugly graph. Think of it has trying to write a program without using any loops – ever. Something like Y0=f(0, X0); Y1=f(Y0, X1); ..., Y50=f(Y49,X50). With a graph this size you run the risk of getting an OOM error – Out Of Memory – when backpropagation takes place, especially as GPU cards are limited in memory, because all the tensor values must be stored for the forward pass so they can be used in the reverse pass to compute the gradients.

Thankfully, we have a solution for that – a function called dynamic_rnn().

Unrolling Through Time - Dynamic

With the dynamic() run function, we use a while_loop() to iterate over the cell the specified number of times. If you want to avoid the OOM errors during backpropagation, you can also tell the model to change from GPU to CPU memory by setting swap_memory=True. Another handy point is that the dynamic_run() function will take one tensor for all inputs at each of the time steps – shape[None, n_steps, n_neurons]. You do not need to use stack(), unstack() or transpose().

This code will create an identical model to earlier with the dynamic_run function – as you will see, it looks a lot better:

```
X = tf.placeholder(tf.float32, [None, n_steps, n_inputs])

basic_cell = tf.contrib.rnn.BasicRNNCell(num_units=n_neurons)

outputs, states = tf.nn.dynamic_rnn(basic_cell, X, dtype=tf.float32)
```

Note

While backpropagation is going on, the while_loop() will do the right stuff – the tensor values for each of the forward pass iterations are stored in the loop and then reused in the reverse pass to compute the gradients.

How to Handle Input Sequences of Variable Length

Up to now, only input sequences of a fixed size have been used, each two steps long exactly. But what if we had input sequences that were variable in length, like sentences for example? For this you would set the parameter called sequence_length when you call the static_run() or dynamic_run() functions. The parameter has got to be a one-dimensional tensor that indicates how long the input sequence is for each of the instances. For example:

```
seq_length = tf.placeholder(tf.int32, [None])
```

```
[...]
```

```
outputs, states = tf.nn.dynamic_rnn(basic_cell, X, dtype=tf.float32,
```

```
sequence_length=seq_length)
```

Let's suppose that there is only one input in the second input sequence, and not two. We would need to use a zero vector to pad it so that it fits in input tensor X – this is because the second dimension of the input tensor is equal to the size of the biggest sequence:

```
X_batch = np.array([
```

```
#   step 0     step 1
```

```
[[0, 1, 2], [9, 8, 7]], # instance 0
```

```
[[3, 4, 5], [0, 0, 0]], # instance 1 (padded with a zero vector)
```

```
[[6, 7, 8], [6, 5, 4]], # instance 2
```

```
[[9, 0, 1], [3, 2, 1]], # instance 3
```

```
])
```

```
seq_length_batch = np.array([2, 1, 2, 2])
```

And now the values of placeholder X and placeholder seq_length must be fed in:

```
with tf.Session() as sess:
```

```
init.run()
```

```
outputs_val, states_val = sess.run(
```

```
[outputs, states], feed_dict={X: X_batch, seq_length:
seq_length_batch})
```

For every time step that is beyond the input sequence length, zero vectors will be output by the RNN – have a quick look at the output from the second instance for the second time step:

```
>>> print(outputs_val)
```

```
[[[-0.2964572 0.82874775 -0.34216955 -0.75720584 0.19011548]
```

```
[ 0.51955646 1. 0.99999022 -0.99984968 -0.24616946]] # final state
```

```
[[-0.12842922 0.99981797 0.84704727 -0.99570125 0.38665548] # final
state
```

```
[ 0.  0.  0.  0.  0. ]] # zero vector

[[ 0.04731077 0.99999976 0.99330056 -0.999933 0.55339795]

[-0.32477224 0.99996376 0.99933046 -0.99711186 0.10981458]] # final
state

[[ 0.70323634 0.99309105 0.99909431 -0.85363263 0.7472108 ]

[-0.43738723 0.91517633 0.97817528 -0.91763324 0.11047263]]] # final
state
```

And the states tensor will have the final states for each of the cells, with the exception of the zero vectors:

```
>>> print(states_val)

[[ 0.51955646 1. 0.99999022 -0.99984968 -0.24616946] # t = 1

[-0.12842922 0.99981797 0.84704727 -0.99570125 0.38665548] # t = 0
!!!

[-0.32477224 0.99996376 0.99933046 -0.99711186 0.10981458] # t = 1

[-0.43738723 0.91517633 0.97817528 -0.91763324 0.11047263]] # t = 1
```

How to Handle Output Sequences of Variable Length

We know what to do with a variable length input sequence, but what about the output sequences? What if they vary in length too? If you know before you start what the length of each sequence will be (i.e. if you know it will be the exact same length as the input sequence) you set the parameter called sequence_length as you did for the inputs. This is not going to be possible all the time; an example would be a translated sentence – often the input sequence is different to the output so the best solution is to define an output. These are called EOS tokens – end-of-sequence – and any output beyond the token is to be ignored – more about this later in this chapter.

We know how to build a recurrent neural network that has been unrolled over time so the next step is to train it.

Training RNNs

Training an RNN involves doing what we just did – unrolling it through time – and then use regular backpropagation in a strategy known as backpropagation through time. As it is in regular backpropagation, we have a forward pass through the network; the cost function C(Y(t min), Y(t min+ 1), ..., Y(t max)) to evaluate the output sequence – t min and t max represent the first and last of the output time steps, not including any ignored outputs. The gradients that result from the cost function are then back-propagated through the network and then, finally, we update the model parameters using the gradients that were computed during the backpropagation through time.

The gradients go backward through the outputs that the cost function uses, not just the last one. For example, let's say that the cost function uses Y(2), y(3) and Y(4) outputs – the last three of the network. The gradients go back through these but they do not go through Y(0) or Y(1). Also, because each time step uses the same parameters of W and b, backpropagation knows that it has to sum over every time step.

Training Sequence Classifiers

Now we are going to train an RNN so that it will classify the MNIST images. Usually, for image classification, the CNN are a better bet but this is going to be a very simple example that you will be somewhat familiar with already. Each image will be treated as a sequence containing 8 rows, each row 28 pixels – we know that the MNIST images are 28 x 28 pixels. We are also going to use cells with 150 recurrent neurons, along with a 10 neurons in a fully connected layer - one neuron for each class, each connected to the output from the previous time step and finish off with a softmax layer.

The construction phase is fairly easy to grasp because it is very like the MNIST classifier we built earlier; the only exception is that the hidden layers are replaced with an unroll RNN. The fully connected layer connects to the states tensor and in that is the RNNs final state, or output number 28. The target classes placeholder is represented by y.

```
from tensorflow.contrib.layers import fully_connected

n_steps = 28

n_inputs = 28

n_neurons = 150

n_outputs = 10

learning_rate = 0.001

X = tf.placeholder(tf.float32, [None, n_steps, n_inputs])

y = tf.placeholder(tf.int32, [None])

basic_cell = tf.contrib.rnn.BasicRNNCell(num_units=n_neurons)

outputs, states = tf.nn.dynamic_rnn(basic_cell, X, dtype=tf.float32)

logits = fully_connected(states, n_outputs, activation_fn=None)

xentropy = tf.nn.sparse_softmax_cross_entropy_with_logits(

labels=y, logits=logits)
```

```
loss = tf.reduce_mean(entropy)

optimizer = tf.train.AdamOptimizer(learning_rate=learning_rate)

training_op = optimizer.minimize(loss)

correct = tf.nn.in_top_k(logits, y, 1)

accuracy = tf.reduce_mean(tf.cast(correct, tf.float32))

init = tf.global_variables_initializer()
```

Now the MNIST data can be loaded and the test data can be reshaped to [batch_size, n_steps, n_inputs], as the network expects. We'll sort out the reshaping of the training data shortly:

```
from tensorflow.examples.tutorials.mnist import input_data

mnist = input_data.read_data_sets("/tmp/data/")

X_test = mnist.test.images.reshape((-1, n_steps, n_inputs))

y_test = mnist.test.labels
```

Now we can train the RNN. For the Execution phase, we will do exactly the same as we did for the MNIST classifier with the exception that each of the training batches is reshaped before it is given to the network:

```
n_epochs = 100

batch_size = 150

with tf.Session() as sess:

init.run()

for epoch in range(n_epochs):

for iteration in range(mnist.train.num_examples // batch_size):

X_batch, y_batch = mnist.train.next_batch(batch_size)

X_batch = X_batch.reshape((-1, n_steps, n_inputs))

sess.run(training_op, feed_dict={X: X_batch, y: y_batch})

acc_train = accuracy.eval(feed_dict={X: X_batch, y: y_batch})

acc_test = accuracy.eval(feed_dict={X: X_test, y: y_test})

print(epoch, "Train accuracy:", acc_train, "Test accuracy:",
acc_test)
```

The output should look like this:

```
0 Train accuracy: 0.713333 Test accuracy: 0.7299

1 Train accuracy: 0.766667 Test accuracy: 0.7977

...

98 Train accuracy: 0.986667 Test accuracy: 0.9777

99 Train accuracy: 0.986667 Test accuracy: 0.9809
```

As you can see, we achieve higher than 98% accuracy, which is pretty good going. Not only that, if you were to tune the hyperparameters, use He Initialization for the RNN weights, train for a little longer or add some regularization, like dropout, for example, you would get even better results.

> **Tip**
>
> If you wanted your RNN to use an initializer, you could specify it by wrapping the construction code for the initializer inside a variable scope, for example, if you wanted to use He Initialization, you would use
>
> variable_scope("rnn", initializer=variance_scaling_initializer().

Training an RNN to Predict a Time Series

Now we should look at how time series are handled, things like stock prices, patterns of brain waves, air temperature, etc. We are going to be training an RNN so it will take a generated time series to predict the next value. Each of the training instances is a sequence containing 20 consecutive values from the series (these instances are selected randomly); the target sequence and the input sequence are the same with the exception that the target sequence is moved on by a step into the future.

First, we will create our RNN. It has 100 recurrent neurons and it will be unrolled over 20 time steps – each of the instances has a length of 20 inputs. Each of the inputs has a single feature, which is the current value and the targets are the same as thing instances – 20 input sequences, each input with one value. The code is almost identical to what we did earlier:

```
n_steps = 20

n_inputs = 1

n_neurons = 100

n_outputs = 1

X = tf.placeholder(tf.float32, [None, n_steps, n_inputs])
```

```
y = tf.placeholder(tf.float32, [None, n_steps, n_outputs])

cell = tf.contrib.rnn.BasicRNNCell(num_units=n_neurons,
activation=tf.nn.relu)

outputs, states = tf.nn.dynamic_rnn(cell, X, dtype=tf.float32)
```

> **Note**
>
> Generally, you will have many more than just a single input features. Take stock prices for example; when you try to predict these you would have multiple input features at each of the time steps, like prices of other stocks, analyst ratings, basically anything that helps your system to make the predictions.

At every time step, there is an output vector, each size 100. What we really want is just one output value at each of these steps and the easiest way to achieve that is to use an OutputProtectionWrapper to wrap the cell. Cell wrappers are much like normal cells; each method call is proxied to an underlying cell but they also add extra functionality. An OutputProtectionWrapper gives us a fully connected layer containing linear neurons, those that don't have an activation function, on top of every output (this has no effect on the state of the cell). Every fully connected layer will share bias terms and trainable weights.

Cell wrapping is really quite simple so let's make some changes to the previous code – let's use an OutputProtectionWrapper to wrap BasicRNNCell in:

```
cell = tf.contrib.rnn.OutputProjectionWrapper(

tf.contrib.rnn.BasicRNNCell(num_units=n_neurons,
activation=tf.nn.relu),

output_size=n_outputs)
```

Ok, that's good. The next thing is, the cost function needs to be defined. To do this, we will use the MSE (Mean Squared Error), like we've done earlier in the book with regression tasks. Then the Adam optimizer is created, along with the training operation and the variable initialization operation, as we always do:

```
learning_rate = 0.001

loss = tf.reduce_mean(tf.square(outputs - y))

optimizer = tf.train.AdamOptimizer(learning_rate=learning_rate)

training_op = optimizer.minimize(loss)

init = tf.global_variables_initializer()
```

Next, the Execution phase:

```
n_iterations = 10000

batch_size = 50

with tf.Session() as sess:

init.run()

for iteration in range(n_iterations):

X_batch, y_batch = [...] # fetch the next training batch

sess.run(training_op, feed_dict={X: X_batch, y: y_batch})

if iteration % 100 == 0:

mse = loss.eval(feed_dict={X: X_batch, y: y_batch})

print(iteration, " \tMSE:", mse)
```

You should see this as the output:

```
0 MSE: 379.586

100 MSE: 14.58426

200 MSE: 7.14066

300 MSE: 3.98528

400 MSE: 2.00254

[...]
```

When the model training is complete, we can start making the predictions:

```
X_new = [...] # New sequences

y_pred = sess.run(outputs, feed_dict={X: X_new})
```

Although the easiest way of reducing the RNNs output sequence dimensionality to a single value for each time step is to use the OutputProtectionWrapper, it certainly isn't very efficient. There is a solution that is far more efficient but it is a but trickier to implement – the RNN outputs that come from [batch_size, n_steps, n_neurons] can be reshaped to [batch_size * n_steps, n_outputs]. Then a single fully connected layer is applied with the correct output size, in this case it is 1, and the result from this is an output tensor of shape [batch_size * n_steps, n_outputs]. Lastly, the tensor is reshaped to [batch_size, n_steps, n_outputs].

Implementation of this solution requires that it is reverted to a basic cell first, minus the OutputProtectionWrapper:

```
cell = tf.contrib.rnn.BasicRNNCell(num_units=n_neurons,
activation=tf.nn.relu)

rnn_outputs, states = tf.nn.dynamic_rnn(cell, X, dtype=tf.float32)
```

Next, the outputs are stacked using reshape(), the fully connected linear layer is applied (with no activation function at this stage) and then we use reshape() again to unstack the outputs:

```
stacked_rnn_outputs = tf.reshape(rnn_outputs, [-1, n_neurons])

stacked_outputs = fully_connected(stacked_rnn_outputs, n_outputs,

activation_fn=None)

outputs = tf.reshape(stacked_outputs, [-1, n_steps, n_outputs])
```

The remainder of the code is as it was in the last code. This can give your model a considerable boost in speed because we have only a single fully connected layer, not one for every time step.

Creative RNN

We now have an RNN model that we can use to predict the future so it can be used to generate a few creative sequences. To do this, we must provide the model with a seed sequence that has n_steps values, i.e. zeros. Then the model can be used to predict what the next value will be; that value is then appended to the sequence, the final n_steps values given to the model so the next value can be predicted, and so on. A new sequence is generated by this and it will look something like the first time series:

```
sequence = [0.] * n_steps

for iteration in range(300):

X_batch = np.array(sequence[-n_steps:]).reshape(1, n_steps, 1)

y_pred = sess.run(outputs, feed_dict={X: X_batch})

sequence.append(y_pred[0, -1, 0])
```

You could, if you wanted, now feed your Meat Loaf albums into an RNN to see if it can predict the next "Bat Out of Hell". You could, but you would need an RNN that is significantly more powerful, that has many more neurons and goes much deeper, which is what we are going to look at next – deep RNNs.

Deep RNNs

To make a deep RNN, you would need to stack up several layers of cells. Implementing a deep RNN using TensorFlow you could create multiple cells and then stack them inside a MultiRNNCell. In the next code, we are going to stack three cells that are identical, although you could use lots of different types of cells with differing numbers of neurons:

```
n_neurons = 100

n_layers = 3

basic_cell = tf.contrib.rnn.BasicRNNCell(num_units=n_neurons)

multi_layer_cell = tf.contrib.rnn.MultiRNNCell([basic_cell] *
n_layers)

outputs, states = tf.nn.dynamic_rnn(multi_layer_cell, X,
dtype=tf.float32)
```

Really, that is all you have to do. The variable called states is actually a tuple and it has a tensor for each layer. Each of these tensors is representative of the final state of the cell for the layer, containing shape [batch_size, n_neurons]. When you create the MultiRNNCell, setting state_is_tuple=False, state will become one tensor and that tensor will have all the states from all the layers and these are concatenated on the column axis. That means the shape is batch_size, n_layers * n_neurons].

Distribution of Deep RNNs Across Multiple GPUs

In the last chapter, we learned that deep RNNs can be distributed efficiently across multiple GPUs and this is done by pinning each of the layers to a different GPU. However, this won't work if you were trying to create each of the cells in different device() blocks:

```
with tf.device("/gpu:0"): # BAD! This is ignored.

layer1 = tf.contrib.rnn.BasicRNNCell(num_units=n_neurons)

with tf.device("/gpu:1"): # BAD! Ignored again.

layer2 = tf.contrib.rnn.BasicRNNCell(num_units=n_neurons)
```

This is not going to work. BasicRNNCell isn't actually a cell, rather it is a cell factory and no cells are created when the factory is created so that means there are no variables created either. So the device block gets ignored, and the cells are created later. When dynamic_run() is called, it will, in turn, call MultiRNNCell and this calls each of the BasicRNNCells in turn; this results in the cells being created with their variables.

However, none of the classes give us any way of controlling the devices that the variables are created on. If you place the dynamic_run() call inside a device block, the entire RNN will be pinned to one device. So where does that leave us? All you need to do is create a cell wrapper:

```
import tensorflow as tf

class DeviceCellWrapper(tf.contrib.rnn.RNNCell):

def __init__(self, device, cell):
```

```
self._cell = cell

self._device = device

@property

def state_size(self):

return self._cell.state_size

@property

def output_size(self):

return self._cell.output_size

def __call__(self, inputs, state, scope=None):

with tf.device(self._device):

return self._cell(inputs, state, scope)
```

Now the method calls will all be proxied to another cell; the _call_() function gets wrapped inside a device block by the cell wrapper and now each layer may be distributed on different GPUs:

```
devices = ["/gpu:0", "/gpu:1", "/gpu:2"]

cells =
[DeviceCellWrapper(dev,tf.contrib.rnn.BasicRNNCell(num_units=n_neuron
s))

for dev in devices]

multi_layer_cell = tf.contrib.rnn.MultiRNNCell(cells)

outputs, states = tf.nn.dynamic_rnn(multi_layer_cell, X,
dtype=tf.float32)
```

Warning

Do not be tempted to set state_is_tuple=False. If you do, all the cell states will be concatenated into one tensor on one GPU.

Applying Dropout to Prevent Overfitting

Building deep RNNs comes with the risk that it will overfit the training set but there is a way to prevent that. One of the most common techniques is to use dropout. All you need to do is add a dropout layer either before or after your RNN; if you want dropout applied between the layers, you must use a DropoutWrapper. In the next piece of code, dropout is applied to the inputs of every RNN layer with each input being dropped with a probability of 50%

```
keep_prob = 0.5

cell = tf.contrib.rnn.BasicRNNCell(num_units=n_neurons)

cell_drop = tf.contrib.rnn.DropoutWrapper(cell,
input_keep_prob=keep_prob)

multi_layer_cell = tf.contrib.rnn.MultiRNNCell([cell_drop] *
n_layers)

rnn_outputs, states = tf.nn.dynamic_rnn(multi_layer_cell, X,
dtype=tf.float32)
```

You can also, if you want, set output_keep_prob so the dropout is applied to the outputs.

There is one big issue with this code; dropout gets applied during testing as well as training - we do not want this because we already know that dropout should only be for the training. At the time of writing, there is no support in DropoutWrapper for is_training, a placeholder. This means you must do one of two things – write a dropout wrapper class yourself or have two graphs – testing and training. This is what option two looks like:

```
import sys

is_training = (sys.argv[-1] == "train")

X = tf.placeholder(tf.float32, [None, n_steps, n_inputs])

y = tf.placeholder(tf.float32, [None, n_steps, n_outputs])

cell = tf.contrib.rnn.BasicRNNCell(num_units=n_neurons)

if is_training:

cell = tf.contrib.rnn.DropoutWrapper(cell, input_keep_prob=keep_prob)

multi_layer_cell = tf.contrib.rnn.MultiRNNCell([cell] * n_layers)

rnn_outputs, states = tf.nn.dynamic_rnn(multi_layer_cell, X,
dtype=tf.float32)

[...] # build the rest of the graph

init = tf.global_variables_initializer()

saver = tf.train.Saver()

with tf.Session() as sess:
```

```
if is_training:

init.run()

for iteration in range(n_iterations):

[...] # train the model

save_path = saver.save(sess, "/tmp/my_model.ckpt")

else:

saver.restore(sess, "/tmp/my_model.ckpt")

[...] # use the model
```

Now you should be able to train any kind of RNN you want. That said, if you want to train over long sequences, it's going to be a bit more complex. Let's have a look at why it is more complex and how it can be done.

The Complexity of Training Over Multiple Time Steps

If you want an RNN trained over long sequences, it must be run over multiple time steps and this will result in a very deep unrolled RNN. Like any of the other DNNs we looked at, there is a good chance that the RNN will suffer from vanishing or exploding gradients and it will take too long to train. To try to mitigate these problems, RNN can also be used with recurrent neural networks, things like good initialization of parameters, using ReLU or other activation functions that don't saturate, Gradient Clipping, Batch Normalization, faster optimizers and so on. However, if your RNN has got to handle sequences that are even a little bit long, say, 100 inputs, for example, the training is still going to be very slow.

There is a very common solution to this, a very simple one. The RNN needs to unroll over just a couple of time steps at a time during the training. This is called truncated backpropagation through time, or TBPTT. This is easily implemented in TensorFlow; all you do is truncate your input sequences. Let's take the time series as an example – n_steps just needs to be reduced during training. The problem will this is that your model will not have the ability to learn any long-term pattern like this so we need a workaround. One way to do it would be to ensure that, in your shortened sequences, you have both old and new data – that way, your model will be able to learn how to use both. For example, you could have a sequence that has monthly data covering five months, weekly data covering 5 weeks and daily data covering five days. However, this is also limited – what if you had fine-grain data from a previous year that could be very useful? What if there was one small event, albeit a very significant one, that has to be taken into account, even if it happens years in the future, such as election results?

Putting aside the issue of the model taking too long to train, there is another problem that long-running RNNs face – in time, the first inputs' memory will fade out. In fact, some data will be lost following each of the time steps, because the data goes through a number of transformations when it travels through the RNN. After a time, the state of the RNN will have almost no traces of the very first inputs. This can be something of a deal breaker. For example, let's say that you have a long movie review that you want sentiment analysis performed on. The review starts with the words, "This movie was great" but the rest of that review is a whole long list of improvements that could have made it an even better movie. If the first four words of that review are gradually lost by the RNN, the review is going to be misinterpreted. Solving this problem has required the introduction of different cell types with long-term memory. These have been such a success that basic cells are rarely used anymore.

We will look next at the LSTM cell, the most popular of these cells.

The LSTM Cell

LSTM stands for Long Short-Term Memory. This cell was first proposed by Jürgen Schmidhuber and Sepp Hochreiter in 1997 and, over time, several more researchers made gradual improvements to it. Some of those researchers include Wojciech Zaremba, Hasim Sak, and Alex Graves. Think of the LSTM as being like a black box; in this way, it could be used in much the same way as a basic cell is but it will have much better performance. Training converges significantly faster and it has the capability of detecting any long-term dependencies in the training data. To implement it in TensorFlow, you would use BasicLSTMCell and not BasicRNNCell.

```
lstm_cell = tf.contrib.rnn.BasicLSTMCell(num_units=n_neurons)
```

LSTM cells have two state vectors to manage and these are, by default, kept apart. This is purely for performance, no other reason. However, this can be changed, just set state_is_tuple=False when you create the BasicLSTMCell.

So, how do LSTM cells work? Well, if you forget about what is inside the box, it looks very much like a regular cell with the exception that the state has been divided into two vectors – h(t) and c(t), with c standing for cell. You can see h(t) as a short-term state and c(t) as a long-term state.

Now, what's inside the box? The basic idea is that the RNN will learn what it needs to store in the long-term state, what it needs to throw away, and what it needs to read from it. The long-term state c(t-1) travels through the network, left to right, going through a forget gate first; at this point, a few memories are dropped and new ones added using the addition operation – these new memories are chosen by an input gate. The result is c(t) and this is sent out straight away with no need for any more transformation.

So, what's happening is that memories get dropped and new ones added at each time step. Once the addition operation has been done, the long-term state is copied and then goes through the activation function, in this case, tanh; that is followed by the output gate filtering the results. We get h(t) the short-term state and this is the same as the output for the time step y(t).

Now we need to have a look at the gates and see where these new memories are coming from.

First, x(t), which is the current input vector, along with h(t-1), the last short-term state, is given to four fully connected layers, each one different. Each has its own purpose.

The main layer outputs g(t). Its role is to carry out analysis of the current inputs x(t) and h(t-1), the last short-term state. If you had a basic cell, this layer would be the only one and the output would go directly to y(t) and h(t). By contrast, with the LSTM cell, the output from this layer does not go directly out; instead, the long-term state partially stores it.

Layers two, three and four are the gate controllers. All three use logistic activation functions so their outputs will be anywhere from 0 to 1. These outputs are fed to multiplication operations that are element-wise so, if the output is 0 the gates are closed while, if the output is 1, the gates are opened. More specifically, f(t) controls the forget gate and this controls what should be removed permanently from the long-term state.

i(t) controls the input gate and this controls what the long-term state needs from g(t) and that is why the output is only partially stored.

Lastly, o(t) controls the output gate and this controls what should be read from the long-term state and the output at the current time step. The output goes to h(t) and to y(t),

In more basic terms, LSTM cells are able to learn how to recognize what is an important input (the input gate), make sure the long-term state stores it, preserve it for however long it is required (the forget gate), and how to know when it needs extracting and do the job. All this tells us why LSTM cells have been so very successful at long-term pattern capture in audio recordings, long pieces of text, time series, and so on.

In the next equation, you can see a summary of how the long-term state of the cell is computed, the short-term state of that cell, and the output of the cell at every time step for one instance. An equation that shows the operations for an entire mini-batch is much the same:

$$i_{(t)} = \sigma(W_{xi}^T \cdot x_{(t)} + W_{hi}^T \cdot h_{(t-1)} + b_i)$$

$$f_{(t)} = \sigma(W_{xf}^T \cdot x_{(t)} + W_{hf}^T \cdot h_{(t-1)} + b_f)$$

$$o_{(t)} = \sigma(W_{xo}^T \cdot x_{(t)} + W_{ho}^T \cdot h_{(t-1)} + b_o)$$

$$g_{(t)} = \tanh(W_{xg}^T \cdot x_{(t)} + W_{hg}^T \cdot h_{(t-1)} + b_g)$$

$$c_{(t)} = f_{(t)} \otimes c_{(t-1)} + i_{(t)} \otimes g_{(t)}$$

$$y_{(t)} = h_{(t)} = o_{(t)} \otimes \tanh(c_{(t)})$$

Equation - LSTM Computations

Breaking this equation down:

- W xi, W xf, W xo, W xg – weight matrices for the four layers; this shows their connection to x(t), the input vector.
- W hi, W hf, W ho, and W hg - weight matrices for the four layers; shows their connection to h(t-1), the last short-term state.
- b i, b f, b o, and b g – bias terms for the four layers. Be aware that, in TensorFlow, bf is initialized to a vector of 1s and not 0s. This is so that nothing can be forgotten at the start of the training.

Using Peephole Connections

With the basic LSTM cells, the only things the gate controllers are able to look at are x(t) (the input) and h(t-1) (the last short-term state). However, it wouldn't be such a bad idea if we gave them more context to work with and we can do that by letting them have a quick look at the long-term state too. In 2000, Felix Gers and Jürgen Schmidhuber proposed a variant of the LSTM, this one containing added connections; these are called peephole connections. The connections are c(t-1) which is the last long-term state, added to the forget and the input gate controllers as an input and c(t), which the current long-term state, added to the output gate controller as an input.

Implementing peephole connections in TensorFlow requires the use of the LSTMCell and not BasicLSTMCell and you need to set use_peepholes=True:

```
lstm_cell = tf.contrib.rnn.LSTMCell(num_units=n_neurons,
use_peepholes=True)
```

There are a lot of other LSTM variants and the most popular of these is the GRU cell, which we will be delving into next.

GRU Cells

GRU stands for Gated Recurrent Unit and it was proposed in a 2014 paper published by Kyunghyun Cho et al. In the same paper, they also proposed the Encoder-Decoder network we talked about earlier.

A GRU cell is nothing more than a simple version of LSTM and it does just as well in performance terms, which is why it is fast growing in terms of popularity. The simplifications are:

- Both if the state vectors have been merged into one h(t)
- The forget and input gates are both controlled by one gate controller. If the controller output is a 1, the input gate will open while the forget gate will close. If a zero is output, we get the opposite happening. What this means is, when a memory needs to be stored, the storage location gets erased first. In itself, this is one of the more frequent LSTM variants.
- GRU does not have an output gate. Instead, with every time step, the output is the full state vector. What we do have is a brand new gate controller; this is one is in control of what bit of the last state the main layer sees.

The next equation shows you the cell's state is computed at each of the time steps for one instance:

$$z_{(t)} = \sigma(W_{xz}^T \cdot x_{(t)} + W_{hz}^T \cdot h_{(t-1)})$$

$$r_{(t)} = \sigma(W_{xr}^T \cdot x_{(t)} + W_{hr}^T \cdot h_{(t-1)})$$

$$g_{(t)} = \tanh(W_{xg}^T \cdot x_{(t)} + W_{hg}^T \cdot (r_{(t)} \otimes h_{(t-1)}))$$

$$h_{(t)} = (1 - z_{(t)}) \otimes \tanh(W_{xg}^T \cdot h_{(t-1)} + z_{(t)} \otimes g)$$

Equation - GRU Computations

It is easy to create a GRU cell using TensorFlow:

```
gru_cell = tf.contrib.rnn.GRUCell(num_units=n_neurons)
```

The GRU or the LSTM cells are one of the biggest reasons why RNNs have been so successful in the last few years, especially for NLP applications, which we will look at now.

Natural Language Processing Applications

These days, most of the state-of-the-art natural language processing applications are based at least partly on RNNs, and this includes applications like sentiment analysis, parsing, automatic summarization, and machine translation, to name just a few. In the final part of this chapter, we will take a look at an RNN model for machine translation. For more information, you should investigate the Word2Vec and seq2seq tutorials provided by TensorFlow on their website.

Word Embeddings

Before we can even think about starting, the first thing to do is pick a word representation. You could have each word represented by a one-hot vector. Let's assume that you have a vocabulary of 25,000 words; a 25,000-dimensional vector is used to represent the nth word; the vector is full of zeros except for the nth position, where there is a 1. However, this is a big vocabulary and it isn't efficient to use a sparse representation like this. What you really want is similar words with representations that are also similar because this would make it much more likely that your model would be able to generalize what it learns about a word to other words that are similar. For example, if you tell your model that "I eat pizza" is a valid sentence, and your model already knows that "burger" is close to pizza but a long way off "crayons" then it will know that "I eat burger" is also a valid sentence while "I eat crayons" isn't. But how do we come up with a representation like this?

The most commonly used solution is to have each of the word represented by a small but dense vector, for example, 150 dimensions. This vector is called an embedding and while training, the neural network will learn embedding for each of the words. When the training starts, these embeddings will be randomly picked, but as the training goes on, backpropagation is used to shift the embeddings in such a way that the network can perform its task properly. What this means is words that are similar to one another will start to cluster near one another and may even finish by being organized in a very meaningful manner. For example, the embeddings may be shifted so that they lie on specific axes, representing adjective/noun, singular/plural, gender, and so on. The result can be nothing short of spectacular.

The first thing you need to do in TensorFlow is create a variable that represents the embedding for all of your vocabulary words and this will be randomly initialized:

```
vocabulary_size = 50000

embedding_size = 150
```

```
embeddings = tf.Variable(

tf.random_uniform([vocabulary_size, embedding_size], -1.0, 1.0))
```

Now let's assume that you want to feed your neural network with the sentence, "I eat pizza". First, the sentence needs to be preprocessed and broken down into known words. You could remove any characters that weren't necessary, replace words that are not known with a predefined token word like [UNK], use [NUM] for numerical values, [URL] in place of URLs and so on. As soon as you have your list of known words, you can then look in a dictionary to find the integer identifier for each of those words – from 0 to 24999. Once you have those identifiers, for example, [58, 47586, 2581], you can use a placeholder to feed them to TensorFlow. Last, the embedding_lookup() function would be applied to get the embedding that corresponds to it:

```
train_inputs = tf.placeholder(tf.int32, shape=[None]) # from ids...

embed = tf.nn.embedding_lookup(embeddings, train_inputs) # ...to
embeddings
```

As soon as good embeddings have been learned by your model, you can reuse them with some efficiency in any of the NLP functions. At the end of the day, regardless of what application you are using, "pizza" and "burger" are still close to one another while being far away from "crayons"!

If you wanted, you could download pre-trained embeddings rather than doing your own training. As you do when you reuse a pre-trained layer, you can decide if the pre-trained embeddings are to be frozen, i.e. use trainable=False to create your embedding variable. Alternatively, backpropagation could be used to tweak them for whatever you need them for. Option one speeds the training up, option two can lead to better performance.

> **Tip**
>
> Embeddings can also be used for the representation of categorical attributes, especially those that take large numbers of values of different types. They are even more useful when the values show complex similarities.

Now you have everything you need to implement your own machine translation system. Let's look at how to do this.

Building an Encoder-Decoder Network for Simple Machine Translation

We're going to look at a machine translation model that translates English into French.

We feed the English sentences into the encoder and the decoder will output them as the French translation. If you use French translations as decoder inputs, they must be pushed back a step. In other words, you can pass the decoder a word as an input that should have been output at the step before, irrespective of what the actual output was. For the first word fed in, a token is supplied that will represent the start of the sentence, for example "<start>". The decoder should then use the EOS (end-of-sequence) token, i.e. "<eos>>" to end the sentence.

Be aware that, when you feed an English sentence to the encoder, they are reversed so "I eat pizza" would become "pizza eat I". What this does is makes sure that the first word of the English sentence is given to the encoder last. Why? Because that is usually what the decoder will translate first.

Every word will be represented initially by an integer identifier, i.e. 2581 for the word "pizza". Then the word embedding is returned by the embedding lookup and the embeddings are fed to the encoder and to the decoder.

The decoder will output a score at every step for each of the output vocabulary (French) words. This is followed by a SoftMax layer which transforms those scores into probabilities. For example, in step one, the word "Je" may have a probability of 15% while, "Tu" may be 5% and so on. The word that is output is the one that has the highest probability. This is something like the classification tasks so you can use the softmax_cross_entropy_with_logits() function to train the model.

It is worth noting that, after training, at inference time, you will not have a target sentence to give to the decoder. Instead, you will give the word that was output at the step before and this will require an embedding lookup.

So now you see the big picture. But if you were to have a look at a large piece of code called rnn/translate/seq2seq_model.py (you can find it on the internet), you would see that there are some very important differences:

First, we have assumed, up to now, that all of the input sequences, to both the encoder and the decoder, have all got constant lengths. However, sentence lengths are not generally all the same and there are a few ways that this can be handled. You could use the argument sequence_length to dynamic_run() or static_run functions; this would be to specify the length of each sentence. There is another way; you could group your sentences together in buckets, each containing sentences of similar length, i.e. one for sentences of one to five word long, one for sentences of six to ten words long and so on. A padding token, such as "<pad>" would be used to pad the shorter sentences.

For example, your sentence, "I eat pizza" would become "<pad> <pad> >pad> pizza eat I" would be translated to "je mange de la pizza <eos> <pad>". What we want to do is ignore anything that is output after the EOS token. To do this, a target_weights vector is used. For example, the sentence "je mange de la pizza <eos> <pad>" would have its weights set to [1.0, 1.0, 1.0, 1.0, 1.0, 0.0] – the 0.0 is for the padding token in the sentence.

If you multiply the losses and the target weights, you will zero out any of the losses that correspond to the words that are beyond the EOS token.

Second, when you have a large output vocabulary, it would be awfully slow if you were to output a probability for each possible word. If you have, say, 25,000 French words, the decoder will output 25,000-dimensional vectors; computation of the softmax function over a vector of this size would be incredibly intensive in terms of the computation. You can avoid this by having smaller vectors output from the decoder, for example, 1,000-dimensional vectors. A sampling technique would then be used for estimating the loss; this allows it to be done without the need to compute it over each and every word in the target vocabulary. To do this in TensorFlow, you would use the sampled_softmax_loss() function.

Third, the implementation makes use of an attention mechanism. This allows the decoder to peek at the input sequence. I won't go any further with this because attention augmented RNNs really are outside the scope of this book but feel free to do your own research.

Lastly, the implementation uses the tf.nn.legacy_seq2seq module. This module gives us the tools we need to build many different models of this type easily. For example, there is an embedding_rnn_seq2seq() function, used to create an Encoder-Decoder model that will automatically sort out all the word embeddings for you.

Now you have all you need to understand the sequence-to-sequence implementation so use your newfound knowledge to train your own translator.

Chapter 14: Using Autoencoders

What are autoencoders? They are artificial neural networks that can learn codings without supervision. A coding is a representation of the input data and the training sets they learn on are unlabeled data. Codings tend to have a dimensionality that is much lower than that of the input data and this is what makes the autoencoder very useful to reduce dimensionality. Perhaps even more important, the autoencoder is an incredibly powerful feature detector, highly suitable to pre-train deep neural networks, unsupervised of course. Finally, autoencoders can generate new data randomly; this new data looks much like the training data and is known as a generative model. You could, for example, use images of faces to train your autoencoder and it would then be able to generate new faces.

Autoencoders work in a surprisingly simple way – they learn to copy the inputs to the outputs. This may sound rather simple but you will see throughout the course of this chapter that, when you constrain the network in some ways, things get more difficult not easier. For example, you could add some noise to the inputs and then have your network trained in recovering the original inputs. Or you could limit how big the internal representation is. Constraints like this stop the autoencoder from copying inputs straight to the outputs and this makes the autoencoder learn better data representation ways. Put simply, codings are nothing more than byproducts from the autoencoder trying to learn identity function when constrained.

Throughout this chapter, we will look in-depth at the way autoencoders work. We'll look at the constraint types that we can impose on them and we will look, as usual, at how to use TensorFlow to implement an autoencoder, be it for unsupervised pre-training, dimensionality reduction, for generative models or for feature extraction.

Efficient Data Representations

Have a look at these two number sequences. Which one is the easiest for you to memorize?

40, 27, 25, 36, 81, 57, 10, 73, 19, 68

50, 25, 76, 38, 19, 58, 29, 88, 44, 22, 11, 34, 17, 52, 26, 13, 40, 20

You would think, and indeed logic would dictate, that sequence one would be easier – it's shorter, after all. However, take a good look at sequence two. Have you noticed? It follows two rules – any even number in the sequence is followed by a number that is exactly half of that even number and the odd numbers are followed by a number that is three times that odd number plus one. This is actually quite a famous sequence and it's called the hailstone sequence.

As soon as your brain picks up on this pattern, you find that sequence two is actually the easiest to remember. Rather than memorizing the entire sequence, all you need is the first number and those two rules, along with the sequence length. To be fair, if you had the ability to memorize long sequences anyway, you wouldn't need to learn the rules and you wouldn't really care much about a pattern; all you would do is learn each number off by heart and that's it, that's all. Pattern recognition comes into its own because it is hard to learn long sequences and remember them. With any luck, this explains why constraint of an autoencoder during training makes that autoencoder find and exploit data patterns.

Early in the 1970's, Herbert Simon and William Chase studied the relationship between perception, memory, and pattern matching. Their observations were on experts in Chess and they found that these experts have the ability to memorize where every piece was on the board just by looking at it for five seconds. This is something that most would find nigh on impossible to do. However, this only happened in cases where each playing piece was in a realistic board position, i.e. from a real game and not when the pieces were randomly placed. Chess experts don't have any better a memory that you or I, but because they have so much experience with the game, they can see the patterns and these patterns are what helps them remember.

In a similar way to the Chess experts in that experiment, an autoencoder will look at all the inputs, convert them to an internal representation and output something that should look very much like those inputs. Autoencoders consist of two parts – the encoder, which is the recognition network, which takes the inputs and converts them to the internal representation, and a decoder, the generative network part, which converts those representations and outputs them.

So, as you see, autoencoders are made up very much like the MLP, or Multi-layer Perceptron, that we discussed earlier in this book but with an exception – the neurons from the output layer must equal the input number. For example, if you have a single hidden layer with two neurons, which is the encoder, the decoder will have three neurons on one output layer. These outputs are sometimes known as the reconstructions – the autoencoder attempts a reconstruction of the inputs and the cost function includes a reconstruction loss that will issue a penalty to a model that has different reconstructions to the inputs.

Compared to the input data, internal representation dimensionality is lower, i.e. it is two-dimensional and not three-dimensional. Because of this, the autoencoder is labeled as under complete and these cannot copy inputs to codings; however, it still has to find a way of outputting a copy of those inputs. The autoencoder is forced to determine what the important features of the input data are and learning them while discarding anything unimportant.

Let's have a look at implementing an under complete autoencoder that will be used for dimensionality reduction.

Using an Undercomplete Linear Autoencoder to Perform PCA

PCA or Principal Component Analysis happens when the autoencoder uses linear activations only and the cost function is the MSE – Mean Squared Error. The next code will build a linear autoencoder. This will be performing PCA on a 3D dataset, with the result that it is projected to 2D:

```
import tensorflow as tf
```

```python
from tensorflow.contrib.layers import fully_connected

n_inputs = 3 # 3D inputs

n_hidden = 2 # 2D codings

n_outputs = n_inputs

learning_rate = 0.01

X = tf.placeholder(tf.float32, shape=[None, n_inputs])

hidden = fully_connected(X, n_hidden, activation_fn=None)

outputs = fully_connected(hidden, n_outputs, activation_fn=None)

reconstruction_loss = tf.reduce_mean(tf.square(outputs - X)) # MSE

optimizer = tf.train.AdamOptimizer(learning_rate)

training_op = optimizer.minimize(reconstruction_loss)

init = tf.global_variables_initializer()
```

This isn't a great deal different from the MLPs that we built earlier. There are two things worth noting:

- There are an equal number of outputs to inputs;
- For PCA to be performed, activation_fn=None must be set – the neurons are linear – and the cost function used is MSE. In a while, we'll look at some more complex autoencoders.

For now, we'll load the dataset in, we'll train our model in this dataset and then use the model to encode the test set, projecting it to 2D:

```python
X_train, X_test = [...] # load the dataset

n_iterations = 1000

codings = hidden # the output of the hidden layer provides the codings

with tf.Session() as sess:

init.run()

for iteration in range(n_iterations):

training_op.run(feed_dict={X: X_train}) # no labels (unsupervised)

codings_val = codings.eval(feed_dict={X: X_test})
```

If you look at the output of the hidden layer, you will see that the autoencoder has found the most efficient 2D plane to project the data onto and has preserved the data variance as much as it could.

Stacked Autoencoders

As it is in other neural networks we've looked at, it is possible for an autoencoder to have several hidden layers. These are known as stacked autoencoders, sometimes as deep autoencoders. By adding more layers in, the autoencoder can learn codings that are more complex. However, you need to take care that you don't make your autoencoder too powerful. Why not? Surely the more powerful it is, the better? Imagine that you have an autoencoder that is so powerful that it can learn simply to map the inputs to one arbitrary number per input. The decoder will obviously learn the reverse of that. Obviously, with an autoencoder like this, the training data will be perfectly reconstructed but the autoencoder has not learned anything useful in terms of data representation and that means when there are new instances, it is not going to generalize very well.

Stacked autoencoder architecture tends to look symmetrical in relation to the hidden central layer – this is the coding layer. You could think of it as being similar to a sandwich. For example, the autoencoder for the MNIST dataset could have 784 inputs. This would be followed by 300 neurons in a hidden layer, followed by 150 neurons in a hidden central layer. Lastly, we have 300 neurons in another hidden layer and a final layer of 784 neurons – the output layer.

Implementing a Stacked Autoencoder with TensorFlow

TensorFlow implementation of a stacked autoencoder looks much like a normal deep Multi-layer Perceptron. More specifically, the techniques that we used earlier to train deep nets can also be applied to these. For example, look at the next piece of code – we build our stacked autoencoder for the MNIST dataset; we use He Initialization, the activation function is ELU and we also use $\ell2$ regularization. You should recognize this code (what you won't see is any labels):

```
n_inputs = 28 * 28 # for MNIST

n_hidden1 = 300

n_hidden2 = 150 # codings

n_hidden3 = n_hidden1

n_outputs = n_inputs

learning_rate = 0.01

l2_reg = 0.001

X = tf.placeholder(tf.float32, shape=[None, n_inputs])
```

```python
with tf.contrib.framework.arg_scope(
    [fully_connected],
    activation_fn=tf.nn.elu,
    weights_initializer=tf.contrib.layers.variance_scaling_initializer(),
    weights_regularizer=tf.contrib.layers.l2_regularizer(l2_reg)):
    hidden1 = fully_connected(X, n_hidden1)
    hidden2 = fully_connected(hidden1, n_hidden2) # codings
    hidden3 = fully_connected(hidden2, n_hidden3)
    outputs = fully_connected(hidden3, n_outputs, activation_fn=None)

reconstruction_loss = tf.reduce_mean(tf.square(outputs - X)) # MSE

reg_losses = tf.get_collection(tf.GraphKeys.REGULARIZATION_LOSSES)
loss = tf.add_n([reconstruction_loss] + reg_losses)

optimizer = tf.train.AdamOptimizer(learning_rate)
training_op = optimizer.minimize(loss)

init = tf.global_variables_initializer()
```

Now the model can be trained as normal; do note that y_batch, the digit labels, are not used:

```python
n_epochs = 5
batch_size = 150

with tf.Session() as sess:
    init.run()
    for epoch in range(n_epochs):
        n_batches = mnist.train.num_examples // batch_size
        for iteration in range(n_batches):
            X_batch, y_batch = mnist.train.next_batch(batch_size)
            sess.run(training_op, feed_dict={X: X_batch})
```

Tying Weights

When you have an autoencoder like this one, neatly symmetrical, one of the most common techniques is to tie the weights in the decoder layers to those of the encoder layers. This will cut the number of weights in your model in half resulting in faster training and a lower risk of overfitting.

Let's say that you have an autoencoder with a total of N layers – disregarding the input layer; the Lth layer's connection weights are represented by W L, i.e. the first hidden layer is layer 1, the coding layer is layer n/2 and the output layer is layer N. The decoder weights would be defined as such:

```
WN-L+1 = WLT (with L  1, 2, …, n/2)
```

However, it is quite cumbersome to use the fully_connected() function in TensorFlow to implement the ties weights. The easiest way is simply to define each layer manually:

```python
activation = tf.nn.elu

regularizer = tf.contrib.layers.l2_regularizer(l2_reg)

initializer = tf.contrib.layers.variance_scaling_initializer()

X = tf.placeholder(tf.float32, shape=[None, n_inputs])

weights1_init = initializer([n_inputs, n_hidden1])

weights2_init = initializer([n_hidden1, n_hidden2])

weights1 = tf.Variable(weights1_init, dtype=tf.float32,
name="weights1")

weights2 = tf.Variable(weights2_init, dtype=tf.float32,
name="weights2")

weights3 = tf.transpose(weights2, name="weights3") # tied weights

weights4 = tf.transpose(weights1, name="weights4") # tied weights

biases1 = tf.Variable(tf.zeros(n_hidden1), name="biases1")

biases2 = tf.Variable(tf.zeros(n_hidden2), name="biases2")

biases3 = tf.Variable(tf.zeros(n_hidden3), name="biases3")

biases4 = tf.Variable(tf.zeros(n_outputs), name="biases4")

hidden1 = activation(tf.matmul(X, weights1) + biases1)

hidden2 = activation(tf.matmul(hidden1, weights2) + biases2)
```

```
hidden3 = activation(tf.matmul(hidden2, weights3) + biases3)

outputs = tf.matmul(hidden3, weights4) + biases4

reconstruction_loss = tf.reduce_mean(tf.square(outputs - X))

reg_loss = regularizer(weights1) + regularizer(weights2)

loss = reconstruction_loss + reg_loss

optimizer = tf.train.AdamOptimizer(learning_rate)

training_op = optimizer.minimize(loss)

init = tf.global_variables_initializer()
```

This is pretty straightforward but there are three things important to note:

- First, weight3 and weight 4 are the transposes of weights2 and weights 1 respectively, not variables. In effect they are tied to them.
- Second, because weight3 and weight4 are not variables, don't waste your time trying to regularize them. The only ones regularized are weights1 and weights2.
- Third, we never tie or regularize biases.

Training Autoencoders One at a Time

Instead of training an entire stacked autoencoder in one hit, like that last code did, it will be a good deal faster if you train them one at a time and then stack them up into one autoencoder. This is a very useful method when you have deep autoencoders.

During the first training phase, the first autoencoder will learn to reconstruct any inputs. In phase two, autoencoder two will learn to reconstruct the outputs of the hidden layer in autoencoder one. Lastly, all these encoders are stacked building a big sandwich. The hidden layers for each of the autoencoders get stacked first, followed by the output layers which go in reverse order. This will give you one large stacked autoencoder. You could train as many as you want in this way, gradually building up a huge stacked autoencoder.

Implementation of a multiphase training algorithm is best done by using a separate TensorFlow Graph for each of the phases. Once an autoencoder has been trained, the training set gets run through it and the output from the hidden layer is captured. This output will then become the training set for the following autoencoder and so on. When all the autoencoders are trained, the weights and the biases from each of the autoencoders is copied and then used to construct the stacked autoencoder. It isn't difficult to implement this so I won't go into detail; you can find code examples in the Jupyter Notebooks though.

Another way would be to use one graph that has the entire stacked autoencoder in it, along with a few additional operations that will be used to perform the training phases. Let's simplify this.

The graph will have a central column, which is the whole stacked encoder – this will be used once training is done. The column on the left is the operations required for the first training phase to be done. An output layer is created that will bypass the second and third hidden layers. The output layer will share the biases and weights that the autoencoder output layer uses. Atop this, we have the training operations that are used to try and make the output as near to the inputs as possible. So, this phase trains the weights and the biases for the first hidden layer and for the output layer – the first autoencoder.

The column on the right of the graph contains the operations required to run training phase two. This will add the training operation that will try to get the output of the third hidden layer as near the output from the first hidden layer as possible. Hidden layer one needs to be frozen while phase two is underway. In this phase, the weights and the biases for the second and third hidden layers are trained – this is the second autoencoder.

The TensorFlow code looks like this:

```
[...] # Build the whole stacked autoencoder normally.

# In this example, the weights are not tied.

optimizer = tf.train.AdamOptimizer(learning_rate)

with tf.name_scope("phase1"):

phase1_outputs = tf.matmul(hidden1, weights4) + biases4

phase1_reconstruction_loss = tf.reduce_mean(tf.square(phase1_outputs
- X))

phase1_reg_loss = regularizer(weights1) + regularizer(weights4)

phase1_loss = phase1_reconstruction_loss + phase1_reg_loss

phase1_training_op = optimizer.minimize(phase1_loss)

with tf.name_scope("phase2"):

phase2_reconstruction_loss = tf.reduce_mean(tf.square(hidden3 -
hidden1))

 phase2_reg_loss = regularizer(weights2) + regularizer(weights3)

phase2_loss = phase2_reconstruction_loss + phase2_reg_loss

train_vars = [weights2, biases2, weights3, biases3]

phase2_training_op = optimizer.minimize(phase2_loss,
var_list=train_vars)
```

Phase one is relatively straightforward; an output layer is created that will skip over the second and third hidden layers. Next we build training operations that will minimize the distance from the output to the input layers and do a little regularization.

Phase two adds the training operations required to minimize the distance from the output of the third and first hidden layers, again with a little regularization. Perhaps more important, we give the minimize() method a list of trainable variables but making sure weights1 and biases1 are omitted; this will freeze the first hidden layer during this phase.

For the Execution phase, all you do is fun the first phase training operations for a given number of epochs and then repeat with the second phase training operations.

Tip

Because the first hidden layer is frozen in the second phase, the output will be identical for all given training instances. So that you don't have to compute the output of this hidden layer for every epoch. Compute it for the entire training set at the end of the first phase. Then, during the second phase, the cached output of the first hidden layer can be directly fed in. The result? A nice little boost in performance.

Visualize the Reconstructions

To make sure your autoencoder has been trained properly, you can compare the inputs and outputs. They should be quite similar with any differences being minor details. We are now going to plot a pair of random digits and their reconstructions:

```
n_test_digits = 2

X_test = mnist.test.images[:n_test_digits]

with tf.Session() as sess:

[...] # Train the Autoencoder

outputs_val = outputs.eval(feed_dict={X: X_test})

def plot_image(image, shape=[28, 28]):

plt.imshow(image.reshape(shape), cmap="Greys",
interpolation="nearest")

plt.axis("off")

for digit_index in range(n_test_digits):

plt.subplot(n_test_digits, 2, digit_index * 2 + 1)

plot_image(X_test[digit_index])
```

```
plt.subplot(n_test_digits, 2, digit_index * 2 + 2)

plot_image(outputs_val[digit_index])
```

Visualize the Features

As soon as your autoencoder has learned a few features, it might be a good idea to look at them. There are a few ways you can do this but the simplest way is to look at every neuron in each of the hidden layers and look for the training instance that activates it more. This is quite useful for the hidden layers at the top because these are more likely to capture the large features that can easily be spotted among a group of training instances. Let's say that a neuron activates strongly when it sees a dog in a picture. This tells us that, obviously, pictures of dogs are what activate it the most. However, this doesn't really work all that well for the lower layers because the features are significantly smaller and more abstract.

Another method is this – for every neuron in hidden layer one, create an image; in this image, the intensity of the pixel corresponds to the connection's weight to the specified neuron. Look at this example; this code will plot the features that five neurons in hidden layer 1 learned:

```
with tf.Session() as sess:

[...] # train autoencoder

weights1_val = weights1.eval()

for i in range(5):

plt.subplot(1, 5, i + 1)

plot_image(weights1_val.T[i])
```

Another way would be to feed a random input image to the autoencoder. You would then measure the activation of the specific neuron you want and then let backpropagation tweak the image a little to get more activation out of the neuron. If you perform gradient ascent, iterating a number of times, the image will start turning into a one that strongly activates the neuron. This is useful to visualize what sort of inputs the neuron wants.

Lastly, if your autoencoder is being used for unsupervised pre-training, like a classification task, one of the simplest ways to verify that the learned features are useful is to measure how well the classifier performs.

Using Stacked Autoencoders for Unsupervised Pre-training

We talked earlier in this book about complex supervised tasks with little in the way of labeled training data. One easy solution is to find a network already trained on a similar task and reuse some of the lower layers. Doing this means that training a higher performance, a more complex model with just a small amount of training data is possible because the model is not going to have to learn the lower-level features. All it needs to do is make use of the feature detectors already learned by another net.

In the same way, if your dataset is large but much of it has no labels, you would first train a stacked autoencoder with all the data and then make use of the lower layers to create the network for your specific task; you would then use the labeled data to train it on. For example, if you wanted to use a stacked autoencoder to do unsupervised pre-training for a network designed for classification. Because the stacked autoencoder will usually train the autoencoders one at a time, if you have little-labeled data to work with you could consider freezing the lower pre-trained layers.

Note

This is quite a common situation because it often is quite cheap to build a large dataset of unlabeled data. For example, one script can download many millions of images from the web. However, reliable labeling can only really be done by a human. It is time-consuming and expensive to label instances so it tends to be common to have just a couple of thousand instances labeled.

One of the biggest triggers of the current high-level of interest in Deep Learning was the discovery by Geoffrey Hinton et al in 2006 that we can pre-train a deep neural network in an unsupervised way. To do this, they made use of restricted Boltzmann machines but a year later, in 2007, Yoshio Bengio et al proved that it could be done just as well with autoencoders.

The TensorFlow implementation isn't anything special. All you do is use all the training data to train one autoencoder and then make use of the encoder levels to create a new network – we talked earlier about reusing pre-trained layers so refer back if you are unsure.

Up to this point, so that the autoencoder is forced to learn good features, the coding layer size is limited, rendering it incomplete. There are several other constraint types that you can use, including those that let the coding layer be as large as or larger than the inputs and this would result in an overcomplete autoencoder. We'll look at some of these methods next.

Denoising an Autoencoder

One way of forcing the autoencoder to learn the good features is to give the inputs a little noise. You would then train the autoencoder to retrieve the original inputs that had no noise. This stops the inputs being copied to the outputs by the autoencoder so it is forced to look for patterns.

The idea behind using the autoencoder to eliminate noise has been known since the 1980's and was, in fact, mentioned in a Master's thesis by Yann LeCun in 1987. Pascal Vincent et al published a paper in 2008 that showed we could use autoencoders for feature extraction too and, in 2010, Vincent et al published a further paper that introduced us to the idea of stacking denoised encoders.

Using TensorFlow to Implement Denoising Autoencoders

It isn't too difficult to implement the denoising autoencoders in TensorFlow. We'll begin with Gaussian noise; it is much like you would train a normal autoencoder with the addition of noise on the inputs and we use the original inputs to calculate the reconstruction loss:

```
X = tf.placeholder(tf.float32, shape=[None, n_inputs])

X_noisy = X + tf.random_normal(tf.shape(X))

[...]

hidden1 = activation(tf.matmul(X_noisy, weights1) + biases1)

[...]

reconstruction_loss = tf.reduce_mean(tf.square(outputs - X)) # MSE

[...]
```

> **Warning**
>
> Because the shape of X only gets partially defined in the construction phase, there is no way to know beforehand what shape of noise we need to add. There is no point to calling X.get_shape() because all we would get back is [None, inputs], which is the partially defined shape and random_normal() requires a shape that is fully defined so an exception would be raised. What we do instead is call tf.shape(X) and this will create an operation that, at runtime, returns the shape of X; at this point it is fully defined.

To implement a dropout version of the code, much more common, really isn't that much harder:

```
from tensorflow.contrib.layers import dropout

keep_prob = 0.7

is_training = tf.placeholder_with_default(False, shape=(),
name='is_training')

X = tf.placeholder(tf.float32, shape=[None, n_inputs])

X_drop = dropout(X, keep_prob, is_training=is_training)

[...]

hidden1 = activation(tf.matmul(X_drop, weights1) + biases1)

[...]

reconstruction_loss = tf.reduce_mean(tf.square(outputs - X)) # MSE
```

[. . .]

During the training, is_training needs to be set to True and we do this with the feed_dict: sess.run(training_op, feed_dict={X: X_batch, is_training: True}. However, is_training does not need to be set to False during testing because that was set as the default when we called placeholder_with_default() function:

Sparse Autoencoders

Sparsity is a type of constraint that can result in good feature extraction and it does this by adding the right term to the cost function. This pushes the autoencoder to lower the number of active neurons that are present in the coding layer. For example, it could be pushed so it has an average of just 5% neurons that are significantly active in the coding layer. What this does is forces the autoencoder to represent every individual input as a mini-set of activations and the result of this is that each of the neurons in the coding layer will end up representing a feature that is useful.

In order that sparse models can be favored, the first thing we need to do is measure how sparse the code layer is for each iteration during training. To do this, we must compute what the average activation is of each of the neurons in the coding layer and this must be done over the whole training batch. The batch size needs to be of a reasonable size – too small and we won't get an accurate mean.

When we have the mean activation for each neuron, we then want the neurons that are overactive penalized and we do this by giving the cost function a sparsity loss. For example, if a neuron is measured as having an average activation of 0.3 but our sparsity target is 0.1, the neuron needs to be penalized so it activates less. One way to do this would be to add (0.3 − 0.1)2, which is the squared error, to the cost function but there is a better way. You could use the Kullback-Leibler Divergence; the gradients are stronger than the MSE.

We can compute the KL divergence between two discrete probability distributions, P, and Q by using the equation below (the divergence is shown as DKL(P||Q):

$$D_{\mathrm{KL}}(P \parallel Q) = \sum_i P(i) \log \frac{P(i)}{Q(i)}$$

Equation – Kullback-Leibler Divergence

What we want to do is measure what the divergence is between p (the target probability that will be activated by a neuron n the coding layer) and q (the actual probability, or the mean activation over the entire training batch.

Our KL divergence example would simplify to the following equation:

$$D_{\mathrm{KL}}(p \parallel q) = p \, \log \frac{p}{q} + (1 - p) \, \log \frac{1 - p}{1 - q}$$

Equation – KL Divergence Between p (target sparsity) and q (actual sparsity)

Once the sparsity loss has been computed for each of the neurons in the coding layer, the next step is to sum up the losses and then add that result to our cost function. So that we have more control over the relative importance of the sparsity and reconstruction losses, the sparsity loss is multiplied by a sparsity weight hyperparameter. If the weight is high, the model will stay close to the sparsity target but the inputs may not be reconstructed properly and this will make the model next to useless. On the other hand, if the weights are low, the sparsity object will be all but ignored by the model and no good features will be learned.

Implementing a Sparse Autoencoder with TensorFlow

Now we have all we need to implement our sparse autoencoder:

```
def kl_divergence(p, q):

return p * tf.log(p / q) + (1 - p) * tf.log((1 - p) / (1 - q))

learning_rate = 0.01

sparsity_target = 0.1

sparsity_weight = 0.2

[...] # Build a normal autoencoder (in this example the coding layer
is hidden1)

optimizer = tf.train.AdamOptimizer(learning_rate)

hidden1_mean = tf.reduce_mean(hidden1, axis=0) # batch mean

sparsity_loss = tf.reduce_sum(kl_divergence(sparsity_target,
hidden1_mean))

reconstruction_loss = tf.reduce_mean(tf.square(outputs - X)) # MSE

loss = reconstruction_loss + sparsity_weight * sparsity_loss
```

```
training_op = optimizer.minimize(loss)
```

There is one very important detail you need to know – coding layer activations need to be between 0 and 1 but cannot be equal to 0 or 1 or NaN (Not a Number) will be returned by the KL divergence. Using the logistic activation function on the coding layer is the easiest solution:

```
hidden1 = tf.nn.sigmoid(tf.matmul(X, weights1) + biases1)
```

There is a little trick you can use for speeding up convergence; rather than MSE, we could use a reconstruction loss that has bigger gradients. Often, the best choice is cross entropy. To use that, we need to normalize our inputs so they take the values 0 to 1 and then use logistic activation in the output layer so that the outputs will also take these values. TensorFlow has a neat function that will efficiently apply the sigmoid (activation) function to the outputs and then compute the cross entropy; that function is sigmoid_cross_entropy_with_logits():

```
[...]

logits = tf.matmul(hidden1, weights2) + biases2)

outputs = tf.nn.sigmoid(logits)

reconstruction_loss = tf.reduce_sum(

tf.nn.sigmoid_cross_entropy_with_logits(labels=X, logits=logits))
```

We do not need the outputs operation during the training, only when we want to take a look at the reconstruction.

Variational Autoencoders

Another category of autoencoders that is very important was first introduced by Max Welling and Diederik Kingma in 2014 and it has quickly become an incredibly popular autoencoder – the variational encoder. These are very different from any autoencoder we have looked at so far:

Variational autoencoders are probabilistic autoencoders and this means that chance plays a part in partially determining the outputs, even when training has finished. The denoising autoencoders, by comparison, will only use randomness throughout the training.

They are also generative autoencoders and this means that new instances can be generated that look as if they have been sampled from the training dataset.

Both of these important properties make them very much like an RBM, but these autoencoders are very easy to train with a much faster sampling process – with RBM, the network has to stabilize into a "thermal equilibrium" before new instances can be sampled.

Let's have a look at how these variational autoencoders work. A variational autoencoder has the same basic structure that all autoencoders have – an encoder, a decoder, sometimes both having hidden layers. But with the variational autoencoder, we have a twist – rather than producing a coding directly for a specified input, the encoder will produce a mean coding of μ and a standard deviation of σ. Then the actual coding will be randomly sampled from a Gaussian distribution that also has a mean coding of μ and a standard deviation of σ.

Next, the decoder will just decode the sampled code as it would normally. A training instance will go through the autoencoder and, as an example, the encoder will produce μ and σ. A random sampling of a coding is done and then the code will be decoded; the final output would look much like the training instance.

The inputs might have a somewhat convoluted distribution, but the variational autoencoder will usually produce encodings that look like they might have been sampled from a Gaussian distribution. In the training phase, the codings are pushed by the cost function to migrate gradually in the coding space, otherwise called latent space so that occupies a region, roughly hyperspherical in shape, that looks like a cloud full of Gaussian points. There is a consequence of this – once a variational encoder has been trained, new instances can very easily be generated; simply do a random sampling of one of the codings from the Gaussian distribution and decode it.

Time to look at the cost function. This is made up of two parts, the first being the reconstruction loss that will push the autoencoder into reproducing its inputs – cross entropy can be used for this.

Second, we have latent loss. This pushes the autoencoder so it has codings that looks like they are sampled from a Gaussian distribution and for this, KL divergence is used between the Gaussian distribution (the target distribution) and the actual coding distribution, The math is quite a bit more complex than it was earlier, mostly down to the Gaussian noise, simply because this will limit the information that the coding layer may have transmitted to it and this is what pushes the autoencoder to learn good features. , Thankfully, the equations for this will simplify for the latent loss to this code:

```
eps = 1e-10 # smoothing term to avoid computing log(0) which is NaN

latent_loss = 0.5 * tf.reduce_sum(

tf.square(hidden3_sigma) + tf.square(hidden3_mean)

- 1 - tf.log(eps + tf.square(hidden3_sigma)))
```

A common variant of this is the train your encoder so it outputs $y = \log(\sigma 2)$ and not just σ. Where we need σ, we can compute $\sigma = \exp(F/2)$. The encoder will find it much easier to capture sigmas that have different scales and convergence is much faster. Not only that, our latent loss code looks considerably simpler:

```
latent_loss = 0.5 * tf.reduce_sum(

tf.exp(hidden3_gamma) + tf.square(hidden3_mean) - 1 - hidden3_gamma)
```

The next code will build a variational autoencoder with the log(σ 2) variant:

```
n_inputs = 28 * 28 # for MNIST

n_hidden1 = 500

n_hidden2 = 500

n_hidden3 = 20 # codings

n_hidden4 = n_hidden2

n_hidden5 = n_hidden1

n_outputs = n_inputs

learning_rate = 0.001

with tf.contrib.framework.arg_scope(

[fully_connected],

activation_fn=tf.nn.elu,

weights_initializer=tf.contrib.layers.variance_scaling_initializer())
:

X = tf.placeholder(tf.float32, [None, n_inputs])

hidden1 = fully_connected(X, n_hidden1)

hidden2 = fully_connected(hidden1, n_hidden2)

hidden3_mean = fully_connected(hidden2, n_hidden3,
activation_fn=None)

hidden3_gamma = fully_connected(hidden2, n_hidden3,
activation_fn=None)

hidden3_sigma = tf.exp(0.5 * hidden3_gamma)

noise = tf.random_normal(tf.shape(hidden3_sigma), dtype=tf.float32)

hidden3 = hidden3_mean + hidden3_sigma * noise

hidden4 = fully_connected(hidden3, n_hidden4)

hidden5 = fully_connected(hidden4, n_hidden5)

logits = fully_connected(hidden5, n_outputs, activation_fn=None)
```

```
outputs = tf.sigmoid(logits)

reconstruction_loss = tf.reduce_sum(

tf.nn.sigmoid_cross_entropy_with_logits(labels=X, logits=logits))

latent_loss = 0.5 * tf.reduce_sum(

tf.exp(hidden3_gamma) + tf.square(hidden3_mean) - 1 - hidden3_gamma)

cost = reconstruction_loss + latent_loss

optimizer = tf.train.AdamOptimizer(learning_rate=learning_rate)

training_op = optimizer.minimize(cost)

init = tf.global_variables_initializer()
```

Generating Digits

Now this autoencoder can be used to generate images that look very much like digits that have been handwritten. We must first train the model and then carry out random sampling on the codings from a Gaussian distribution; last, we decode them:

```
import numpy as np

n_digits = 60

n_epochs = 50

batch_size = 150

with tf.Session() as sess:

init.run()

for epoch in range(n_epochs):

n_batches = mnist.train.num_examples // batch_size

for iteration in range(n_batches):

X_batch, y_batch = mnist.train.next_batch(batch_size)

sess.run(training_op, feed_dict={X: X_batch})

codings_rnd = np.random.normal(size=[n_digits, n_hidden3])

outputs_val = outputs.eval(feed_dict={hidden3: codings_rnd})
```

That's all there is to it; we can now see what these so-called handwritten digits that the autoencoder produced look like:

```
plt.subplot(n_digits, 10, iteration + 1)

plot_image(outputs_val[iteration])
```

The majority of the weights here look realistic but some are a little on the creative side. Don't place too much blame on the autoencoder though; it hasn't been learning for long so give it more training time and you will see that the digits get better over time.

Other Autoencoders

Supervised learning has seen great successes in the areas of image and speech recognition, translation and much more and this has tended to overpower the unsupervised learning – behind the scenes, though, it is actually a booming success. We are regularly seeing new inventions and architectures for unsupervised learning algorithms like autoencoders, so many in fact that there isn't time to write about them all. However, I can give you a very brief overview of some autoencoders that you might want to look up:

- **Contractive autoencoder** - the autoencoder gets constrained while training happens so that codings derivatives are small – regarding the inputs. What this means is that two inputs that are similar must also have similar codings.
- **Stacked convolutional autoencoder** – a type of autoencoder that reconstructs images that have been processed through a number of convolutional layers to learn how to extract visual features.
- **Generative stochastic network** – this is a generalization of the autoencoders to denoise but it has the addition of being able to generate data.
- **Winner-Take-All autoencoder** – once the activations of the neurons from the coding layer have been computed during training, the top k% of the neuron activations over the training batch get preserved with the remainder being set to zero. This results in sparse codings. An approach much like this can also be used to produce a sparse convolutional autoencoder.
- **Adversarial autoencoders** – a network gets trained so its inputs are reproduced and, simultaneously, another is trained to find the inputs that can't be properly reconstructed by the first network. This will push the autoencoder to learn very robust codings.

In the last chapter, we will look in-depth at Reinforcement Learning.

Chapter 15: Reinforcement Learning

The last subject of this book is Reinforcement Learning or RL. It is probably the most exciting field in machine learning and it also happens to be one of the oldest. Reinforcement Learning. It first came about in the 1950s and over the years, it has been responsible for many interesting applications, games in particular. One of the most popular was a Backgammon playing program called TD-Gammon. Reinforcement Learning has also excelled in the machine control area but rarely made the headlines. However, things changed in 2013 when DeepMind got involved. Researchers from the English startup demonstrated their own system that had the capability of learning to play almost any Atari game right from scratch. Eventually, their system went on to outperform any human being in most games using nothing more than some raw pixels for inputs and with no upfront knowledge of the rules of any game.

This was just the start. Over the next three years, their system performed a lot of "miracles" and, in 2016, their system AlphaGo beat the world champion of the game Go, Lee Sodol. No program until now had even come close to beating a game's Master, let alone a world champion. Today, the world for RL is brimming with ideas for a whole range of different applications.

As an aside, Google purchased DeepMind in 2014 for more than 500 million dollars.

How did AlphaGo beat a world champion? When you look at it now, it all seems so simple and so obvious – all they did was combine the power of Deep Learning with Reinforcement Learning and the result was more than they could ever have imagined.

In this chapter, we will look at what Reinforcement Learning is, what it is good for, and then we will look at two very important deep Reinforcement Learning techniques – policy gradients and deep Q-networks or DQN. We will also discuss MDP, the Markov decision processes. We will make use of the techniques to train a model in balancing a pole on a cart that moves and another model to play those Atari games. These self-same techniques can easily be used for many other tasks including fully mobile robots right up to the self-drive car.

Learning How to Optimize Rewards

In Reinforcement Learning, software agents are used to make observations. They take a certain action within the environment and it receives rewards as a result. It has an objective of learning to act in such a way that its long-term rewards will be maximized. Think of these rewards as pleasure if they are positive and pain if they are negative (in this case, the term "reward" is somewhat misleading). In simple terms, the agent will act in the environment and use trial and error to learn to minimize the pain and maximize the rewards.

RL really is quite broad and it can be applied to many different tasks. A few examples:

- The agent could be a program that controls a mobile robot. The environment, in this case, would be the real world; the agent will use a set of sensors to observe the environment – these could be touch sensors or cameras, for example – and the agent's actions will be to send signals that activate specific motors. It may be programmed so that, whenever it gets to its target destination it gets a positive reward and when it goes wrong, falls over or just wastes time, it will get a negative reward.

- The agent may be a program that controls Ms. Pacman. The environment, in this case, would be a simulation of the game played on the Atari. The actions would be the possible positions of the joystick (there are nine of them) and the observations would be screenshots. The rewards, in this case, would be the points earned in the game.
- The agent could be a program that plays a board game like Chess or Go.
- The agent is not required to control something that moves virtually or physically. It could be used to control a smart thermostat, for example; the positive rewards would be given when it gets close to the specified target temperature, resulting in energy savings, and negative rewards would be given when the temperature has to be tweaked by a human. Thus, the agent needs to learn to anticipate the needs of the human.
- The agent could be a program that observes prices on the stock market and makes a determination how much should be bought or sold every second. The rewards, in this case, are financial gains and losses.

In some cases, there may be no positive rewards. An example of this would be the agent moving around a maze. Negative rewards are given at each time step so the agent must find the exit as quickly as it can.

There are plenty of other tasks where RL could be used: self-drive cars, putting ads onto a web page, or even controlling where image classification needs to focus attention.

Policy Search

The algorithm that the software agent uses to determine what actions to take is called a policy. For example, that policy may be a neural network that takes in observations in the form of inputs and outputs what the action is going to be. The policy could be any algorithm and it needn't be a deterministic algorithm. For example, you have a robotic vacuum cleaner; its reward is how much dust it can pick up in half an hour. Its policy may be to move forward with probability p each second or to rotate left or right randomly with a probability of $1 - p$. The angle of rotation would be random, somewhere between -r and +r. Because we have an element of randomness in the policy, it is known as a stochastic policy. The trajectory of the robot will be erratic and this guarantees that, at some point, it will get to every place that it can reach and it will pick up all the dust. But how much dust can it pick up in that half-hour? Who knows?

So, how do we train a robot like this? You can only tweak two policy parameters – p (the probability) and r (the angle range). One learning algorithm that you could try would be to experiment with multiple values for each parameter and then choose the combination that has the best performance. This is called policy search and, in this case, it's a brute-force approach.

However, when there is too much policy space, which is usually the case, it isn't easy to find the right set of parameters; rather like searching for a minuscule needle in a ginormous haystack.

There is another way. You could use genetic algorithms to explore the policy space. For example, you could come up with a random creation of a first generation containing 100 policies and then try all of them out. You would then kill off the top 80 worst policies, leaving you with 20. Next, you would make these surviving policies each produce four offspring, which is nothing more than a copy of the parent plus a little random variation. These 20 survivors together with their offspring would create a further 100 policies that make the second generation. You can keep on like this, iterating through generation after generation until you find a decent policy.

There is one more way. Use optimization techniques to evaluate the gradients of each reward with respect to the parameters and then you would tweak the parameters. To do that you follow the gradient, using gradient ascent, up to the higher rewards. This is called policy gradients and we'll talk more about that later. As an example, we'll go back to our robotic vacuum cleaner; you could increase p slightly and then evaluate if that increase results in more dust being picked up in the 30 minutes. If yes, increase it a little more. Or you could reduce p. Very shortly we will be using TensorFlow to implement one of the more common policy gradient algorithms. Before we do that, we need an environment that the agent can live in; let's talk about OpenAI gym.

Introducing OpenAI Gym

One of the single biggest Reinforcement Learning challenges is this – to train your agent, you must first have a working environment. If you wanted an agent programmed to learn how to play an Atari game, you would need to build the environment of a working Atari game simulator. If you wanted a moving robot programmed, the real world is your environment and your robot can be trained directly in it but there are limits to this – if your robot walked under a car, there isn't an "undo" button you can click. Time can't be speeded up either; it doesn't matter how much computing power you add, you can't make your robot go any faster. Generally, it would be far too costly to train 1000 robots in parallel. Simply put, in the real world training is very hard and very slow so you need an environment that has been simulated at the very least to bootstrap training.

OpenAI gym provides a large number of different simulated environments, such as 2D or 3D physical simulations, board games, Atari games and more. This allows you to train your agent, compare it or come up with brand new Reinforcement Learning algorithms.

First, we need to install OpenAI gym. For a minimal installation you can get away with using pip:

```
$ pip3 install --upgrade gym
```

Now you can open a Python shell or a Jupyter notebook – your choice – to get your first environment created:

```
>>> import gym
>>> env = gym.make("CartPole-v0")
[2016-10-14 16:03:23,199] Making new env: MsPacman-v0
>>> obs = env.reset()
>>> obs
array([-0.03799846, -0.03288115, 0.02337094, 0.00720711])
>>> env.render()
```

We create the environment using the make() function; in our case, it is a CartPole environment, a 2D simulation, where you can accelerate a cart left or right to keep a pole balanced on top of it. Once the environment has been created, it must be initialized and this is done with the reset() method. This will return the very first observation and each observation will depend entirely on the environment.

In the CartPole environment, each of the observations is a 1D NumPy array with four floats. The floats are used to represent:

- The horizontal position of the cart – 0.0 = center
- The velocity of the cart
- The vertical position of the cart – 0.0 = vertical
- The angular velocity of the cart

Lastly, to display the environment we use the render() method. If you wanted the rendered image returned as a NumPy array, you would need to set the mode parameter as rgb_array (be aware that different environments are likely to support different modes:

```
>>> img = env.render(mode="rgb_array")
>>> img.shape # height, width, channels (3=RGB)
(400, 600, 3)
```

What you will find is that the CartPole, along with some other environments, will render the image to screen despite you setting the mode to rgb_array. There is only one way you can avoid this and that is to use a false X server, like Xdummy or Xvfb. For example, you could install Xvfb and then use the following command to start Python:

```
Xvfb-run -s "-screen 0 1400x900x24" python
```

Alternatively, you could use the xvfbwrapper package.

Let us see what actions the environment says are possible:

```
>>> env.action_space
Discrete(2)
```

Discrete (2) tells us that there are two possible actions and both are integers called 0 and 1. They represent left acceleration (0) or right acceleration (1). There may be more discrete actions in other environments and there may be different types of action. Because our pole is leaning to the right, let's tell the cart to accelerate to the right:

```
>>> action = 1 # accelerate right
>>> obs, reward, done, info = env.step(action)
>>> obs
array([-0.03865608, 0.16189797, 0.02351508, -0.27801135])
>>> reward
1.0
>>> done
False
>>> info
{}
```

The step() method will execute the specified action and it will return four values:

- **obs** – this represents a new observation. The cart is moving to the right, (obs[1]>0) and the pole remains tilted to the right, (obs[2]>0). However, the angular velocity is now a negative, (obs[3]<0) so it is likely that, after the next step, the pole will tilt left.
- **reward** – with this particular environment, we get a reward of 1.0 at each step, regardless of what we do; the goal here is to keep on running for as long as possible.
- **done** – when the episode is finished, this particular value is True, and this will happen if the pole is tilted too much. Afterward, we need to reset the environment before it can be used again.
- **info** – this is a dictionary that could give debug information in some other environments. It would be cheating if you used this data for training so don't.

It's time to hardcode a policy that will accelerate to the left when the pole tilts to the left and accelerates to the right when the pole tilts right. This policy will be run over 500 episodes to see what the average rewards are:

```python
def basic_policy(obs):

angle = obs[2]

return 0 if angle < 0 else 1

totals = []

for episode in range(500):

episode_rewards = 0

obs = env.reset()

for step in range(1000): # 1000 steps max, we don't want to run forever

action = basic_policy(obs)

obs, reward, done, info = env.step(action)

episode_rewards += reward

if done:

break

totals.append(episode_rewards)
```

This code should be fairly self-explanatory. Let's see what the result is:

```python
>>> import numpy as np

>>> np.mean(totals), np.std(totals), np.min(totals), np.max(totals)

(42.125999999999998, 9.1237121830974033, 24.0, 68.0)
```

Even iterating over 500 episodes, the policy didn't keep the pole standing upright for any more than 68 consecutive steps. Not too good. If you take a look at the simulation of this in Jupyter Notebooks it will show you that the cart lurches right and left with increasing regularity until the pole is tilted too much.

Let's see if we can get a better policy using a neural network.

Neural Network Policies

Now we're going to create a neural network policy and, much like the policy we just coded, this network will have the input of an observation and an output of the action to be done. Perhaps more precisely, for each action, the network will estimate a probability, after which we will randomly choose an action according to those probabilities. With the CartPole environment, we have two actions that are possible – right or left – so that means we only need a single output neuron. This neuron will output p (probability) of action 0, which is left and 1 – p will be the probability of action 1, which is right. For example, if 0.7 were output, we would choose action 0 with a probability of 70% and action 1 with a probability of 30%.

Why are we choosing random actions based on these probabilities output by a neural network? Why aren't we choosing the action that has the highest score? Because, by using this approach, we can allow our agent to find the optimum balance between the exploration of new actions and the exploitation of those actions already known to work very well.

Let's build the network using TensorFlow:

```
import tensorflow as tf

from tensorflow.contrib.layers import fully_connected

# 1. Specify the neural network architecture

n_inputs = 4 # == env.observation_space.shape[0]

n_hidden = 4 # it's a simple task, we don't need more hidden neurons

n_outputs = 1 # only outputs the probability of accelerating left

initializer = tf.contrib.layers.variance_scaling_initializer()

# 2. Build the neural network

X = tf.placeholder(tf.float32, shape=[None, n_inputs])

hidden = fully_connected(X, n_hidden, activation_fn=tf.nn.elu,
weights_initializer=initializer)

logits = fully_connected(hidden, n_outputs, activation_fn=None,
weights_initializer=initializer)

outputs = tf.nn.sigmoid(logits)

# 3. Select a random action based on the estimated probabilities

p_left_and_right = tf.concat(axis=1, values=[outputs, 1 - outputs])
```

```
action = tf.multinomial(tf.log(p_left_and_right), num_samples=1)

init = tf.global_variables_initializer()
```

Let's break this down.

The neural network is defined after the imports. The observation space size dictates the number of inputs of which there are four for CartPole. We also have four hidden units and we don't need anymore, and we have a single output probability, which is that of going left.

Next, the neural network is built. For this example, we are using a standard Multi-layer Perceptron (MLP) with one output. Note that the sigmoid, or logistic activation function is used on the output layer and this is to ensure that we get a probability between 0.0 to 1.0. If we had more than two actions, we would have an output neuron for each one and use the SoftMax activation function instead.

Finally, a random action is picked using the multinomial function() . Given the log probability of the integers, the multinomial function independently samples at least one of them. For example, if you called the function using an array of [np.log(0.5, np.log(0.2, np.log(0.3)], using num_samples=5, the output would be five integers, each one having a probability of 50% for being 0, 20% for being 1 and 30% for being 2. We only require one integer to represent which action should be taken. Because the outputs tensor has only got a probability of turning left, 1-outputs must be concatenated to it so that we get a tensor that contains the probability of the left and the right actions. If we have more than two actions, one probability would need to be output for each one so the concatenation step would not be necessary.

Okay, we got all that and we have a neural network policy that takes observations as inputs and outputs actions, but how do we go about training it?

Action Evaluation: Credit Assignment Problem

If we already knew what the best step was going to be for each step, we would be able to train the network as normal, with cross entropy minimization between the estimate and the targeted probabilities. It would be much like plain old supervised learning. The problem with Reinforcement Learning is that the agent only receives guidance through rewards and these tend to be delayed and sparse. For example, let's say that your agent achieved a rate of 100 consecutive steps to balance the pole; how will it know which of these 100 actions were any good and which were not good? All it does know is that, at the last action, that pole fell off but surely, this action couldn't have been totally responsible, could it? This is known as the credit assignment problem; when the agent gets the reward it isn't easy for it to determine which of the actions should be given credit for positive rewards or blamed for negative ones. Think about a dog; it does something right but it doesn't get rewarded for it until a few hours later. Will it actually realize why it is being given the reward?

There is a common strategy used to tackle this issue and that is to base an action evaluation on the sum of every reward that followed it; usually, a discount rate r will be applied at each of the steps. For example, we have an agent that opts to go right on three consecutive turns and, after the first step, it gets a reward of +10, after the second step the reward is 0 and after the third step, the reward is -50. Assuming that we apply a discount rate of r 0.8, the first action gets a score of 10 + r x 0 + r 2 x (-50) = -22. If we use a discount rate near to 0, rewards that come in the future will count for little compared to the immediate ones. By contrast, if the discount rate is near to 1 the rewards that come far into the future will be almost as valuable as the immediate rewards.

Typically, discount rates tend to be either 0.95 or 0.99. If you use a rate of 0.95 then rewards 13 steps ahead will count for approximately 50% of the immediate reward while using a rate of 0.99 rewards 69 steps ahead will count for approximately 50% of what the immediate rewards do , In the CartPole environment, the effects of the actions are relatively short-term so a reasonable rate would be 0.95.

Of course, it goes without saying that one good action could easily be followed by a few bad ones that could make the pole fall very quickly; this results in a low score for the good action. However, if the game were played enough times, the good actions will, on average, get a better score than the bad ones so that's the trick – to get reasonably reliable scores for the actions we need to run multiple episodes and all the action scores must be normalized – subtract the mean, divide by standard deviation. We could then assume, quite reasonably, that positive scores indicate a good action while the negative indicates a bad one.

Great, now we know how each action should be evaluated we can think about training the first agent with the policy gradients. Let's see how we do this.

Using Policy Gradients

We talked earlier about how the policy gradient algorithms are used to optimize the policy parameters by following the gradients up toward the higher reward using gradient ascent. One of the more commonly used classes of the policy gradients is the REINFORCE algorithm and this was brought to us by Ronald Williams in 1999. This is one of the more common variants of it:

First, the neural network policy should be allowed to play the game a few times; at each step, the gradients that would make a chosen action the most likely one are computed but not applied at this stage.

Second, when a few episodes have been run each action score can be computed using the method we described in the last couple of paragraphs.

Third, if the score is positive, it indicates a good action and the gradients you computed can now be applied to make it more likely that this action is chosen in the future. However, if the action score is a negative one the action is bad, you need the opposite gradients applied so it is less likely that the action will be chosen in the future. The answer is to take each gradient vector and multiply it by the score of the corresponding action.

Lastly, the mean is computed of all the gradient vectors that result and then it gets used to perform the Gradient Descent.

We can now use TensorFlow to implement the algorithm. The neural network policy we already built will be trained to learn how to balance the pole on the cart. We will begin by finishing the construction phase we started coding earlier to add the cost function, the target probability, and the training operation. Because we are going to act as if the chosen action is the best action, we must have a target probability of 1.0 if the action is left (0) and 0.0 is the action is right (1):

```
y = 1. - tf.to_float(action)
```

We now have a target probability so we can go ahead and use cross entropy to define our cost function and compute the gradients:

```
learning_rate = 0.01

cross_entropy = tf.nn.sigmoid_cross_entropy_with_logits(

labels=y, logits=logits)

optimizer = tf.train.AdamOptimizer(learning_rate)

grads_and_vars = optimizer.compute_gradients(cross_entropy)
```

Note that the compute_gradients() method from the optimizer was called and not the minimize() method. We did this because, before the gradients get applied, we need to tweak them. With the compute_gradients() method we get a list of the gradient vector and variable pairs, one pair for each of the trainable variables. Now we can put all the gradients into one list so getting their values is more convenient:

```
gradients = [grad for grad, variable in grads_and_vars]
```

Now we get to the part that is a little more tricky. When the Execution phase runs, the algorithm runs the policy. For each step, it will evaluate the gradient tensors and then stores the resulting values. After several episodes have run, the algorithm tweaks the gradients by multiplying them by the actions scores and then normalizes them and then the mean of those tweaked gradients will be computed.

Next the gradients are fed back to the optimizer so that an optimization step can be done. For this we need a placeholder for each of the gradient vectors. We also need to create the operation that is going to apply those updated gradients. To do this, we call apply_gradients(), a function in the optimizer; this takes the list of the vector/variable pairs. Rather than the original vectors for the gradients, we'll give it a list that has the updated gradients instead – these are the ones that went through the placeholders:

```
gradient_placeholders = []
```

```python
grads_and_vars_feed = []
for grad, variable in grads_and_vars:
gradient_placeholder = tf.placeholder(tf.float32,
shape=grad.get_shape())
gradient_placeholders.append(gradient_placeholder)
grads_and_vars_feed.append((gradient_placeholder, variable))
training_op = optimizer.apply_gradients(grads_and_vars_feed)
```

We'll just step back for a minute and look at the entire construction phase:

```python
n_inputs = 4
n_hidden = 4
n_outputs = 1

initializer = tf.contrib.layers.variance_scaling_initializer()
learning_rate = 0.01

X = tf.placeholder(tf.float32, shape=[None, n_inputs])
hidden = fully_connected(X, n_hidden, activation_fn=tf.nn.elu,
weights_initializer=initializer)
logits = fully_connected(hidden, n_outputs, activation_fn=None,
weights_initializer=initializer)
outputs = tf.nn.sigmoid(logits)
p_left_and_right = tf.concat(axis=1, values=[outputs, 1 - outputs])
action = tf.multinomial(tf.log(p_left_and_right), num_samples=1)
y = 1. - tf.to_float(action)
cross_entropy = tf.nn.sigmoid_cross_entropy_with_logits(
labels=y, logits=logits)
optimizer = tf.train.AdamOptimizer(learning_rate)
grads_and_vars = optimizer.compute_gradients(cross_entropy)
gradients = [grad for grad, variable in grads_and_vars]
```

```
gradient_placeholders = []

grads_and_vars_feed = []

for grad, variable in grads_and_vars:

gradient_placeholder = tf.placeholder(tf.float32,
shape=grad.get_shape())

gradient_placeholders.append(gradient_placeholder)

grads_and_vars_feed.append((gradient_placeholder, variable))

training_op = optimizer.apply_gradients(grads_and_vars_feed)

init = tf.global_variables_initializer()

saver = tf.train.Saver()
```

Now we'll look at the Execution phase. We will require some functions so that the total discounted rewards can be computed in relation to the raw rewards and then the results must be normalized across several episodes:

```
def discount_rewards(rewards, discount_rate):

discounted_rewards = np.empty(len(rewards))

cumulative_rewards = 0

for step in reversed(range(len(rewards))):

cumulative_rewards = rewards[step] + cumulative_rewards *
discount_rate

discounted_rewards[step] = cumulative_rewards

return discounted_rewards

def discount_and_normalize_rewards(all_rewards, discount_rate):

all_discounted_rewards = [discount_rewards(rewards)

for rewards in all_rewards]

flat_rewards = np.concatenate(all_discounted_rewards)

reward_mean = flat_rewards.mean()

reward_std = flat_rewards.std()

return [(discounted_rewards - reward_mean)/reward_std
```

```
for discounted_rewards in all_discounted_rewards]
```

Let's check that this works:

```
>>> discount_rewards([10, 0, -50], discount_rate=0.8)
array([-22., -40., -50.])
>>> discount_and_normalize_rewards([[10, 0, -50], [10, 20]],
discount_rate=0.8)
[array([-0.28435071, -0.86597718, -1.18910299]),
array([ 1.26665318, 1.0727777 ])]
```

When we call discount_rewards(), we get what we expect to get. We can easily determine whether discount_and_normalize_rewards() does return the normalized scores for each of the actions in both of the episodes. The first episode does a lot worse so it has negative normalized scores. This means any actions from that episode are considered to be bad and all those from the second are considered to be good.

We now have everything we need to train the policy:

```
n_iterations = 250 # number of training iterations
n_max_steps = 1000 # max steps per episode
n_games_per_update = 10 # train the policy every 10 episodes
save_iterations = 10 # save the model every 10 training iterations
discount_rate = 0.95

with tf.Session() as sess:
init.run()
for iteration in range(n_iterations):
all_rewards = [] # all sequences of raw rewards for each episode
all_gradients = [] # gradients saved at each step of each episode
for game in range(n_games_per_update):
current_rewards = [] # all raw rewards from the current episode
current_gradients = [] # all gradients from the current episode
obs = env.reset()
```

```python
for step in range(n_max_steps):
action_val, gradients_val = sess.run(
[action, gradients],
feed_dict={X: obs.reshape(1, n_inputs)}) # one obs
obs, reward, done, info = env.step(action_val[0][0])
current_rewards.append(reward)
current_gradients.append(gradients_val)
if done:
break
all_rewards.append(current_rewards)
all_gradients.append(current_gradients)
# At this point we have run the policy for 10 episodes, and we are
# ready for a policy update using the algorithm described earlier.
all_rewards = discount_and_normalize_rewards(all_rewards)
feed_dict = {}
for var_index, grad_placeholder in enumerate(gradient_placeholders):
# multiply the gradients by the action scores, and compute the mean
mean_gradients = np.mean(
[reward * all_gradients[game_index][step][var_index]
for game_index, rewards in enumerate(all_rewards)
for step, reward in enumerate(rewards)],
axis=0)
feed_dict[grad_placeholder] = mean_gradients
sess.run(training_op, feed_dict=feed_dict)
if iteration % save_iterations == 0:
saver.save(sess, "./my_policy_net_pg.ckpt")
```

Each of the training operations begins with the policy being run for a total of 10 episodes. Each episode has a maximum of 1000 steps so that they don't run on and on forever. At each of the steps, the gradients are computed assuming that the chosen action was indeed the best one. Once these episodes have run, the action scores are computed using discount_and_normalize_rewards(); each of the training variables is gone through across each episode and all the steps; the gradient vectors are each multiplied by their respective action score and the mean of the gradients that result from this is computed. Lastly, the training operation is done; we feed the mean gradients to it, one for each variable and the model gets saved after every 10 operations.

That's it! This code will now train your neural network policy so that it learns to balance the pole successfully on the cart. Be aware; the agent can lose this game in one of two ways – the pole tilts too far or the cart disappears off the screen completely.

Over the course of 250 iterations, our policy managed to learn to balance the pole very well but it cannot yet avoid disappearing off the screen; to fix that, simply do a few hundred more iterations.

The algorithm may look simple but this is deceptive. This is actually very powerful and it can be used for harder tasks than pole balancing. AlphaGo was based on an algorithm much like this one.

Next, we will look at another algorithm family. While the policy gradient algorithms attempt to optimize the policy directly so the rewards can be increased, this next family of algorithms is not quite so direct. The agent will still be learning how to estimate the sum of the discounted future rewards of every state or for every action in every state but this time, they will be the expected sums. It will then use the knowledge it gained to decide how it will act. Understanding these algorithms requires an introduction to the MDP – the Markov decision processes.

Markov Decision Processes

Early in the 20th century, Andrey Markov, a mathematician, started to study stochastic processes that had no memory. These were called Markov chains. A process like this has a fixed number of states and at each step, it randomly evolves from one state to another. It has fixed probability of evolving from state s to state s' and that will only depend on the s s' pair and not on any past states – remember, it has no memory so it can't remember the past states.

Imagine a Markov chain that has four states. We'll assume that the process will begin in state s 0 and that there is a 70% probability that it will stay there for the next step. It will leave the state eventually and it will not return because there is no other state that points back to s 0. If it moves on to state s 1, there is a 90% probability that it will go on to state s 2 and a 100% probability of going back to state s 1. It may go between these states a few times, but at some point, it will go to state s 3 and stay there forever. This is called the terminal state. Markov chains can be considerably different in dynamics and they tend to be used a great deal in chemistry, thermodynamics, statistics, and more.

The Markov decision processes were first described to us by Richard Bellman in the 1950s. They are much like the Markov chain but they have a bit of a twist – at each of the steps, the agent can choose between multiple actions and that decision will dictate the transition probabilities. Some of the state transitions will return a positive or negative reward and the goal of the agent is to find the best policy to maximize the rewards over time.

As an example, we'll assume we have an MDP with three states and a possible three discrete actions at each of the steps. If it begins in state s 0, the agent makes the decision on three actions - a 0, a 1, or a 2. If a 0 is its choice, it will stay in state s 0, with no reward and with certainty. It has the choice of staying there forever but if a 0 is chosen there is a 70% probability that a reward of +10 will be gained and that it will stay in state s 0.

Then it can try for as much reward as it can possibly get over and over again. However, there will come a point when it moves to state s 1 and there it will have just two possible actions – a 0 or a 1. It can decide to stay where it is by choosing action a 1 over and over again or it can decide to move to state s 2 and be given a negative reward of -50 – painful! In state s 3, there is no choice – it must take the action a 1 and this is likely to take it back to state s 0, along the way picking up a reward of +40. Are you starting the see the picture now? Which action do you think is going to gain the highest rewards over time? With state s 0, we know that action a 0 is the best decision and, with state s 3, the agent doesn't have a choice; it must take action a 1. However, with state s 1, there is no obvious demarcation as to whether the agent should take action a 0 and stay where it is or take action a 2 and head on.

Bellman managed to find a way to estimate what the optimal state values of any state s was – noted V*(s). This is the sum of all the future discounted rewards the agent may expect, on average once it gets to a state s, always assuming that it acts in an optimal manner. He showed that provided the agent does act optimally, the Bellman Optimality Equation will apply – see below. This is a recursive equation and it states that, provided the agent is acting optimally, the current state has an optimal value that is equal to the reward it will attain on average after it takes a single optimal action, with the addition of the optimal value expected for all the possible next states that the action may lead on to:

$$V^*(s) = \max_a \sum_{s'} T(s, a, s')[R(s, a, s') + \gamma . V^*(s')] \quad \text{for all } s$$

Equation - Bellman Optimality Equation

Let's break this down:

- T(s, a, s') – the probability of transition from state s to state s'; the agent decided on action a.
- R(s, a , s') – the reward the agent will get for going from state s to state s'; again the agent opted for action a.
- Y – the discount rate

This equation will take us straight to an algorithm that is able to estimate precisely what the optimal state value is of each possible state. First, the state value estimates are initialized to zero then the Value Iteration algorithm, shown in the equation below, is used to update them iteratively. Given sufficient time, these estimates include a guarantee that convergence will happen at the optimal state values and will correspond accordingly to the optimal policy:

$$V_{k+1}(s) \leftarrow \max_a \sum_{s'} T(s, a, s')[R(s, a, s') + \gamma . V_k(s')] \quad \text{for all } s$$

Equation - Value Iteration Algorithm

Vk(s) – the value estimated for state s at the kth iteration in the algorithm.

Note

This algorithm shows us an example of Dynamic Programming. This breaks complex problems down into sub-problems that are tractable and can be iteratively tackled. In our case, we are estimating a sum of discounted future rewards that could potentially be infinite and, for the iterative problem-tackling it must find the action that will maximize the average reward plus the next discounted state value.

It is very useful to know what the optimal state values are, especially when it comes to evaluating a policy. However, knowing this doesn't explicitly tell an agent what it should do. Bellman did find an algorithm that was quite similar to estimate what the optimal state-action values would be – these are usually called Q-Values. Take the state-action pair of (s, a); the optimal Q-Value would be the sum of the average discounted future rewards that the agent could receive on reaching state s and deciding on action a before the outcome of the action is seen – this all assuming that, following that action, the agent acts optimally.

How it works is this – the Q-Values are all initialized to zero then the Q-Value Iteration algorithm updates them:

$$Q_{k+1}(s, a) \leftarrow \sum_{s'} T(s, a, s')[R(s, a, s') + \gamma . \max_a Q_k(s', a')] \quad \text{for all } (s, a)$$

Equation – Value Iteration Algorithm

When you have got the optimal Q-Values, it is really quite easy to define the optimal policy: when the agent gets to state s, the action chosen should be the one with the highest Q-Value for the state - $\pi^*(s) = \text{argmax}_a Q^*(s, a)$.

Now the algorithm can be applied to the MDP but first, that MDP needs to be defined:

```
nan=np.nan # represents impossible actions

T = np.array([ # shape=[s, a, s']
```

```
[[0.7, 0.3, 0.0], [1.0, 0.0, 0.0], [0.8, 0.2, 0.0]],

[[0.0, 1.0, 0.0], [nan, nan, nan], [0.0, 0.0, 1.0]],

[[nan, nan, nan], [0.8, 0.1, 0.1], [nan, nan, nan]],

])

R = np.array([ # shape=[s, a, s']

[[10., 0.0, 0.0], [0.0, 0.0, 0.0], [0.0, 0.0, 0.0]],

[[10., 0.0, 0.0], [nan, nan, nan], [0.0, 0.0, -50.]],

[[nan, nan, nan], [40., 0.0, 0.0], [nan, nan, nan]],

])

possible_actions = [[0, 1, 2], [0, 2], [1]]
```

The Q-Value Iteration algorithm is now run:

```
Q = np.full((3, 3), -np.inf) # -inf for impossible actions

for state, actions in enumerate(possible_actions):

Q[state, actions] = 0.0 # Initial value = 0.0, for all possible
actions

learning_rate = 0.01

discount_rate = 0.95

n_iterations = 100

for iteration in range(n_iterations):

Q_prev = Q.copy()

for s in range(3):

for a in possible_actions[s]:

Q[s, a] = np.sum([

T[s, a, sp] * (R[s, a, sp] + discount_rate * np.max(Q_prev[sp]))

for sp in range(3)

])
```

The Q-Values that come from it this look like:

```
>>> Q
array([[ 21.89498982, 20.80024033, 16.86353093],
[ 1.11669335, -inf, 1.17573546],
[ -inf, 53.86946068, -inf]])
>>> np.argmax(Q, axis=1) # optimal action for each state
array([0, 2, 1])
```

We now have the optimal policy for the MDP using a 0.95 discount rate. In state s 0, action a 0 should be chosen; in state s 1, the action a 2 should be chosen; in state s 2, the action a 1 should be chosen because it is the only action possible. However, what is interesting is if you were to lower the discount rate to 0.9, the optimal policy will change; in state s1, action a becomes the best one – stay where you are. It does make sense; if you put more value on the present than you do on the future, the reward prospect is really not worth the pain.

Q-Learning and Temporal Difference Learning

If you have a Reinforcement Learning problem that has discrete actions, often it can be modeled as a Markov decision process. However, to start with the agent will not have a clue what the transition probabilities will be – it doesn't know what T(s, a, s') is and it has no clue as to what the rewards will be either – it doesn't know R(s, a, s'). Instead, it will need to go through and experience every state and transition at least one time if it is to learn the rewards, and many more times if it is to learn a reasonable estimation of the probabilities for the transition.

TD Learning or the Temporal Difference Learning algorithm is much like that of the Value Iteration one but it is capable of taking into account that the agent only partially knows the MDP. Generally, we would assume that the agent knows just the possible states and values to start with, no more. To explore through the MDP, the agent will use an exploration policy, such as a random policy, and, as it goes through, the TD Learning algorithm will update the state value estimates based on what rewards and transitions are seen, as you can see from the equation below:

$$V_{k+1}(s) \leftarrow (1 - \alpha)V_k(s) + \alpha(r + \gamma . V_k(s'))$$

Equation - TD Learning Algorithm

- a – learning rate

For every state s, the algorithm will track the running average of the rewards an agent gets immediately it leaves the state, together with the rewards expected to be given later, provided it has acted optimally.

In much the same way, the algorithm for Q-Learning is adapted from the algorithm for Q-Value Iteration but the probabilities for the transitions and the rewards are not known to start with. That equation can be seen below:

$$Q_{k+1}(s, a) \leftarrow (1 - \alpha)Q_k(s, a) + \alpha\left(r + \gamma.\max_{a'} Q_k(s', a')\right)$$

Equation - Q-Learning Algorithm

For each of the state-action pairs (s, a), that algorithm tracks the running average of r, the rewards are given to the agent when it leaves state s with action a, together with the rewards expected to be given later. Because the target policy acts optimally, the maximum Q-Value estimates can be taken for the next state.

This is how we implement Q-Learning:

```
import numpy.random as rnd

learning_rate0 = 0.05

learning_rate_decay = 0.1

n_iterations = 20000

s = 0 # start in state 0

Q = np.full((3, 3), -np.inf) # -inf for impossible actions

for state, actions in enumerate(possible_actions):

Q[state, actions] = 0.0 # Initial value = 0.0, for all possible
actions

for iteration in range(n_iterations):

a = rnd.choice(possible_actions[s]) # choose an action (randomly)

sp = rnd.choice(range(3), p=T[s, a]) # pick next state using T[s, a]
```

```
reward = R[s, a, sp]

learning_rate = learning_rate0 / (1 + iteration *
learning_rate_decay)

Q[s, a] = learning_rate * Q[s, a] + (1 - learning_rate) * (

reward + discount_rate * np.max(Q[sp])

)

s = sp # move on to the next state
```

Provided there are sufficient iterations, the algorithm converges to the Q-Values that are optimal. This is known as an off-policy algorithm; we are not executing the policy we train. It is actually quite surprising that the algorithm is even capable of learning what the optimal policy is purely by watching the random actions of an agent. So, what could we do that would be better?

Exploration Policies

Q-Learning will work only if the exploration policy has given the MDP a thorough look through. It is pretty much guaranteed that a purely random policy will make a visit to every state and every transition multiple times but it will take a very long time to do it. A better method is to use the ε-greedy policy. This policy will act randomly with the probability ε at every step' this is also known as acting greedily, i.e. picking the action that has the highest Q-Value, with a probability of 1- ε. The ε-greedy policy has an advantage over a random policy in that it will spend as much time as needed exploring the environment, as the Q-Value estimates improve, while still managing to spend time visiting some of the unknown regions in the MDP. It isn't uncommon for a high value to be used for ε at the start, for example, 10, and then have it reduce gradually down to, for example, 0.05.

Instead of relying on chance for the exploration, another way would be to provide encouragement to the exploration policy, get it to try some actions that it has little to no experience of. You can implement this as a bonus to Q-Value estimates, as you can see in the next equation:

$$Q(s, a) \leftarrow (1 - \alpha)Q(s, a) + \alpha\left(r + \gamma.\max_{\alpha} f(Q(s', a'), N(s', a'))\right)$$

Equation - Q-Learning With An Exploration Function

- $N(s', a)$ – will count how many times action a got chosen in state s'.
- $f(q, n)$ – an exploration function, like $f(q, n) = q + K|(1 + n)$. In this, K is a hyperparameter (curiosity type) that will measure the level of attraction the agent has to the unknown.

Approximate Q-Learning

There is one inherent problem with this Q-Learning though; it isn't very good at scaling to medium or large MDPs, particularly when there are multiple states and actions. Let's say that you wanted to train an agent in laying Ms. Pacman and you used Q-Learning to do it. Ms. Pacman has more than 250 pellets available to eat, each being present (on the screen) or absent (already eaten). Even considering just the possible states of the pellets only, there are more than $2^{250} \approx 10^{75}$ possible states. That number is much greater than that of the atoms in the observable universe so you could not possibly track the estimates for every one of the Q-Values.

What is the solution? We need a function that will use a manageable number of parameters to approximate the Q-Value and this is known as Approximate Q-Learning. For many years, the recommendation was to use linear combinations full of features that were hand-crafted and extracted out of the state, for example, the distance of the nearest ghost, direction and more, to estimate the Q-Value. However, DeepMind shows us that DNNs work a good deal better particularly where we have complex problems, and it requires nothing in the way of feature engineering. We call a DNN that is used to estimate the Q-Values a deep Q-network or DQN; to use a DQN for the Approximate Q-Learning is known as Deep Q-Learning. For the remainder of the chapter, we will train an agent so that it plays Ms. Pacman and we'll do it using the Deep Q-Learning. This code is tweakable so it can be taught to play most Atari games to a good level. It can also gain superhuman skill in most of the action games but it isn't much good when it comes to games that have long stories.

Using Deep Q-Learning to Learn How to Play Ms. Pacman

Because our environment will be an Atari simulation, first we need to install the Atari dependencies from OpenAI gym. While we do that, we'll install the dependencies for some other environments in case you want to use them.

On the Mac, you will need Homebrew installed and then you can type this command:

```
$ brew install cmake boost boost-python sdl2 swig wget
```

On Ubuntu, type this command (if you are using Python 2, type in python and not python3:

```
$ apt-get install -y python3-numpy python3-dev cmake zlib1g-dev
libjpeg-dev\

xvfb libav-tools xorg-dev python3-opengl libboost-all-dev libsdl2-dev
swig
```

Then you need the extra modules:

```
$ pip3 install --upgrade 'gym[all]'
```

If all goes according to plan, we should be good to go on creating the environment for Ms. Pacman:

```
>>> env = gym.make("MsPacman-v0")

>>> obs = env.reset()

>>> obs.shape # [height, width, channels]

(210, 160, 3)

>>> env.action_space

Discrete(9)
```

As you see, we have nine discrete actions all of which relate to the nine joystick positions:

- Up
- Down
- Left
- Right
- Center
- Upper left
- Upper right
- Lower left
- Lower right

The observations are nothing more than screenshots showing the Atari screen, each represented as a 3D NumPy array. These are quite large so we need to create a preprocessing function, just a small one. This crops the image and reduces it down to 88 x 80 pixels. The image is then converted to grayscale and the contrast of Ms. Pacman is improved. This, in turn, reduces the number of computations that the DQN needs and training is speeded up:

```
mspacman_color = np.array([210, 164, 74]).mean()

def preprocess_observation(obs):

img = obs[1:176:2, ::2] # crop and downsize

img = img.mean(axis=2) # to greyscale

img[img==mspacman_color] = 0 # improve contrast

img = (img - 128) / 128 - 1 # normalize from -1. to 1.

return img.reshape(88, 80, 1)

from tensorflow.contrib.layers import convolution2d, fully_connected
```

```python
input_height = 88
input_width = 80
input_channels = 1
conv_n_maps = [32, 64, 64]
conv_kernel_sizes = [(8,8), (4,4), (3,3)]
conv_strides = [4, 2, 1]
conv_paddings = ["SAME"]*3
conv_activation = [tf.nn.relu]*3
n_hidden_in = 64 * 11 * 10 # conv3 has 64 maps of 11x10 each
n_hidden = 512
hidden_activation = tf.nn.relu
n_outputs = env.action_space.n # 9 discrete actions are available
initializer = tf.contrib.layers.variance_scaling_initializer()
def q_network(X_state, scope):
    prev_layer = X_state
    conv_layers = []
    with tf.variable_scope(scope) as scope:
        for n_maps, kernel_size, stride, padding, activation in zip(
                conv_n_maps, conv_kernel_sizes, conv_strides,
                conv_paddings, conv_activation):
            prev_layer = convolution2d(
                prev_layer, num_outputs=n_maps, kernel_size=kernel_size,
                stride=stride, padding=padding, activation_fn=activation,
                weights_initializer=initializer)
            conv_layers.append(prev_layer)
        last_conv_layer_flat = tf.reshape(prev_layer, shape=[-1,
n_hidden_in])
```

```
hidden = fully_connected(

last_conv_layer_flat, n_hidden, activation_fn=hidden_activation,

weights_initializer=initializer)

outputs = fully_connected(

hidden, n_outputs, activation_fn=None,

weights_initializer=initializer)

trainable_vars = tf.get_collection(tf.GraphKeys.TRAINABLE_VARIABLES,

scope=scope.name)

trainable_vars_by_name = {var.name[len(scope.name):]: var

for var in trainable_vars}

return outputs, trainable_vars_by_name
```

To start with, this code is defining the DQN architecture parameters. Then the DQN is created using the q_network function, taking X_state as the input (the state of the environment) and the variable scope name. Note that the state of the environment is represented by a single observation because there is virtually no hidden state, with the exception of the directions for the ghosts and blinking objects.

Next, the dictionary, trainable_vars_by_name takes in all the DQN variables that are trainable. It will be useful in the next step when the operations are created to copy the critic to the actor DQN. The dictionary keys are the variable names, stripping the prefix part that only relates to the name of the scope. It will look like this:

```
>>> trainable_vars_by_name

{'/Conv/biases:0': <tensorflow.python.ops.variables.Variable at
0x121cf7b50>,

'/Conv/weights:0': <tensorflow.python.ops.variables.Variable...>,

'/Conv_1/biases:0': <tensorflow.python.ops.variables.Variable...>,

'/Conv_1/weights:0': <tensorflow.python.ops.variables.Variable...>,

'/Conv_2/biases:0': <tensorflow.python.ops.variables.Variable...>,

'/Conv_2/weights:0': <tensorflow.python.ops.variables.Variable...>,

'/fully_connected/biases:0':
<tensorflow.python.ops.variables.Variable...>,
```

```
'/fully_connected/weights:0':
<tensorflow.python.ops.variables.Variable...>,

'/fully_connected_1/biases:0':
<tensorflow.python.ops.variables.Variable...>,

'/fully_connected_1/weights:0':
<tensorflow.python.ops.variables.Variable...>}
```

Now the input placeholder can be created, along with the pair of identical DQNs and the operation required to copy the critic DQN to the actor:

```
X_state = tf.placeholder(tf.float32, shape=[None, input_height,
input_width,

input_channels])

actor_q_values, actor_vars = q_network(X_state,
scope="q_networks/actor")

critic_q_values, critic_vars = q_network(X_state,
scope="q_networks/critic")

copy_ops = [actor_var.assign(critic_vars[var_name])

for var_name, actor_var in actor_vars.items()]

copy_critic_to_actor = tf.group(*copy_ops)
```

Let's just stop for a minute. We have two DQNs, both able to take the environment state or preprocessed observation as the input; the output for both is an estimation of the Q-Value for every possible action within that state. We also have the operation called copy_critic_to_actor which will copy the trainable variables from the critic DQN over to the actor DQN. The TensorFlow function tf.group() is used to group the assignment operations together into one single operation.

The actor DQN will play Ms. Pacman, albeit badly to begin with. The idea is to have the actor DQN carry out a thorough exploration of the game so you would need some kind of exploration strategy combined with it, such as the ε-greedy policy.

That's all very well and good but how is the critic DQN going to learn to play Ms. Pacman? Put simply, it will attempt to have its own Q-Value predictions match up with those values the actor estimates as it experiences the game. More specifically, we'll allow the actor time to play so all its game experiences can be stored in a replay memory.

Each of these memories is a 5-tuple, containing the state, the action, the next state, the reward and the continue. The final item, the "continue", is equal to 0.0 when the game finishes or to 1.0. At regular points, a batch of memories from that replay memory will be sampled and the

Q-Values will be estimated. Lastly, the critic DQN is trained to predict the Q-Values. To do this, it will use standard techniques for supervised learning. After every few iterations, the critic DQN gets copied over to the actor DQN.

And that really is it. The next equation shows you the cost function that was used to train the critic DQN:

$$J(\theta_{\text{critic}}) = \frac{1}{m}\sum_{i=1}^{m}(y^{(i)} - Q(s^{(i)}, a^{(i)}, \theta_{\text{critic}}))^2$$

$$\text{with } y^{(i)} = r^{(i)} + \gamma . \max_{a'} Q(s'^{(i)}, a', \theta_{\text{actor}})$$

Equation - Deep Q Learning Cost Function

- s(i), a(i), r(i) and s'(i) – the state, the action, the reward and the next state of the ith memory that was sampled from our replay memory.
- m – the memory batch size.
- θ critic and θ actor – the parameters for actor and critic.
- Q(s(i), a(i), θ critic) -the prediction from the critic DQN of the Q-Value from the ith memorized state action.
- Q(s'(i), a', θ actor) – the Q-Value prediction from the actor DQN; this is what it expects from the next state s'(i) if action a' is chosen.
- y(i) – the ith memory's target Q-Value. This is equal to the reward that the actor observes and the prediction from the actor of the rewards it expects in the future if it were to play optimally.
- J(θ critic) – the cost function to train the critic DQN. This is the MSE between the actor DQN-estimated target Q-Values and the predictions of the values from the critic DQN.

Note

The replay memory is totally optional but it is recommended. If you don't have it, the critic DQN would be trained in consecutive experiences that are likely to be highly correlated. The result of this would be a high-level of bias and convergence of the training algorithm would be considerably slower. When you use a replay memory, you can ensure that the memories the training algorithm is fed are uncorrelated as far as possible.

Now we can add the training operations to the critic DQN. First, the predicted Q-Values for each of the state-actions in the memory batch need to be computed. Because the DQN will output a Q-Value for each of the possible actions, the only Q-Value we need to retain is the one that relates to the action chosen in the memory. To do this, the action is converted to a one-hot vector (a vector that is full of zeros and a 1 at the ith index). This is then multiplied by the Q-

Values which will result in the Q-Values being zeroed out except for the one that relates to the memorized action. Lastly, we obtain the Q-Value prediction we want for each memory by summing over the first axis.

```
X_action = tf.placeholder(tf.int32, shape=[None])

q_value = tf.reduce_sum(critic_q_values * tf.one_hot(X_action,
n_outputs),

axis=1, keep_dims=True)
```

Next, the training operations are added; the assumption is that a placeholder is used to feed the target Q-Values through. We will also create global_step, a variable that cannot be trained; incrementation will be done by the minimize() operation. The init operation is also created, along with the Saver.

```
y = tf.placeholder(tf.float32, shape=[None, 1])

cost = tf.reduce_mean(tf.square(y - q_value))

global_step = tf.Variable(0, trainable=False, name='global_step')

optimizer = tf.train.AdamOptimizer(learning_rate)

training_op = optimizer.minimize(cost, global_step=global_step)

init = tf.global_variables_initializer()

saver = tf.train.Saver()
```

That's the construction phase completed, on to the Execution phase. Before we go there though, we are going to need some tools. First, the replay memory needs to be implemented. We'll do this using a dequeue list because these push items to a queue efficiently and pop them from the end when we reach the maximum memory size. We also need a function that will carry out random sampling of a batch of replay memory experiences:

```
from collections import deque

replay_memory_size = 10000

replay_memory = deque([], maxlen=replay_memory_size)

def sample_memories(batch_size):

indices = rnd.permutation(len(replay_memory))[:batch_size]

cols = [[], [], [], [], []] # state, action, reward, next_state,
continue

for idx in indices:
```

```python
memory = replay_memory[idx]

for col, value in zip(cols, memory):

col.append(value)

cols = [np.array(col) for col in cols]

return (cols[0], cols[1], cols[2].reshape(-1, 1), cols[3],

cols[4].reshape(-1, 1))
```

Next, the actor must explore the game so we will make use of the ε-greedy policy, decreasing ε gradually from 1.0 down to 0.05 over 50,000 training steps:

```python
eps_min = 0.05

eps_max = 1.0

eps_decay_steps = 50000

def epsilon_greedy(q_values, step):

epsilon = max(eps_min, eps_max - (eps_max-eps_min) *
step/eps_decay_steps)

if rnd.rand() < epsilon:

return rnd.randint(n_outputs) # random action

else:

return np.argmax(q_values) # optimal action
```

Now we have everything we need for the training to start. There isn't anything too complicated in the Execution phase but it is quite long. So, take a deep breath and dive in. We start by initializing some variables:

```python
n_steps = 100000 # total number of training steps

training_start = 1000 # start training after 1,000 game iterations

training_interval = 3 # run a training step every 3 game iterations

save_steps = 50 # save the model every 50 training steps

copy_steps = 25 # copy the critic to the actor every 25 training
steps

discount_rate = 0.95
```

```
skip_start = 90 # skip the start of every game (it's just waiting
time)

batch_size = 50

iteration = 0 # game iterations

checkpoint_path = "./my_dqn.ckpt"

done = True # env needs to be reset
```

Then we open a session and get the main training loop running:

```
with tf.Session() as sess:

if os.path.isfile(checkpoint_path):

saver.restore(sess, checkpoint_path)

else:

init.run()

while True:

step = global_step.eval()

if step >= n_steps:

break

iteration += 1

if done: # game over, start again

obs = env.reset()

for skip in range(skip_start): # skip the start of each game

obs, reward, done, info = env.step(0)

state = preprocess_observation(obs)

# Actor evaluates what to do

q_values = actor_q_values.eval(feed_dict={X_state: [state]})

action = epsilon_greedy(q_values, step)

# Actor plays

obs, reward, done, info = env.step(action)
```

```
next_state = preprocess_observation(obs)
# Let's memorize what just happened
replay_memory.append((state, action, reward, next_state, 1.0 - done))
state = next_state
if iteration < training_start or iteration % training_interval != 0:
continue
# Critic learns
X_state_val, X_action_val, rewards, X_next_state_val, continues = (
sample_memories(batch_size))
next_q_values = actor_q_values.eval(
feed_dict={X_state: X_next_state_val})
max_next_q_values = np.max(next_q_values, axis=1, keepdims=True)
y_val = rewards + continues * discount_rate * max_next_q_values
training_op.run(feed_dict={X_state: X_state_val,
X_action: X_action_val, y: y_val})
# Regularly copy critic to actor
if step % copy_steps == 0:
copy_critic_to_actor.run()
# And save regularly
if step % save_steps == 0:
saver.save(sess, checkpoint_path)
```

If there is a checkpoint file, we start by restoring the models. If there isn't one, the variables are initialized normally. The main loop then starts; the iteration will count how many game steps have been gone through since the start of the program and the total number of training steps since the training began. Note, if a checkpoint gets restored, the global step also gets restored. Next, the game is reset and the initial game steps, the boring ones where nothing happens are skipped. The actor will then evaluate what needs to be done and then plays the game; the experience will be memorized into the relay memory.

After an initial warm-up period, at regular points, the critic will go through a training step. A batch of memories is sampled and the actor is asked for an estimation of the Q-Values for all the next state's actions; the Deep Q-Learning algorithm is applied so that y_val can be computed; this is the target Q-Value. There is only one tricky part – the Q-Values for the next state must be multiplied by the continues vector. This will zero out any Q-Values that correspond to memories relating to when the game is finished. Next, we improve the prediction ability of the critic by running the training value and, lastly, the critic is copied to the actor at regular points and the model is saved.

Tip

Training is not going to be fast and, if you are doing the training on your laptop, be prepared for it to take many days for Ms. Pacman to become any good at the game. Also, the learning curve shows a great deal of noise when the average rewards per episode are measured. Sometimes, there will appear to be no progress for such a long time and then the agent will suddenly learn how to survive the game for a longer period of time. One way that we could speed the training would be to add in as much prior knowledge to the model as we possibly could – this could be done through preprocessing, through rewards, and so on. You could also try bootstrapping the model – simply train it in the first instance to imitate a very basic strategy. Whatever you do, Reinforcement Learning will require a lot of time, patience and plenty of tweaking – the end result is well worth it though.

Conclusion

Thank you for taking the time to read this guide. I know it was a long one, but machine learning is not a five-minute wonder and there is no way that you would grasp any real knowledge of machine learning in just a few thousand words.

Throughout this guide, we've covered as much as possible to give you a decent basis in machine learning, the topics that you need to know and, from here, it's up to you to take your learning further and to put what you learned into practice.

Follow this quick checklist to get you through any machine Learning Project you opt to take on:

- Framing – work out the scope and look at the project as a whole
- Get your data
- Get insights from your data
- Prepare your data so the algorithms can see the data patterns
- Explore models and compare the best ones
- Fine-tune and put your models together in a fantastic solution
- Present that solution
- Launch it

Adapt as needed for each project.

It isn't possible to give you a comprehensive overview of Deep Learning, hopefully, I've done enough to raise your interest enough to go further.

Thank you, once again, for taking the time to read this guide.

References

https://medium.com

https://techburst.io

https://www.datacamp.com

https://www.analyticsvidhya.com

https://pythonprogramming.net/

https://machinelearningmastery.com

https://hackernoon.com

https://towardsdatascience.com

https://moz.com

http://scikit-learn.org

http://www.dataschool.io

https://docs.scipy.org

https://blog.csdn.net/

https://qiita.com

https://github.com/ageron/handson-ml/blob/master/book_equations.ipynb

http://www.cnblogs.com/yaoz/p/6918467.html

https://trainingdatascience.com/workshops/linear-regression/

https://scholar.google.com/citations?view_op=view_citation&citation_for_view=DJ8Ep8YAAAAJ:hkOj_22Ku90C

Made in the USA
Lexington, KY
11 August 2018